A SEA WITHOUT A SHORE:

SPIRITUAL REFLECTIONS FOR THE BROKENHEARTED, WEARY, AND LONELY

Jeannie Ewing

Jeannie Ewing
68353 Main Street
P O Box 652
New Paris, Indiana 46553
fromgrief2grace.com

Ordering Information: Quantity sales and special discounts are available to corporations, associations, and others. For details, contact the publisher at the address above.

Cover Photo: © 2016 Ruth J. Smucker, Artist + Designer
Cover Design: © 2016 Ruth J. Smucker, Artist + Designer
Book Layout © 2015 BookDesignTemplates.com

A Sea Without A Shore | Jeannie Ewing - 1st edition

ISBN-13: 978-1-5136-1461-8
ISBN-10: 1513614614

For all of the brokenhearted, weary, and lonely people who struggle to maintain their faith: may you be strengthened and renewed in hope and healing on your life's journey.

CONTENTS

INTRODUCTION

There are thousands of devotionals on the market today, all serving various religious and spiritual schools of thought. Some are daily devotionals, while others provide more of a study guide with introspective questions and prayers at the end of each topic. With this in mind, I didn't set out to write a devotional. I'm an avid reader of spiritually enriching books, including daily devotionals, but writing one was never on my radar until this book fell into place.

My prayer routine changed significantly at one point, and I saw that God was inspiring me to reflect on particular phrases from Scripture, homilies, or quotes from saints. As I did, a pattern emerged that appeared similar to the format of a devotional reader. Still, this compilation isn't a true devotional, in the sense that it's not specific to a theme or daily readings. Rather, this is a collection of my own musings about particular mysteries or liturgical seasons. In sharing what I've felt and heard from my heart, my hope is that you will glean some insight, consolation, and encouragement in your own journey to Heaven.

This poem by Brother Jacopone da Todi, O.F.M., captures the essence of this devotional:

THE MIRACLE OF THE TRANSFIGURATION

He who witnesses Your splendor
Can never describe it.

On achieving their desired end
Human powers cease to function,
And the soul sees that what it thought was right
Was wrong. A new exchange occurs
At that point where all light disappears;

A new and unsought state is needed:
The soul has what it did not love,
And is stripped of all it possessed, no matter how dear...

The soul, made new again,
Marveling to find itself
In that immensity, drowns.
How this comes about it does not know.

It is within and sees no exit;
It no longer knows how to think of itself
Or to speak of the wondrous change.
It knows only that it finds itself
Clothed in new garments.
Fused with God, it ventures forth
Onto a sea without a shore
And gazes on Beauty without color or hue...

The soul becomes one with God,
Possesses what He possesses. It hears
What it did not hear, sees what it did not know,
Possesses what it did not believe,
Savors that which has no taste...

In losing all, the soul has risen
To the pinnacle of the measureless;
Because it has renounced all
That is not divine,
It now holds in its grasp
The unimaginable Good
In all its abundance,
A loss and a gain impossible to describe.

To lose and to hold tightly,
To love and take delight in,

To gaze upon and contemplate,
To possess utterly,
To float in that immensity
And to rest therein –
That is the work of unceasing exchange
Of charity and truth.

CHAPTER ONE

The Our Father

OUR FATHER

Our Creator, the Alpha and Omega, You commanded for all living things to be, and they came to be. We exist because of Your power, but most of all, because of Your love. You are our Father, because you care for every detail of our lives. Nothing happens without Your perfect or permissive will. When we are in danger, You are in the midst of it and protect our souls from harm.

As a father provides for his family, so You provide for us as Your adopted children. Your protection and provision shelter us from the enemy's snares. You never let us go, stop pursuing us, or give up on us. You are our Father, because You rescue us time and again. You instruct us, admonish us, and pour Your mercy upon us.

You breathed life into our souls – Your life. We live, because You govern all of creation. O Triune God who created us, redeemed us, and sanctified us, remind us that above all, Your love never fails.

WHO ART IN HEAVEN

Lord, I know You are everywhere and that Heaven is not the only place You reside. Perhaps each human soul is a small taste of Heaven, for this is the indwelling of Your Spirit and the home for Your tabernacle. Is my heart a true tabernacle? I wait for you, Lord, in that quiet place within. It is the place where Heaven and Earth meet – in an embrace of love each time I encounter You in the Holy of Holies in my heart.

Yet Heaven is my eternal home and the place for which I

long. Heaven is where no evil can touch me – no disease, no temptation, and no sin. It is my final destination, where You permanently hold a place of perfection and peace. You are in Heaven, because it is the only state that exists in any reality that is entirely unblemished and unstained.

You prepare a place for me. May You find me to be a good and faithful servant to the end of my days on Earth.

HALLOWED BE THY NAME

I hear Your name spoken in vain nearly every day, Lord, and it pierces my heart. When I hear Your name, I want for it to be a loving proclamation or gesture of acknowledging Your sanctity. For if Your name alone is holy, then certainly everything You are and everything You encompass is holy.

What's in a name? An identity, a mission, a personhood. Your name – Father, Son, and Holy Spirit – reveals some aspect of Yourself. When we read "Yahweh" or "Emmanuel," we cannot deny the power of who You are – the eternal, Triune God. Yet so often we utter Your name in fear, as an expletive, or even in casual conversation. The truth is that these are blasphemous ways to speak Your name. Only when we desire to connect with You or share Your love with another person should we say Your name – and with a gentle persuasion that surpasses colloquial triviality.

Your name is the Name above all names. You are Hosanna in the highest. You are the King of kings, Lord of lords, Priest of all priests. You are the Messiah who saved us from sin and eternal death. You are the Paraclete who continues Your mission on Earth through Your Church and in each baptized person. Your Name – spoken or read – reveals Your infinity, Your majesty. You are I AM.

You are God, and I am not.

May Your name be uttered with gratitude, wisdom, awe, and humility. Remind me that Your name alone bears the power to give and the power to take away. Blessed be Your holy name.

THY KINGDOM COME

You never called Yourself a king. You were not born in a palace but in a stable with barn animals. You did not wear a crown of gold but instead were given a crown of thorns. It is true that Your entire humanity was a condescension. How sweet Your humiliation is to me, Lord! Your abasement grants me strength in my afflictions. I know my humiliations – when bestowed upon me for a heavenly purpose – are sweet and delightful to You, as well.

Your kingdom is not of this world, yet You created this world. All material matter reflects Your intelligence and Your love. I cannot help but bask in the beauty of my natural environment, because it is only one of many ways You whisper to my heart: "I created all of this for you." Can love be revealed in such a way? It would seem so. I walk outside and hear Your voice in the songbird. I see Your face in the unfurling flowers. Everything is a reflection of Your kingdom. Truly, there are times when the riches of the Earth in its simplicity fill my heart to capacity. This is Your kingdom.

When we ask for thy kingdom come, we pray with joyful anticipation. We await the promise of the new Heaven and new Earth. We ask for Your kingdom to come both now and in the future. It is a plea, not of desperation, but of earnest hope. We know that You are faithful and will fulfill every promise You have made. We also know that we may not be perfectly happy in this life, but we are guaranteed supreme happiness in the next. This is how Your kingdom comes: in the here and now as we care for our natural environment and appreciate its beauty and bounty, but also in the afterlife, where a never-ending kingdom awaits us.

May I praise and glorify You now and forever. Amen.

THY WILL BE DONE

I pray for Your will in all things, Father, even if it leads to my demise. Sometimes I feel I am in peril, and I attempt to flee from my cross and give into the temptation to pray for my will, which involves certainty and comfort. But Your will challenges me, Father. Your will refines me in the crucible of Your love with every concession I make to You. I accede to You. I defer to You – not always willingly or entirely, but the desire is present in my heart.

I know You possess both a perfect and permissive will. I know You actively will the good for all of humanity and all of creation, but You permit suffering to afflict us all in various forms. You did not will for death to befall us, but You permitted it as a consequence of original sin.

And I know with certitude that what You permit to happen to me is for my ultimate benefit, though it may never be revealed to me in this life. If I yield to Your will with confidence that Your love encases me and all that happens to me, save for sin, will bring me closer to You and to Heaven, then I must pray over and over, *thy will be done*.

Thy will be done – this day and every day – not just to me, but to all people everywhere, to all of the world and works of Your hands. Yes, Lord, Thy will be done. May it be done to me according to Your word.

ON EARTH AS IT IS IN HEAVEN

I imagine Heaven in celestial terms and sublime visions. It is a place of peace and perfection – a utopia. It is where virtue reigns, and those who dwell there are privileged to gaze upon the Heavenly Hosts and bask in Your love for eternity. I pray the love found in Heaven and the Church Triumphant may also exist on Earth. As Your will is in Heaven, may it also be on Earth.

Yet Earth is still restrained by the bonds of the enemy – for a time. It shall not be so forever. One day the reign of Heaven will indeed fill the world – a new Earth – and the enemy's control will end permanently. As the prophet Isaiah envisioned, the lion will rest with the calf and all shall be peace on Your holy mountain.

Peace is where Heaven and Earth converge. It is our goal as Christians to serenely resolve differences and to respect all of life. But the earth is still ravaged with disease and war. Peace does not supersede the mess and chaos that remains from original sin. Yet today and every day, I can choose to be a person of peace and justice. I can somehow be a small segment in the grander scheme of eternity that makes an indelible mark on this world to unite it to Heaven.

Uniting Earth and Heaven is how we, as Christians, bring You to a world that does not know or welcome You – a world entrenched in atheism, postmodern ideas, and other residual heresies and philosophies from the Enlightenment.

The day Heaven and Earth come together in purpose and peace will truly be a day of triumph and glory. I await that day with thanksgiving and joy.

GIVE US THIS DAY

This day I am compelled to remain here in this moment with You, Lord – not to look far into the future or be distracted by the past. Even entertaining thoughts from moments ago robs me of the gift of this moment – *this day*. I ask You to give me this day and nothing more, though also nothing less. In so doing, Your will can be done in and through me. For this day is full of promise and opportunity. This day bears all things new. This day awakens my soul after the night of slumber.

I am refreshed at the dawn. When You give me this day, You hand me *life*. You breathe Your Spirit in me and offer me Your grace. When You hand me this day, I know the gift You bring – no matter what perceived misfortunes or disappointments may occur – is holy and for my sanctification.

Reveal to me *this day* Your plan and purpose for my life,

but only for today, for if I lose sight of this moment, I lose it entirely. Sufficient is a day for its own evil – and good.

OUR DAILY BREAD

What is our daily bread? It is our sustenance, that which fuels and fortifies us for the day's battles and conquests. It is our source, for You are the beginning from which I came to be and the end to which I will return. It is the summit, the apex, the highest feast upon which I will partake. It is the culmination of my life's work. This is *Eucharist*.

It is thanksgiving, perpetual gratitude for this heavenly food, offered to me when my soul is in a state of grace or repentance. It is where I greet You in the recesses of my heart – solitude – yet it is also where I come together as one portion of the Mystical Body of Christ.

Eucharist is *unity*. Our daily bread draws us in communion with all of humanity: those who have lived and died, those currently alive, and those yet to come.

Our daily bread is *boundless*. When we are weary from the journey, You refresh and revitalize us with the nourishment of Yourself, Your very essence.

And what is meant by daily? A day transcends a twenty-four-hour time period, though we certainly exist within the framework of time. And a day is all we need to focus our energies for the tasks You have allotted for our mission.

But days represent our lives, our earthly existence. The cycle of day and night represent birth and dying, respectively. Our daily bread, therefore, is every breath we inhale throughout our entire earthly existence – breathing Your breath, Your Spirit – *life*.

You sustain us under the guise of simple food, poor food, common food. Yet in our daily bread, You give us everlasting life.

AND FORGIVE US OUR TRESPASSES

How many times have I sinned against You, Lord, without a second thought? I have lived free of mortal sin for many years, yet my venial sin I do not reproach. I justify it as mere weakness or "not really that bad." But my venial sins accumulate. Even one small transgression is cause for Your wounds.

And Your wounds I wish to assuage rather than afflict. I long to participate in Your healing rather than scourging. Yet I cannot do this without Your forgiveness and my self-amendment. *Forgive us, Lord, for we know not what we do.* In Your day, sinners were tax collectors, prostitutes, and Pharisees. Today they are pederasts, pornographers, and oppressive politicians.

But am I so set apart from the sinners, simply because I do not participate in the same sins as they do? Am I somehow different – superior – because I attempt piety in my daily life? I do not believe so, because I have met these sinners. I have encountered them in their brokenness, and there I have been flooded with a genuine sense of Your mercy that all of us seek.

Set all of Your people free from sin as the floodgates of Your mercy burst open and You cleanse us with the Living Water, Your Spirit. Forgive us, Father, for we are all sinners alike. No one is inferior or superior to another person based on sin or security. Let Your mercy rise, therefore, and Your redemption promptly overcome our concupiscence.

AS WE FORGIVE THOSE WHO TRESPASS AGAINST US

Lord, how often do I neglect this part of the Our Father in my actions and attitudes? You know me. You've probed me and know my heart. Many times unforgiveness and resentment reside there after having settled in when a grievance was committed against me. I now consider these grievances and those who perpetrated them. It is truthfully my pride that has clutched the lack of forgiveness toward them, for true humility would have me embrace the wounds they afflicted upon me. Humility would welcome them sweetly, knowing that these are opportunities for self-abasement and subsequently for self-amendment.

But pride has somehow ensnared me in its clever trap. I have justified my unforgiveness. I have often wallowed in it, yet still I seek Your mercy and love. How can I – out of justice – be granted forgiveness if I remain unwilling to forgive? First, I must reconcile with my brothers and sisters before placing my offering of sacrifice at Your altar.

Lord, I believe wholeheartedly that You recognize my desire to forgive. Now I pray for the grace of humility that will crumble the walls of unforgiveness around my heart. Teach me to love, even and especially when it hurts or costs me greatly. Teach me to risk all for the sake of gaining all.

AND LEAD US NOT INTO TEMPTATION

Lord, the darkness of my sin engulfs me in shame. I fear I may be swept away by the evil surrounding me. I know the enemy awaits his chance to snatch me from You, and this terrible thought draws me nearer to You, desperately pleading for Your mercy!

I know You permit me to undergo temptations for the sake of strengthening virtue and increasing my love for You. But at times these temptations assail me so fervently that I feel I cannot withstand their fire alone. That is why I appeal to You, Lord, for my weakness will surely devour me. I will fall without Your saving grace.

I know it is the enemy – not You – who leads me into temptation, but You do permit it. Will You let me become trapped and doomed by my foes, or will You rescue and deliver me? I have confidence in Your mercy. Though I may be tried by the fire and tested through many trials, I know my appeal to You will not go unheeded. You will not forsake me in my distress.

O Deliverer, deliver me from the temptations I face today. Walk with me, that I may not face them alone. Then when I cry out to You for help, I know You will swiftly come to my aid.

BUT DELIVER US FROM EVIL

Lord, You called Moses out of the desert to lead Your enslaved people to the Promised Land. How am I enslaved by my sin? I cannot overcome the evil of sin that consumes me. I cannot save myself from myself or from the enemy.

Evil comes in many forms: distractions, diversions, busyness, narcissism, self-righteousness, sanctimoniousness, and impurities of all kinds. Sin, too, can be a spiritual laxity, a lukewarm apathy – a cold heart of stone. Perhaps I am a slave to the master of sloth or money or worldly enticements.

My very flesh traps me, Lord, yet You have delivered me from all evil through the blood sacrifice of Your only Son, and I am cleansed – my flesh and soul made new – in the Sacrament of Baptism. But the battle for my soul does not end – rather it begins – when I am claimed as Your adopted child. So many times I have fallen prey to the enemy's snares. So often do I neglect the discipline necessary that the "Spirit may overcome" my flesh.

In my daily weakness, I turn to You. My sin keeps me coming back to You. I am rendered lost and empty without Your saving grace. My sin, ironically and necessarily, keeps me dependent on You – to be my all, for the sake of all.

AMEN

I conclude my prayer to You with a renewed confidence and earnest fervor. My "Amen" means *I believe* – from the depths of my innermost being. I say *I believe* to all that You ordain in my life – the natural blessings, divine grace and providence, the mysteries, the darkness, and the perceived misfortunes.

I say *I believe*, because I know You are at work in all the circumstances of my life, so I open my arms, outstretched in faith, to invite You to transform my trepidation into authentic faith. Faith – my *amen* – requires me to step away from the committee in my head that attempts to divert me from focusing on Your voice. The *amen* is a bold declaration, not simply punctuation for my prayers.

Each time I say *amen*, I renew my faith and proclaim it unabashedly, imploring that You may increase it evermore.

CHAPTER TWO

Advent & Christmas

DISPELLING THE DARKNESS

"There is no gloom where there had been distress." ~ Isaiah 8: 23

While we linger in cold and dreariness, our hearts await the dawn of light, which breaks forth on the horizon of our souls. Jesus, You are the One we anticipate with earnest and unwavering ardor. You dispel the darkness. Your birth reminds us that we, too, are born in You through Mary.

Birth signifies newness, springtime of victory, and eternal hope. Now we hold still in the pregnant waiting of Advent for Winter's Rose to bear the Son of God and Man. In our pregnancy, our latent longing, we realize that labor pains must precede our own birth in You, Jesus. We cannot dwell within Your heart without our necessary struggle of labor and delivery.

But what brings this agony upon us? It is not merely the dark night of winter, but it is also essentially that jostling with ourselves – our sins, our habits, our possessions, our earthly attachments, our egos, and our relationships. All that is not You or of You must be eradicated, which is why we must labor in our hearts for a time such as this – a time of patient and perseverant waiting that weighs heavily with the overwhelming, but transitory, pain.

Advent, then, is our own spiritual pregnancy. It is a well-defined period of time in which the Son of God and Man grows within the womb of our hearts until one day – Christmas Day – He is born in and through us. Christmas Day symbolizes our ongoing, lifelong conversion, then, in which we invariably display the Christ Child through our burgeoning childlike simplicity and purity of heart. When we, too, revert to innocent babes in a spiritual sense, we will have, at last, been born into eternal life.

GOD IS WAITING FOR US
"God is love. God is waiting for us." ~ Pope Francis[i]

During Advent, we're told that this is a period of inner retreat into the "cells of our hearts," as St. Alphonsus Liguori once stated, so that we purposefully wait in anticipation for the birth of our Savior – in recollection and remembrance, yes, but also as a mystical birth or rebirth in our lives. This creates a holy tension within us, which is the anticipation soaring to an unbearable climax that is only allayed by the gift and grace of the Incarnation.

Do we consider that God is also waiting for *us*? All this time we focus inward, which is a beautiful and necessary discipline, but we are inclined to neglect the reality that God has been waiting for us all along, all of our lives. He is the ever-patient One who quietly, but persistently, pursues us. We falsely believe it is we who exclusively wait for Jesus, when truly He has been waiting for us while we prepare and plan.

Pause to kneel before the Christ Child, at least in your heart. A baby – Himself unable to speak or feed Himself, incapable of much except to gaze upon you in love – *waits for you*. He longs for you to hold and caress Him in your arms, but even more does He long to hold you in His. Stay with the Child Jesus in the solitude of sunset, so that His birth will bear the dawn of love in your heart.

SILENCE OF THE HEART
The wind blows where it will, and often my heart follows suit. Even if I, in my deliberate attempt to seek solitude, root out all

external noise in some makeshift hermitage, my heart is still chattering about with emotions and sentiments. I find that quieting my mind often corresponds with silencing my heart, but both are nearly impossible in this Information Age so full of sounds and stimuli and the promise of instant gratification.

Life was born from and into silence. God Himself operates in the rhythm of order, not chaos. So why is it that my interior realm remains messy and confounded? Be calmed, dear mind; be quiet and cease your distractions. Pause to enter into the peace of this moment, this season of waiting. And, dear heart, resume your cadence of beating the lifeblood into my veins, but no more than that is necessary, because you must prepare a way to welcome the Christ Child in His manger soon. He will rest His little head upon you, beating heart, so allow Him to dwell there, sleeping in you.

THE FLESH AND HINGE OF OUR SALVATION

"The flesh (caro) of Christ – which, as Tertullian says, is the hinge (cardo) of our salvation – was knit together in the womb of Mary." ~ Pope Francis[ii]

Jesus, the little infant Savior, has taken on the flesh of humanity. His flesh is our salvation, but He is also like a hinge on a door – connecting us to the Father. His flesh bridges the gap between Heaven and Earth. What peace! What unity! To believe that Jesus, by His very birth, joined mere matter together – limited creation – to its infinite Creator is, indeed, the blessing of the Incarnation.

Our Lady provided the temporary home of the little Christ-Child. Her womb became a house of preparation, waiting, and silence. It was in her unblemished, sinless body that Jesus first experienced bodily and earthly things. Our Lady's body protected and nurtured Jesus, so that His condescension to humanity would not be as harsh as it would have been without her. She, the Mediatrix, softened the inevitability of

Jesus' humiliation because of her great love for God and for all of us. This is why Jesus became a bridge between Heaven and Earth, because He first experienced it through His mother.

GIVE BIRTH TO WISDOM

We awake to new light as the sun ascends the horizon, and the temptation for us is to make this day like the one before or the one after. Yesterday and tomorrow, although similar to today, are either past or not yet come. We cannot dwell in either place, which is illogical. Today is the place and space, the time in which we dwell, so we must make it such that our presence and attitude also awake with the dawn. Then we will embrace a fresh perspective on everything that has become stale and stagnant.

Wisdom is the infant within our wombs, a faceless child whom we have not yet greeted on this side of Heaven. Yet she grows each passing day with vigor and candor. She lives in us at the core of our existence, though she may feel distant and foreign to us at times. We have not yet birthed wisdom, which is to say that wisdom incarnate has not yet entirely been fulfilled in us.

How, then, can wisdom spring forth from our hearts? We await her arrival with earnest expectation, though the waiting agonizes us. Do not delay, wisdom! She will hasten, but we must wait a little longer to greet and meet her in us. When she exits our womb, and the darkness therein becomes the dawn of today, we will at last rejoice in the One who is Light, and she, the Dawn, who bears the Light in her.

REVEALED TO THE CHILDLIKE

"At that very moment he rejoiced [in] the Holy Spirit and said, 'I give you praise, Father, Lord of heaven and earth, for although you have hidden these things from the wise and the learned you have revealed them to the childlike. Yes, Father, such has been your gracious will.'" ~ Luke 10: 21

For some of us, it is easier to approach Jesus or even relate to Him as an adult rather than as a baby. He spoke in parables, cured and healed, and traversed on foot. But how do we approach our Savior as a child, one who is so small and delicate? God's Incarnation as a human through infancy is a source of profound humility. When we speak to Jesus as a baby, we do not use lofty language but instead the language of the heart.

If we learn to not only love the Christ Child but also to pray to Him as an infant, we are well on our way to discovering a childlike faith, which is untainted, pure of heart, abandoned in total trust of our Heavenly Father, and open to grace. It takes a baby who is incapable of complex reasoning to remind us who we really are and who we are meant to be.[iii]

This Christmas, approach the Child Jesus as a child yourself. Rediscover the wonder that childhood offers, and find Jesus lying in the manger of your heart. His eyes beckon and bid you to merely watch Him, ponder His simple grandeur, and love Him with natural affection and devotion. It is never difficult to love a child with one's entire being. Love Him as a child, and your heart will become childlike again.

EVERY DAY IS CHRISTMAS DAY

Jesus chose to go where no one else wanted to go. ~Fr. Dan Scheidt[iv]

The pomp we express and joy we exude on Christmas Day tends to wane as we enter a new calendar year with hopeful intentions for change but no authentic interior transformation. We then resume our frenetic lives, full of busyness and distractions, and the zeal that grace bore on Christmas somehow becomes muddled or altogether lost in the fray.

But every day can be Christmas if we live by a changed nature. The very purpose of festivities and feasts around this Solemnity is to draw us back to the gratitude of God's immense mercy for having gifted humanity with His Son to redeem us. All is lost, dark, and barren without this promise fulfilled, and that is the cause of our merriment.

What if we lived in a perpetual state of this humbling gratitude? Every time we ponder the First Christmas and acknowledge the humiliation of God becoming man and lying in a feeding trough, we face our own poverty.

At times this poverty saddens us, because we realize what we lack: peace, kindness, charity, etc. We are spiritually impoverished, so we long for the fulfillment of that First Christmas to be born in us, to dwell in slumber in our hearts, and to rise in us after we have first died to ourselves.

After this occurs, a new type of poverty replaces the first – one that is intentional and chosen. This evangelical poverty is a charism we may seek to imitate after the ever-present poverty in which Jesus contentedly lived. We follow the Star when we relinquish our strongholds on our creature comforts and earthly pleasures. Material acquisition is no longer our goal. It is replaced by the practice of simplicity, engaging in matters seemingly small but staggeringly significant.

Letting go of wealth and possessions liberates us, so that we are no longer enslaved by these temporal diversions. Instead, our minds and souls – even our dwelling space – is available to receive the gift of God Himself. We become less inclined to earthly matters and more receptive to responding and encountering God when we live with less.

This deliberate lifestyle then provides a springboard for us to do as Jesus did – to go where no one else wanted to go, to be among the smelly, sinful, decrepit, and marginalized people. When we live like them, we understand them with greater empathy, so we then realize we are already just like them. When all the lavish and ostentatious excess is shed, the transparency of one's heart is exposed. This kind of poverty is necessary for every heart to receive Jesus in totality. Love requires openness, not mere fondness. Love requires all.

So this is how Christmas Day is not only possible but preferable to the otherwise mundane way we go about our lives. Christmas Day is born anew in us every morning as we greet the Dawn, the Morning Star, the Light, the Way. We remove the existential and exterior obstacles to Him, and then He rises in us again and again. This is how Christmas Day can be expressed in us every day of our lives.

LIVING YOUR ANOINTING

As Christians, our baptism unites us with the mission of Jesus as Priest, Prophet, and King. He is anointed – the Anointed One – and we, too, receive the chrism of anointing when we are baptized. How do we live this anointing?

Our lives somehow must halt as we face the answer to this question. It may reappear during particularly confounding or laborious times in our lives. But the question remains, as does the answer, at the ready: "Come, Lord Jesus."

He has anointed us for some specific call, which is fulfilled in both the magnanimous and menial. Living our anointing is synonymous to the call of Peter and Matthew, and we must leave everything worldly behind – at least for a time – in order to realize and fulfill our particular anointing.

Go today, then, dear brethren. Cast off the distractions and diversions of this chaotic culture, and sit for a while in solitude with the Anointed One, the Priest of all priests, King of kings, and Lord of lords. Sit at His feet with this Advent expectation, eager to respond when He replies with a whisper or a brick. Do not be dismayed if you do not realize your anointing immediately, but do not delay, either, when the time has arrived for you to rise up and enter your element.

The time has now come for the message of Emmanuel, God-with-us. God is in our midst and indeed within us. Let us live, then, as incarnations of the Incarnate One, as people of light who give way to the Light of the World.

THE GIFT OF BAPTISM

"Jesus immersed Himself in our human condition [when He was baptized]. Baptism is our Christmas gift." ~ Fr. Dan Scheidt[v]

Do we view Baptism as a gift, as more than a mere ritual or Rite of Initiation? On this last day of the Christmas season, we are given the chance to ponder the immense value – the *gift* – of our Baptism. Certainly Jesus began His earthly existence as a condescension and contradiction. But His Baptism somehow finalized His decision to not only be born in humiliation, but also to begin His public ministry this way, as well.

Jesus was not merely leading us to be baptized, but He was telling us more – how much He loves us, so much that He was willing to be submerged in water – an earthly element, but symbolizing heavenly realities – so that His immersion in our life might indicate the kind of total self-giving we should make for His sake.

Our baptism calls us to this total and free act of love as we are bathed in the water and anointed with oil. We declare ourselves (or our parents do) to do all for Jesus, to die of human desire and be born into the resurrected life of Christ. Our baptism is evidence that we are willing to go where Jesus goes, and to undergo a life of submission to His will, to be immersed in His grace but also in His humiliation. When we live this way, we emerge from the water as people anointed by the Father and blessed by His Spirit: "This is my son/daughter, with whom I am well pleased."

Our Christmas gift is to live the call of our baptism so that our life, our love, is a gift to Him.

THE CHRISTMAS SPIRIT

If we truly wish to emulate the Christmas spirit all year round, we must imitate - but first ponder – the disposition of every figure present at that first Christmas, starting with Our Lady. Unpretentious and meek, she accepted and embraced the impossible as the "Theotokos," or God-bearer, because she knew her littleness and God's vastness. Like her, we must accept the good and bad alike, knowing God's love never fails us. Every difficulty is an opportunity for spiritual growth.

Let us next consider St. Joseph, a poor craftsman, really a "nobody" betrothed to this glorious woman who was immaculately conceived. He is the most humble of all men. He never spoke in Scripture, so he is very much a hidden figure. Perhaps we, too, should be content when we are invisible and when our acts of charity are not acknowledged or even perceived by others. Like St. Joseph, our greatness is not in grandiosity or extravagance but instead in obedience and submission.

The shepherds were poor and inferior herders, often living reclusively or even ostracized into exile. They had nothing in their possession to claim as their own, except a grand hope. Their gift to us is contemplation. In their solitude, they saw and heard the angel, St. Gabriel, who proclaimed the good tidings of great joy. Had they been distractible or harried businessmen, they likely would have missed the greatest message of all history. Are we privy to the murmurings of God's messengers? Do we wait quietly for the herald who announces what is to come? Like the shepherds, we watch by night and wait for the wonder revealed by Heaven's angels.

We may not believe we can learn from Herod, but it was his pride that led him to sin. He knew well the prophecy of the Messiah and even believed it to the point of being threatened. So Herod's faith in the prophecy sadly was overshadowed by wickedness. We must examine ourselves for our particular sins and ask the Baby Jesus to mercifully pardon us, drawing us nearer to Him.

The Magi – three sages, three representations of the Triune God – traveled through uncertainty, desert storms, threats, and setbacks. Though the star was their guide in the sky, it was truly their faith that led them to the tiny stable at Bethlehem.

The Magi remind us of our own share in Jesus' mission by virtue of our baptism. As priests, prophets, and kings, we participate in the ongoing work of the Church.

The Christmas star was the beacon that illuminated the Christ Child's birth. Do we seek the light in this dark and perverse world? Where is the Christmas Star that shines in and through our souls? We know the Light of the World has entered space and time in human flesh. Truly He has overcome the darkness. The star is our hope, and the Light is our joy.

And no words can exhaust the immenseness of the Incarnate Word, for He who condescended Himself for love of us was born of a woman in the crudest of places. His palace was a stable, and his throne, a manger. We desire glory and honor, laud and accolades in this life, which is derived from the esteem of people. The infant Jesus, unable to yet speak to us, who can neither walk nor defend Himself, has indeed spoken by His very birth. We remember the tenderness of God when we approach the Child Jesus, the love that can only be reflected through the soft gaze of an infant.

As He sleeps, we remember the value of resting in His bosom. We pause in the stillness of night, holding in this moment the power of silence and solitude. We can and must approach Him in silence, since He came to us in such a way. Out of chaos, God made order, and His design was so beautifully – though only partially – revealed on that first Christmas night.

Let Him sleep in you, dear brethren, as you rest in Him. His slumber will awaken in you the Christmas virtues to be lived each day, all year.

FOLLOW THE STAR

"When the king of heaven was born, the heavens knew that he was God, because they immediately sent forth a star..."

~ *St. Gregory the Great*

What a journey for the Magi! Truly it was a pilgrimage, because they embarked on an unknown path in pursuit of a prophecy fulfilled. What incredible faith! If only we could do as the Magi did, leaving everything behind, holding nothing back from God. Though they brought treasures of gold, frankincense, and myrrh, the real treasure was what they gave to baby Jesus upon their arrival to Bethlehem: their hearts.

Perhaps it was instant conversion, perhaps gradual, but the Magi put no barriers between themselves and their Savior. Socioeconomic status made no difference to these kings, because their wisdom – the wisdom from following the star – recognized Jesus' kingship beyond His poverty.

Like the Magi, we are called to follow the Christmas star, to begin a journey of faith that involves sacrifice of worldly comforts, self-offering of who we are and of the treasures God has given us. We are called to give God everything, and nothing less than that.

Following the star requires us to look beyond what is visible and to acknowledge the miracle of light in what appears to be an ordinary or coincidental arrangement of stars. The star points the way to the hope we have in the true Light – a beacon shining in the darkness and hope for all humankind. When we follow the star, we're essentially following Jesus Himself, and when we arrive at His dwelling place, we leave behind our narcissism and selfishness, instead embracing His meekness and poverty.

Follow the star, and you will find yourself reflected in the eyes of the newborn Jesus.

THE FIRST BUDS OF MARTYRDOM

All children are close in spirit to God, whether or not they have been baptized. This is because they are not far removed from their Source; that is, they have not spent so many years on Earth outside of the womb, as adults have. Their hearts and minds easily absorb all things spoken of eternity, so they heartily and readily believe in and turn to God.

They are the Holy Innocents.

All children remind the rest of us what matters most – an open and eager heart that is both receptive to and an agent of love, a life that thrives on simple joys and experiences, and a mind that is drawn to the wonder of creation. Their pure, untainted lens of life is often starkly contrasted with our jaded, cynical one. But children reflect God to us in many ways spoken and unuttered. They herald His presence and birth through their giggles and delights.

But children also model sin, as evidenced by their tempers, disobedience, and tendency toward sensory pleasures or comforts. They can be impatient and, at times, unpleasant, but this is because of their need for instruction and guidance.

The dichotomy between sin and holiness is nowhere more prevalent than in a small child (even though they aren't accountable for sin before the age of reason). Because of this, we know that they are both born into a sinful nature and also cherished by God. When Herod commanded the boys under age two to be slaughtered because of his own fear of a Divine King, we can assume that the Christ Child delivered these children immediately to Heaven.

As the first martyrs, we can pause to consider the irony: Jesus, whose blood was destined to be shed for expiation of our sins and for our redemption, had not yet shed any blood at all. His purity of infancy was palpable to all who encountered Him. Yet the other children, conceived in sin, shed their blood, despite their innocence.

The martyrdom of children is horrific but possibly contributes to God's salvific plan. Is it possible that all aborted babies today are truly martyrs who enter Heaven as saints to pray for us? It is possible and quite likely. Notwithstanding specific theology, all holy innocents are God's beloved, and He desires that they join the Heavenly Hosts, even without baptism.

The red martyrdom of pure, guileless babies points the way for our white martyrdom – a dying to self and all temporal attachments. They are, indeed, the buds of martyrdom that blossom in our hearts so that one day we may join them in Heaven.

CHAPTER THREE

Lent & Easter

YOU ARE MY STRONGHOLD

"For you are my fortress, my refuge in time of trouble." ~Psalm 59: 17

My body grows weaker with an unknown affliction. It seizes me from time to time and renders me incapable of any physical strength. At times it's as if my entire being has been swallowed by a ravaging disease, but no one has identified it, so I suffer in silence – a burden known only to You and me.

But You are my stronghold, because from You I draw my strength for the day. I cling to You, grasp for You, searching always for that firm grip so that I may find my sustenance in You. Once I do, I experience a liberating release, for You are my refuge, fortress, and home. In You, I've discovered my resting place – both here on Earth and my eternal resting place in Heaven. You safeguard me from the enemy of my soul, and at last, I can be at peace, dwelling with and in You always.

Help me never to loosen my grip from You, lest I stumble and crumble into a heap of defeat. Lord, You know my bodily weakness, as well as my emotional and spiritual weakness. I am nothing without You. I wither and fade into dust. I perish. I am empty, fruitless, and devoid of vitality.

With Your strength, I can accomplish all, despite any challenging circumstances. For Your Spirit overcomes my flesh always. Have You made me infirm so that You alone may be visible to others through my life? Is it that Your greatness might be attributed to some wondrous act on my part, were it not for my obvious weak character and afflicted body?

It must be so that I become nothing in order that You alone are glorified in and through and for me. This is why I cling to You, my stronghold and safety, because from my malady You heal, and from my sin you deliver, and from my nothingness You create a glorious masterpiece.

THE CHARITY OF THE CROSS

To look at the Crucifixion pragmatically, one would necessarily conclude that it was cruel, confusing, and evil. On a base level, this is all very true, because the Son of God and Man should never have subjected Himself to such unthinkable punitive torment – that is, unless He Himself was Love Incarnate. Love alone overcame sin and death by dying and rising again.

In that case, the Cross has become a symbol of the utmost charity, but it is more than a mere token of what historically took place two thousand years ago. The Cross is where we find ourselves and thrust our ills and spiritual maladies, as well as all our sin, so that He who is Love may heal us interiorly by His ultimate sacrifice.

And when I encounter the crucified Christ, whose charity chose the Cross, I am forever changed. Then I, too, am commissioned to walk the path of Calvary and carry my own crude piece of wood. I choose this. I choose the cross, not because I am drawn to masochism or a martyr's crown, not out of presumption or false humility, but out of love for Him who first showed me Love.

And love for its own sake is what saves.

A WATCH IN THE NIGHT

"A thousand years in your eyes are merely a day gone by, before a watch passes in the night, you wash them away; they sleep, and in the morning they sprout again like an herb." ~Psalm 90: 4 – 5

My life is so fleeting, yet I do not always remain vigilant to the sneaky snares of temptation. In my bone-weariness, I am often inclined to tune out the intensities of spiritual living. But like a breath – like a watch in the night – everything could vanish or be extinguished.

A watchman keeps vigil, waiting throughout the night for both friend and foe. He sits quietly, patiently, and acutely aware of the stealthy acts of the enemy who is waiting to devour him. But the watchman also acts as guard and gatekeeper. He defends the fortress of his body, mind, heart, and soul. He also protects others whom he observes may fall into the pit of fire before his very eyes.

Be on guard.

Stay vigilant.

Remain faithful.

Persevere with patience.

These are all words of encouragement to us, the Church Militant, who grow battle-weary from time to time. Jesus refreshes us with His promise and presence. He never leads us astray nor forsakes us as orphans. We are His adopted brothers and sisters, sons and daughters of the Father. Even in the thick black of night, we keep our posts as faithful watchmen, because we know we are prone to sin, yet we also watch for the One who is to come again.

THE FOOTWASHING

My feet are dry and weary from the journey, Master. My feet carry the burden of my body, but they also bear witness to the pilgrim way of life – my traversing to bear witness to Your love. My feet have grown accustomed to the rhythm of walking. Why must they now remain still as You tenderly wash them?

This act of love not only cleanses my feet, but it also washes my soul clean. You knew the death You were about to endure. You know, also, that my weary feet require revitalization to take me where I do not want to go. So, then, I welcome this act of humiliation on Your part with passive resignation and humility on my part. For I know the journey is long and has only just begun.

WHY JUDAS WAS NECESSARY

Why would a man like Judas – who eventually became possessed by the devil before betraying Jesus in the Garden of Gethsemane – be selected by Jesus as one of the original twelve apostles? We are well aware of the contrast between Judas and Peter – both betrayed Him, yet Judas despaired and Peter repented. So why was Judas necessary as one of the apostles? Why wasn't he more of a peripheral figure who appeared suddenly for the sole purpose of handing Jesus over to His betrayers?

Judas personifies our concupiscence. He represents our potential to despair. He reminds us that we are all Judases – all called by God to follow Him, to abandon our evil ways and repent of our sinfulness, yet ever-lured by worldly fanfare. Judas the betrayer is easily John or Jane the betrayer. I am Judas each time I turn my back on God's beckoning. I have the potential to fall into mortal sin and eternal death.

Judas forces us to look at the reality of the human condition – the call, the awakening to new life, the temptation, the wrestling, the succumbing to sin, and the possibility of our souls being lost eternally. Judas signifies the rise and fall of humanity – the back-and-forth we often experience between truth and falsehood, good and evil, darkness and light.

Through Judas's decision to betray and despair, we are humbled by the acknowledgment that we have the capacity to fall into perdition. We are capable of permanently losing our souls to the fires of Hell. Judas jolts us away from our Pharisaical delusion that we would never fall from grace and certainly never despair if we did. But the tragedy of Judas' end lingers in our hearts today as the gravity of the Triduum approaches. He reminds us of the lost souls of our day, the suffering souls in Purgatory, and sadly, those who have chosen eternal damnation.

His choice reverberates today as a warning to us – "be vigilant," "keep watch" – for the enemy seeks to devour us. He never sleeps and always waits for his opportunity to invade our psyche, emotions, and ultimately our souls. Let us not fall prey to the enemy and his guile. Instead, we cling evermore to Jesus, offering Him our sins, offering Him the evil that pervades our lives and society. We cleave to Jesus, knowing He is our only hope for salvation.

DEVOUR AND SAVOR

"Do not work for food that perishes, but for the food that endures for eternal life." ~John 6:27

What is "true food," Lord? It is the everlasting manna I receive in the hidden host of the Eucharist that fortifies me. It is also the food of Your will, to be devoured and savored. When I consider the act of devouring, it seems entirely contrary to savoring. Devouring appeals to an animalistic sense, a barbaric consumption that is both mindless and grotesque. Could it be that You do, in fact, desire for us to devour Your flesh, Your word, and Your will? Perhaps this is so that we may more easily grasp the true hunger You wish for us to exhibit as we approach Your holy altar.

If we are empty, not just in body but also in spirit, then we pine for You. Nothing else will satiate us, except the food of Your flesh and Your will. When we approach You with this inimitable hunger, we necessarily devour all that You offer, which is all we have been lacking our entire lives – fulfillment, wholeness, and holiness.

Devouring implies an extreme act of our will to consume You so that You, in turn, consume us. You want nothing less than our all, offered and presented to You with a ravenous zeal. Then savoring follows devouring, because it is the act of processing this food, which we have consumed all too eagerly and hastily. In savoring, we pause and contemplate the gift of Your food and to thus offer our gratitude and praise to You for this supernatural sustenance.

Savoring is an act of contemplation itself. It is the discipline that must be subsequent to the devouring. Only when we first devour and then savor the food You give us are we able to become this food, and therefore, go into the world to offer it to others who are starving for salvation.

You are the bread of life; whoever comes to You will never hunger and whoever believes in You will never thirst (paraphrased from John 6:35).

AN EMPTY CUP

God requires that we present to Him an empty cup. We may falsely conclude that emptiness signifies the finality of death, as the water has finally run dry in us. Have we taken the last sip from our cup, or have we offered the Living Water to our parched brothers and sisters?

Only when our cup is empty can we wholeheartedly and authentically hand it to God. Only then are we finally free of self, of the world's enticements, of sin. Only then have we truly become poor in spirit.

When we have nothing to offer God except our poverty, He fills our cup up with Himself. God then hands our pauper's cup back. But it has become a chalice, overflowing and never running dry, for it is filled with God Himself. God has filled our chalice with the gift of His sacrifice – His blood shed for our sins.

We are asked to drink from this chalice, to actively participate in His Passion. We are each presented with our own journey to Calvary. Our prayer, too, then becomes, "Father, if it is possible, let this cup pass from me; yet not as I will, but as You will."

We pray with Christ after our subsequent acceptance of this chalice, for our lives and future no longer belong to us. They are, at last, in God's hands, for He holds our chalice – full of Himself, empty of our self – in the night of life when death approaches.

PASSING AWAY

"He escaped from their power." ~ *John 10: 39b*

How mysterious that, as His Passion nears, Jesus slips away quietly from the crowd's wrath. Many times He encounters the precipice of death, yet He passes through without notice. The mob, in their fury, are roused by unjust anger, confusion, and division, and in this chaotic spirit of the enemy, they do not notice that Jesus subtly vanishes.

Jesus knew when it was time to capitulate to human power, and His time had not yet arrived. Though many rose against Him and sought His death, it was not quite time, and Jesus was acutely aware of this. God's timing is everything.

We, however, miss the message of God's timing. We may use the phrase, "All in God's time" as a cliché more than a declaration of faith, but truly, God's timing is the perfect revelation and fulfillment of His promise.

We who exist within the confines of time do not fully value this truth. Jesus could have allowed Himself to be stoned, but His hour had not yet come for death. The precise moment of surrendering Himself to His captors was orchestrated ahead of what we know as time. God, Who is not limited by the constraints of time, chose to enter it and continues to enter it for our sakes.

Timing reveals God's power, presence, and perfection. We know God provides for the details of our lives, because He knows the outcome of every circumstance or misfortune we encounter. His timing is a revelation of His love.

WEAKNESS AND STRENGTH

"Watch and pray that you may not undergo the test. The spirit is willing, but the flesh is weak." ~ Matthew 26: 41

As I desire to grow closer to God, it seems as if everything else is against me – the world and society, of course the devil, and now especially my flesh. So often my body cries out for its previously comfortable state, as if I could resume a life of pleasure again. It's not that following God more fervently is devoid of pleasure, but fleshly pleasure is replaced by supernatural and sublime delights – the joys of the Spirit.

As the days progress toward Good Friday, my spirit rejoices in instant zeal, but my flesh dreads what is to come – more penance, sacrifice, and self-denial. Will I possess the strength to pass the test? All of God's tests have instilled a stronger will for my soul, rather than my body, to survive. Thus, I have longed for virtue to be perfected in me, and this exposes my lack. God enters my lack with Himself, thus replacing my weakness with His strength.

The joy of the Lord is my strength, as Nehemiah so aptly reminds me today (chapter 8, verse 10).

PETRA AND SKANDALON

"Petra and Skandalon – the rock of God and a stumbling block." ~ Pope Benedict XVI[vi]

In a sense, we all have two faces, like St. Peter – holy *and* sinful, seeking God *and* turning away from Him, a heavenly agent *and* one who causes others to fall. We are all Petra and Skandalon, the "rock of God and a stumbling block," a piece of stone that can be used to build or destroy. Rocks, though callous and tough, can be used to shelter or to kill. We, too, are such instruments, and we consciously choose to be God's rock (used for good) or the enemy's tool (used for evil).

How often do we deny Christ? Daily. We do this when we

neglect to defend Him as we overhear or participate in offensive or scandalous speech against religion. When we block out His voice with our devices that feed us world news and blaring music, we deny Him. And we deny Jesus when we choose ourselves over His love.

But St. Peter gives us hope, because his faith, though shaken and tattered, was renewed and eventually glorified. He chose love. He chose to believe that, despite His sin, Jesus would allow him – *welcome* him – back into the fold. We can hope, as Easter approaches, that God's mercy will eclipse our sin as it did Peter's on that first Good Friday.

SIMON THE CYRENIAN

Imagine being thrust into a realm of chaos and suffering while you happened to be sojourning for ordinary, daily things. What do you do as the Roman soldiers hand you a wooden cross? Your inclination is to panic and run away, but before you assess the scene, your fear of the consequences forces you to accept this crude piece of wood.

In the midst of jeering and constant mocking, your eyes meet Jesus' gaze, and you realize that you were chosen for this task – to ease, if only temporarily, the burden of the Cross that carried the weight of the world's sins on it. For a time, you walk side-by-side with Jesus in silence, contemplating the sudden madness into which you were hurled. Unassuming and unpretentious as a bystander, you all at once became a permanent and crucial person in this story.

You realize that this story and scene reach far beyond the scope of your comprehension, so you are instantly humbled as you wonder, "Why me? Why was I chosen for this ghastly, unwanted chore?" But as Jesus offers a weary smile to you in gratitude for your help, your heart softens, and you become grateful for the opportunity to help alleviate His pain.

To some degree, we all have been in Simon of Cyrene's shoes. We have perhaps been chosen to lift or carry someone else's burden, or we may be asked to participate in the sufferings of Christ through our personal trials and hardships. Whatever the case, Simon's acceptance of the Cross may have been initially reluctant – as ours is – but his faithfulness and love was the strength that allowed him to bear its weight. And he found that strength in Jesus' weakness. He found himself on the road to Calvary.

O HAPPY FAULT

"O happy fault…O truly necessary sin of Adam." ~ Exsultet

People often casually comment on why sin was brought into the world, or rather, what would have occurred had Adam and Eve never sinned at all. Naturally, Jesus would never have been necessary if all of humanity remained truly guileless.

At times I have lamented over original sin. I have (regrettably) wished it never took place, so that I (along with every human of every era) would never again fight so insistently and persistently against my own concupiscence. In an idyllic world, we all would dwell untainted, unblemished, and sin-free.

But I consider the Easter Proclamation, "O happy fault." Why is the sin of Adam and Eve a *happy* fault? Why was it the *necessary* sin? Because Jesus is greater than our sin. He is the greater gift. From the evil in the Garden of Eden, an eternal plan of redemption was born by the Father in Heaven. How can it be possible that we so easily overlook this obvious mercy? The very act of love to swiftly save all of humanity through the blood sacrifice of God's only Son was not necessary due to justice.

Yet Mercy was compelled to find a much grander way around evil, suffering, and sin. Mercy swells at the sight of our plight. With every intense temptation or horrific act of evil (or even seemingly cruel acts of nature, as is the case with my daughter's condition), Love engulfs us into its womb, where we wait in darkness. We are refined in the womb of Love as we await our birth in Christ: a new life, a new chance at eternal indwelling with Love Incarnate.

The question should not so much be, "Why did Adam and Eve sin so as to ruin it for the rest of us?" or "Why would an all-loving God permit incomprehensible suffering?" Rather, our hearts should rise to the truth that *Mercy is alive*! The love and mercy of our Creator did not abandon us in our shame. He did not permit us to all perish eternally with no chance of spiritual liberation!

The God of mercy rescued us by sending us a Savior. And this Savior was no random selection, but was the Word-Made-Flesh, the Incarnation of Love. How could we wish away the sin of Adam and Eve when Jesus is the greater outcome?

Eastertide leaves us not with lingering agony, but with a promise fulfilled and an indelible punctuation of hope on our misery. *Love has conquered all!* This is our song that supersedes our sorrows. This is the song of Easter.

THE GIFT OF HOLY SATURDAY

"Waiting is an experience of redemption." ~ Fr. Gary Caster

Where is the Light in this dark abyss? All seems lost in this cocoon of death, mere shadows of what has come to pass. I cannot see – with my eyes or the inner vision of my heart. Have You truly extinguished everything I came to hope? Where, O Light, have You gone?

In this tomb, I wait with earnest expectation, though I am sorely tempted to despair in haste. Could it be that Truth lies in not what is beholden by vision, but rather nestled somewhere in the womb of my soul – safely encased and sheltered in hope – that what lies latent there may, indeed, be born through You, O Light, and in me?

The darkness permeates my being as I lie still, waiting for Your manifestation, Your rebirth. Where, O Light, is the promise for which I have longed? Shall I neglect to let it slip through my frail grasp? In this darkness and waiting, I find that You meet me in the unknown, uncertainties, and mysteries of my indwelling with You. Your glory I await, for though the stillness of night overshadows my reality for a flicker of time, the flame of Your light has never fully been extinguished.

For a time, I dwell with You in the stillness, the silence of the tomb, the nothingness, and the waiting. For the magnitude of Your glory will be more brilliantly revealed at the perfect moment. In this day, I learn to respond to Your gentle withdrawal of Light. I learn to wait with You and for You at the appointed time, for all will be fulfilled according to Your word. I know You meet me in this holy tension.

I await Your divine illumination.

WHY DO YOU WEEP?

"Woman, why are you weeping? Whom are you looking for?" ~ *John 20: 15*

I weep for all that is lost and gone forever. I weep from the inexhaustible, unquenchable pain that is imprisoned inside me. I weep for being separated from You on this side of Heaven. Though I consume Your flesh and receive Your Spirit, it is not enough to cease the longing to finally – at last, forever – be united with You, never to part and never cease praising You in Heaven.

You ask me why I weep, because sorrow and death do not have the final say. Yours is a Resurrection love, and You have called me to be a Resurrection person. "Rise, my beloved, my beautiful one, and come. For see, the winter is past, the rains are over and gone. The flowers appear on the earth" (Song of Songs 2: 10-12).

Yes, indeed, I must arise from this place of perpetual mourning. I cannot stay here. I do not belong to the enemy or the world. My home, my haven, my refuge is in You and You alone. There is hope in life after death. There is always Resurrection hope when something or someone passes away. It is hope that fills the void of loss always.

Today I am a new creation, or rather, I live as the new creation I've been since my baptism and confirmation. No more weeping in vain. No longer will I be stagnant in suffering, for that is the enemy's attempt at deceiving and luring me into despondency. Today, despite my continual setbacks, I choose hope. I choose new life and Resurrection glory.

I HAVE SEEN THE LORD

"I have seen the Lord." ~ *John 20:18*

Most people today request outward signs as proof of God's existence, yet Jesus said, "Blessed is he who has not seen and yet believes." Is it safe to assume that we truly have seen the Lord – not with our fleshly eyes, but rather with the eyes of the soul? In this regard, we can boldly and accurately proclaim, "I have seen the Lord" as accurately as Mary Magdalene claimed when she first saw Jesus in His glorified body.

To see God is to know Him most intimately, to dwell within His mystery and drown ourselves in the abyss of His mercy, as St. Faustina described. To *see* God is to *seek* God, the One whom our hearts love. It is to look beyond the world with our limited lenses and instead look within ourselves and within the hearts of others.

We see God in every tabernacle but also in every human face. All of humanity and, indeed, all of creation, perfectly reflects God's glory and beauty. Each tells a story about God and reveals a different aspect of His personhood.

We have truly seen the Lord, and for this we must rejoice!

SECRET RESURRECTIONS

"In every life there are many secret resurrections." ~ Caryll Houselander[vii]

Just as I am secretly scourged by Your wound of love, and just as every day necessitates dying to self and other deaths, so, too, does my life entail the secret resurrections. These are the hidden hopes that reemerge unexpectedly. Sometimes my secret resurrections arrive in the form of spiritual healing, so subtle that I cannot pinpoint the moment it occurred. Yet I notice something different about myself, something new and renewed.

The secret resurrections are gifts of Your providence and grace. They are in the joys of daily living, the simple moments of capturing a sunrise or pausing to watch a butterfly dance on a nearby daisy. These are healing moments, movements of Your Spirit to my heart. They are transient, yet they heal the chronic pain from the wound of grief.

Like the fluttering butterfly, I am transformed by these secret resurrections. They change the substance of my pain from despondency and discouragement to love – authentic, redemptive love that is united to Your Most Sacred Heart.

I can and will embrace the hidden scourges and deaths of everyday life, because I also know the secret resurrections will assuredly come.

LIVING STONES

"Come to him, a living stone, rejected by human beings but chosen and precious in the sight of God, and, like living stones, let yourselves be built into a spiritual house to be a holy priesthood to offer spiritual sacrifices acceptable to God through Jesus Christ." ~ 1 Peter 2:4-5

My heart is the stony heart of which You spoke, Lord, but I desire that it be made into a feeling, living entity – a heart of flesh. Could this be what it means to be "living stones?" You alone have enlivened everything, and every part of Your creation has risen from the grave and been made new. Yes, even stones, which have no life, are motionless, and do not engage or encounter, are made into vital and vibrant active forces that transform the world.

It is because You are the first Living Stone, the Stone rejected by the builders, the cornerstone. Because You live, so do I. I have also become a living stone, for You set my heart ablaze and move me by Your Spirit of life.

May the stony indifference so prevalent in our day become the fleshly love, the indwelling of Your Spirit. For nothing is impossible for you, Jesus, not even giving life to a stone that has no movement on its own. We once were mere rocks, dry and motionless, without purpose, but You have made us into living stones, so that we may reflect Your glory by our changed lives in You.

PEOPLE OF THE LIGHT

"What you decide shall succeed for you, and upon your ways light shall shine." ~Job 22:28

My father used to say, "Nothing good happens after midnight" when I was in high school, seeking a late curfew to be with my friends. At the time, I didn't take heed to his wisdom, but naturally everything is clearer in retrospect. Choosing to stay up late, it was clear to me that darker acts were committed as night fell. I witnessed many sins in my youth – for the sake of curiosity, stubbornness, and desperation to find a social circle of my peers.

The Lord, in His interminable mercy, protected me and even my very life from harm. Somehow I was enveloped by grace, even though I had easily tempted fate by plunging myself into the near occasion of sin.

During Eastertide, I consider what it means to be a

Resurrection people, a people of light. It seems God has offered many spiritual lessons using the metaphor of light and darkness, but also by the natural cycles of day and night. Our bodies are wired to follow these rhythms. We are made to follow the light, to live and work in the day. We are most accomplished and efficacious when we follow the natural, innate patterns of day and night – work during the day, sleep at night.

Even more, we are drawn to light. Fires somehow lure us with their mesmerizing glow, and we are enraptured by the cadence of each flame's flicker. We were not designed to be witnesses of God's love in the shadows of evil, but instead we were designed to seek and follow truth, which resides in the light.

Truthfully, Jesus is the Light, for He is the Son who calls us to the Father. And He is the Sun who lights our way, so He is also Truth. If we seek the Son, we seek Light Incarnate. We are immersed in the heat, the warmth, the illumination that the Light provides us as sustenance for our life's odyssey. Even when our feet tread in darkness, amid trouble and tragedy, the Light is present to us, illuminating our path.

All works are more clearly visible in the light, for nothing is hidden from He who is Light. We may more easily conceal our sins under the cloak of darkness, but everything eventually is brought to the light of day.

Every dawn reminds us of this truth: that we are called to be a Resurrection people, to be children of light. In such a dismal world and during such dreary social and economic climates, we carry hope in our hearts that radiate the rays of the Son. We are given the flame of Truth through the Holy Spirit, and as a people of dawn and day, we share the light of love to a broken, hurting, weary world that has succumbed to the enticements of night.

As people of day, our hearts awaken and enliven with each fresh dawn – the newness and reminder that night never prevails. "We may weep for a time, but joy comes in the morning" (see Psalm 30:5).

SEEK THE LORD

During the Octave of Easter, we focus on pursuing the risen Christ in our lives. For forty days we've journeyed with the crucified Christ, and now it is a time of celebration and rejoicing. As Scripture says, "There may be weeping at night, but joy comes with the dawn." For us, the night is all-consuming darkness, manifested in sin, weakness, death, grief, and corruption. The night surrounds us, and at times we live as people of darkness.

But the dawn reveals our true longing – that night is overcome by light and that light dissipates our shadows as it approaches the horizon of our fears and expectations. Once the light engulfs the darkness completely, we live as children of day, because we see ourselves more honestly, but in the light of God.

Jesus permeates our entire being when we wholeheartedly look for Him. But we must remember to search in the most unlikely of places – in the shadows, the darkness, through our frailties and flaws. The point of Jesus' wounds and afflictions was to show us that scars can be poignant reminders of what once was and is no longer. He bore our wounds for the sake of love, and so must we bear our share of hardships.

To seek Jesus every day, then, is to be willing to bear His sacred scars in our own lives, to go where no one else dares to go, and to bring the hope of healing in the Resurrection to those unlikely places and people, including the crevices of sin we'd rather ignore within ourselves.

If He is truly risen, then we, too, must rise above the shadows of night. We must run to the Dawn and meet Him there, eager to be consumed by His light.

PENTECOST

"Come, Holy Spirit, fill the hearts of your faithful and enkindle in them the fire of your love." ~*Traditional Prayer*

O Spirit of Life, so often You do not manifest Yourself as a splendid spectacle but rather in breath – soft, warm, and rhythmic. You breathed all things into existence, and You set my heart into motion for love of You.

O Spirit of Fire, now set my heart ablaze. May the fire within me quicken so as to reach the masses of people whose fires turned to embers and cinders, and then all that remains are cold ashes. Rise up from the ashes and renew us in the fire of divine charity.

O Spirit of Water, baptize me with ardor and fervor. Grant me newness of life when my bones become parched. There are times I feel lifeless and useless. Then refresh me with the Living Water that cleanses, purifies, and nourishes.

O Spirit of Wind, like Your quiet yet powerful breath, You speak to me in the whispers of the wind. Teach me to discern Your voice among the many fallacies that blow where they will in the breeze.

O Spirit of Justice, break forth like the dawn, that You may reclaim victory for souls through my life – which I pray is a life lived in patient perseverance and silent witness. May I walk in justice and my steps never falter in fear.

O Spirit of Truth, Your word is truth. All that brings me to sanctification in truth reflected in the myriad ways You select for me. May I know, live, follow, and spread truth in a world filled with apathy.

CHAPTER FOUR

Mary & The Angels

ANGEL OF GOD

My sweet angel, you have rescued me from foolish decisions, petulant folly, and even recklessness. All my life I owe to your protection, which, at times I have noted with gratitude and other times I have neglected to acknowledge.

But your presence, whether felt or not, remains with me. You walk where I trod. You rest with me, watching over me in the night. You surround me by day and guard me to listen closely. I watch and wait.

You who dwell among the heavenly hosts have never abandoned me, though I have often felt forsaken and alone. I consider how you are constantly in God's presence, and your efforts to bridge the gap between Heaven and Earth have not been wasted on me.

I am ashamed that I have ever doubted or become discouraged and hot with envy and anger. Because of God's mercy, I am entrusted to your care, and I have often ignored this gift. But I will no longer be deceived by the enemy's plot against me, for you will be my steady and sure guide to remind me of truth, to live in it and proclaim it with my life.

THE WINGS OF THE WIND

"You make the clouds your chariot; traveling on the wings of the wind. You make the winds your messengers." ~ Psalm 104: 3 – 4

St. Michael, long ago did I find you at my side as my defender against evil. You are a true soldier of the Lord, fighting for good and against the adversary.

St. Raphael, I prayed to you for many years that I might find a husband and have children one day. Though it seemed like a lifetime, you came to my aid, and I will praise God as Sarah and Tobias did on their wedding night for the gift of my family.

St. Gabriel, the messenger to our dear heavenly mother and the messenger to the world, you are truly God's herald of mercy and peace.

All you angels of Heaven and Earth, you reach us on the wings of the wind. The wind brushes against us, grazing our skin, and we are reminded of your presence and unfailing help. Your fidelity to God shames what little faith we have, and we are drawn to your obedience and humility. You never cease praising God.

So now we beseech you – with longing and desperation – guide us, teach us, reach us on the wings of the wind to turn our eyes and hearts always to the One who created and loves both angels and humans.

FULL OF GRACE AND TRUTH

"And the Word became flesh and made his dwelling among us, and we saw his glory, the glory as of the Father's only Son, full of grace and truth." ~ John 1: 14

My Lady and dear Jesus, how You have taught me about mystical marriage! To be fully united in heart – two lives, two hearts, but a unified cadence of each beat. Your rhythm is always in sync, and therefore your love for us is one and the same. This is so, because the Son was born of Spirit and woman, so He is biologically part of woman's flesh. His love for His mother and her love for her son cannot be dissolved.

This is why Our Lady, like her son, Jesus, is full of grace and truth – because she who carried her child in her womb was full of His grace. Her quiver was filled with light and love.

Because Jesus is Light, Love, and Truth, Our Lady has always inexorably been filled with Him – with Light, Love, and Truth. This is why she is full of grace, not because she is divine, but because she is infused with the divine…not because she is the redeemer, but because she birthed Redemption.

Her journey with Jesus began at that first fiat and extended into eternity.

No one can separate a mother from her children, at least not in the heart. For what the child feels – torment, frustration, confusion, elation, - the mother, too, very much experiences. So the united hearts of Jesus and Mary always have one mission: to freely, totally, faithfully, and fruitfully offer themselves in love, mercy, and truth to us so that we, in turn, may be full of grace and truth.

PIERCED BY A SWORD

My dear Lady, this Feast of the Presentation has grown closer to my heart in recent months, though I didn't fully realize the reason until today. In my mind's eye, I was making the connection between Jewish presentation and Christian baptism, focusing on Your sacrifice and obedience to God. But today I saw and recalled those words of Simeon, "You yourself a sword shall pierce, so that the thoughts of many hearts shall be revealed" (see Luke 2: 35).

Most Sorrowful Mother, you knew the fate of your child, "destined for the rise and fall." You believed this foreshadowing and internalized it in your maternal heart. It was at the Presentation of your only son that your passion – the crucifixion of your heart – began.

And so today I am strangely consoled by Simeon's haunting prophecy, because I am now more certain than ever before that you experience my heart-agony with me. You are my mother, the only mother of my heart. I have before given you all I thought I possessed, but today I also consecrate my interior sufferings to you.

Perhaps the swords that lance my heart somehow unite my heart and life to yours more completely and deeply. Perhaps this type of heart-agony is the gateway to Jesus' crucified heart. You are the gateway, dear Mediatrix. You've led me to this place where I've fought against the daily struggle. You led me here, because your maternal heart longed for my undefined torment to unite with the wounds of Jesus and hide there. You did this for love of my soul and to also console your son in His Passion.

SOMETHING NEW AND BEAUTIFUL

In the desert, a solitary rose blooms in the arid sand. A desert rose: such a magnificent reflection of beauty is she! In the midst of the watching and waiting of life, in the thick of struggle and nothingness, we are reminded that God is always doing something new and beautiful.

We are that desert rose, or rather, we look to the August Princess who was the first Desert Rose. She is our hope, our Lady of Light. She blooms always to reflect the beauty of her Creator. Her life glorifies His majesty.

We look to the Desert Rose blooming in the drought. She points the way to something new and beautiful for us. She is strong and resilient. She defies the empty wellspring, for even in the driest, darkest, and most unfruitful of times and places can something new and beautiful flourish.

In my own desert, I am tempted to doubt and despair. But I see her, and I long to become a desert rose, too. I know I am incapable of this on my own, but hope surges in my heart, and I run to my Desert Rose. There she plants me under her shade, and I begin to grow, slowly but deliberately, under the nourishing Son.

THE HOLY NAME OF MARY

Mother of all, it is you who has soothed the ache in my soul that could be alleviated by neither food nor sleep. When I hear your name spoken, my restless voice within is calmed as a child is calmed in his mother's presence.

When asked what my favorite title for you would be, I always respond, Mystical Rose. You are the miracle of the rose blooming in the midst of winter, the one sign of hope to which we can cling in such uncertain times as these.

But above all, you are essentially my mother and my lady – Our Lady. I cannot imagine merely calling you Mary, the Mother of God (though you are), because it seems too impersonal and distant.

So when our girls began adopting the term of endearment, "Mama Mary" for you, I let them, because they need to be reminded often that you are our refuge, our oasis, our source of hope. You comfort our ills and soothe us with the holy balm of your love.

You are our mother – *my* mother – and I am eternally grateful for your maternal help and perpetual presence in my life.

THE PORTAL OF YOUR INTERCESSION

Dear Lady, my mother, open wide the portal of your intercession. Have pity on me – a Pharisee, a scribe, a hypocrite – because I know your mercy is boundless, and you are a sweet and generous Mediatrix.

My life is in shambles, and I often feel that the mess is irreparable. But then you come to mind – your kind face and open arms – and I am instantly at ease. My confidence in your son's providence is bolstered by the power of your intercession. I know that even the worst of sinners, like me, can find favor with you.

You are approachable, amicable, and admirable. You beckon me to trust evermore in Jesus's divine mercy, but I often feel deep regret and shame when I consider approaching the King of Heaven. That is why I come to you first. When I am broken and weak, you soften the blow and somehow strike within me the desire for humble contrition so that I may be reconciled to your son.

All of this occurs through the portal of your intercession. Oh, where would I be without your soothing balm, your cool refreshment, and your calm presence in my life?

My dearest mother, I know that as long as I look to you, I will see the face of Heaven near you. And as long as I keep my sights on you, I will never be far from my beloved Jesus.

THE WAY OUT OF DARKNESS

"Dawn is the end of the foregoing night and is the beginning of the day that follows...The light puts an end to night and starts the day, shines, and does not fall into corruption..." ~ *St. Thomas Aquinas*

For so long I've resigned myself to the improbability of ever seeing light again. This spiritual darkness has nearly become my companion, since it has journeyed with me for several years. Even so, I thirst for the light again and wonder if I can catch but a glimmer of the dawn.

Perhaps I've kept myself unnecessarily caged in this darkness longer than what could have been if I had only known what is so obvious today: that the dawn draws near, and all I need to do is run to the arms of the Dawn of Day, who is Our Lady.

Our Lady is the way out of darkness, for she points the way more quickly and easily to the Light of the World. She is the Dawn, and He is the Light, and yet I have been hiding in the shadows of darkness, waiting to be rescued.

As our Mediatrix, Our Lady's mercies flow abundantly, for she has the compassionate heart of a mother for us all. She cannot bear to witness our misery as we continually seek to live in the light by following truth but never knowing for certain if we've discovered it or not.

We must never stop searching for the light, irrespective of

our time spent in darkness. The temptation of becoming familiar with darkness is, of course, that we no longer believe we will see the light, and perhaps we stop searching for it altogether.

But the Dawn of Day reignites that perseverance in us, so we continue to follow her lead, knowing she will lead us out of the darkness and into the light.

WAIT FOR THE DAWN

"My soul looks for the Lord more than sentinels for daybreak."
~ *Psalm 130: 6*

"Longing for light, we wait in darkness..." begins the well-known hymn, "Christ Be Our Light." It is true that the darkness feels long, and we may lose hope as time draws on with no sign of the light of day. What we wait for is not so much to see everything in our lives with certainty and clarity, for all of life is enshrouded in mystery one way or another. Instead, we wait for Our Lady to appear, the Dawn who leads us to the Sun of Day. We wait in silence. We wait in patient expectation.

We await the Dawn. And she will not disappoint us, because she knows we need refreshment from this long and lonely night. She knows we need her Son, our Sun who radiates the warmth of His Spirit into a world grown cold and hearts hardened by ice and stone.

Our hearts will never grow cold as long as we fix every sentiment they express on the horizon and do not lose sight of it. Our focus must be on endurance, perseverance, and fortitude. We must gain strength from the promise of our God Who never fails, and then hope will spring forth in us as the Dawn of day breaks into fresh hope and a new chance to start again.

WHAT IS UNSEEN

"Faith is the realization of what is hoped for and evidence of things not seen." ~ Hebrews 11: 1

I seek You, Lord, but You are hidden from my sight right now. Could it be that You so desperately desire nothing less than my endless search for You? Yes, You are hidden in the host, but I hunger for more, for entire union with You, because nothing in this world satiates my spiritual appetite.

All I've come to understand about You, life, death, faith, Catholicism, etc. is all unseen, blissful Mystery. The darkness of the Holy Saturday *tomb* has become a darkness of the *womb*: safe and sure, yet unseen. This level of faith requires all – every fragment of fragile hope, every iota of confidence and certainly total trust in You. I cannot remain in the womb of Your heart without faith, and faith certainly is not visible.

Yet You ask me to believe You, to expect great miracles and wonders. What a bold confidence! Do I possess such a faith – to believe Your promises when all seems lost and banished to oblivion? Nothingness, day after day, is my visible compass. Ordinary, routine monotony is the fruit I see.

But what remains unseen? Is there far more that lies dormant and still? It's the *more*, the hope for fulfillment of Your sacred Word, that maintains this meager and wounded hope. Yes, I have been disappointed, and many of my dreams have been shattered, but I am captivated by Your mystery.

What is unseen remains my interior compass, for it is truly faith that guides my life, not sight. Yes, I am a fool, but foolishness in You is wiser than human wisdom. Noah was labeled crazy for obeying Your command to build an ark, but he followed the hidden path – which was the certain path – of faith in Your word.

I must be like Noah and carry on with this mission that I truly want to abandon some days. I see no fruits. There is no visible evidence that this time – of all other efforts I've tried and failed – will bear lasting fruit for Your kingdom. This requires a deeper trust in what is unseen, and I must believe that Your hand guides me on right paths in the darkness.

And what of Our Lady's fiat? This was the greatest act of faith in human history. She, though poor in spirit and little known to the world, said *yes* to bearing the only begotten Son of God. She said this with no inkling of doubt, only confidence in God's promise of salvation through her.

And as she carried You in the darkness of her womb, Jesus, so she carries me. This is why You have beckoned to me in this dark place, where my inclination is to flee in fear. You call me to her holy womb, because You, too, found Your earthly beginnings nestled safely in the unknown, in total dependency on Your beautiful mother for every breath.

Hide me in her womb, Jesus, and in Your tomb, for I've learned that tombs are not devoid of hope, and wombs are not to be feared. Grant me the birth of faith in this dark place of waiting.

CHAPTER FIVE

Darkness & The Meaning of Suffering

A RECORD OF MY TEARS

"Are my tears not stored in your flask, recorded in your book?"
~ Psalm 56: 9

Some say tears are like holy water – an offering of pure cleansing, a gift of healing, or a plea for redemption. My tears have been my daily bread, for they flow regularly and have often fed the ache in my bones and my soul.

How immeasurable is Your love, then, to keep record of every tear I have shed? If I offer my tears each time they manifest, then truly my offering becomes a welcome gift.

Take my tears, Lord, and transform not just me, but my family, and not just my family, but my community, and not just my community, but my nation, and not just my nation, but the entire world. My tears become Your love. My tears mingle with Yours and those of Your Sorrowful Mother. Because of this, they are purifying, cleansing, healing, and renewing.

My suffering must be united to Your Passion if anything meaningful or hopeful will become of it. I cannot hold fast to my tears or my sorrow. Joy is everlasting. It is the fruit of tears well nurtured by love.

Tears of sorrow are the seeds I plant in Your hands today. With each that falls, I know You collect them all and care for each reason they existed. And then beautifully, majestically, You plant hope that bears lasting fruit from the seeds of suffering.

CONQUER MY HEART

My heart is its own prison, and everything I am is shackled inside. In cannot breathe. I cannot escape, for who can escape oneself? How is it that a heart once open and available has become so wounded and disappointed over time that it has closed in on itself? I feel its retreat and imminent defeat. It's giving up on love, and my will and intellect cannot contain this impending downfall.

Dear heart, please come back from the grave. Do not become cold as ice or hard as stone. The world needs more bleeding hearts, the ones willing to be hurt for the sake of love. Do not fear pain, dear heart, but invite God to meet you there in your wounds. Your pain will catapult you to a kind of love that surpasses the worldly definition, which is a love that understands death and yet embraces life, a love that demands sacrifice of itself, a love eternal.

Jesus, will you conquer my heart, beginning today? Only Your love can penetrate my callousness and cynicism. I may be well-intentioned, but I know I cannot save myself. This is why You suffered torment – to conquer hearts, to win souls for Heaven – so teach me, Master of Love, that dying isn't something I should fear, and pain in my heart isn't reason enough to protect it from the crushing blow of loneliness and rejection. My heart has made its decision to protect itself from further hurt, but I want You to crumble the fortress I have built there, and rescue me from fear and doubt into a place of love and trust.

Only an open heart like Yours can be salvaged. Only then will I love, not by removing myself from suffering or hiding behind a barricade, but only in the transparency of love, from Your heart to mine. The exposure is daunting but necessary. I am exposed to You, and my heart cannot hide from You. Take it in Your loving hands and tenderly repair it, nursing it back to life, so that I may live more fully for You.

CRUSHED IN SPIRIT

"The Lord is close to the brokenhearted, saves those whose spirit is crushed. Many are the troubles of the righteous, but the Lord delivers him from them all." ~ Psalm 34: 19 – 20

I've known for some time that more would be required of me – a "more" I could not fully give without permanent death to all I have ever known, seen, or experienced. To be crushed by You is sweet misery: misery in the sense that my humanity cries out in protest, but sweet because You chastise those whom You love.

All suffering eventually tastes sweet to a saint before she passes into eternal bliss. I have the promise of this, too, if only seconds before I take my last breath. I carry a quiet confidence that my death will be holy and reveal many surprising truths that expand and perfect humility and charity in my heart – two virtues that are sorely lacking in me.

To some degree, we are all crushed in spirit: worn, weary, frustrated, exhausted, depleted, and defeated. All of us have, at some time or another, believed the end is destined to be bitter. We are tempted to despair.

But You remind us that, though the righteous will experience countless trials in this life, You revive their broken spirits. It is a foretaste of the Resurrection: to die interiorly, perhaps daily even, but to cling to the hopeful promise that You will revive all that has become shattered or desolate.

Revive our crushed spirits. Revive and renew our resolve to persevere to the end.

HUMAN ANGUISH SHAPES THE HEART

Pain is not my enemy. It is my teacher, my mentor. But so often I wince in pain. I hate it, abhor it. I want nothing to do with it, even though I know that tremendous beauty and growth can be born from pain.

Suffering shapes and molds my heart toward goodness or

darkness. If I choose the light, suffering becomes tolerable at first, then sweet. This is because I have chosen the path of love, which first requires a reservoir of trust in God.

How can I trust Him whom I cannot see, hear, or touch? How can trust be possible when I am faced with a cross I do not want to carry? Trust is possible through a desire to love Him who became Love and suffered all for the sake of love.

I do not want the path of bitterness and resentment, though I know my suffering can lead to these. Anger is always a temptation for me when life gets harder. I want to give up and lash out.

But to choose love is a more difficult (yet also fruitful) path. Love is never easy, because it involves dying to all that holds me back from choosing to suffer with and for Jesus out of love for Him.

I AM DARK BUT LOVELY

"I am dark but lovely, daughters of Jerusalem..." ~ *Song of Songs 1: 5*

In the New Testament, Jesus juxtaposes many images and metaphors, not to perplex us, but to increase our awe in the truth of His mystery. Irony is prominent in Scripture, so we've concluded that it's too confounding and may be weak in spiritual merit. But this is why we have theologians and Scripture scholars, who marry the history of Judaism and culture with some semblance of modern understanding and relevance.

This verse from the Old Testament is one of those that can befuddle us. How can God be dark? Darkness is often a metaphor used for evil and absence of light. Jesus calls Himself the Light of the World, so how can He also be dark? Consider here the subsequent phrase, "but lovely." This suggests that darkness – if it is a *holy* darkness – is actually quite beautiful. It also suggests that God Himself is so vast and incomprehensible that He is Mystery. Yes, God is known, especially through Jesus and the Holy Spirit. But we have to accept that One who is infinite and has no beginning or end cannot be entirely understood by those who are anything else, which is all of us.

God is Mystery, because there are things He permits that we may never understand in this life. He asks us to trust Him, to walk with Him in the darkness. Isn't it comforting to know that He calls Himself "dark but lovely?" We can be reassured by this statement that the darkness will not swallow us, but that somewhere in it is the God of Mystery who chooses to make Himself invisible to us from time to time. Still, He wants us to stop fearing the desert moments of our faith journey, the dry and desolate times of nothingness and waiting.

He is telling us here that darkness itself (holy darkness) can be magnificent and stunning when we dwell in it with faith and trust. The spiritual fruitfulness and fecundity that result are what make it lovely, and He who is can be nothing less than lovely.

So stop fearing the unknown and resisting uncertainty. Do not abhor or ignore the aridity you experience in prayer, however long it may last. Instead, remember the beauty and gift of the darkness and that God Himself dwells most intimately with you in it. Do not be afraid, but persevere through the darkness and in it so that you will again see the God of light.

LEARNING OBEDIENCE

"He learned obedience from what he suffered." ~ Hebrews 5: 8

Perhaps suffering is a gift that is intended to lead me to submission to God in all things, to believe that obedience to the humiliation of the Cross is, indeed, my saving grace.

Why do I continually run from my cross and the Cross? It's as if my reflex is to turn away in horror rather than to cling to the Cross in love and adoration. When I see a crucifix, my eyes are fixated on the corpus of Jesus rather than the wood of the Cross. It is impossible for me to imagine a cross without Jesus on it.

But when I consider the cross tailor-made for me and my journey to Heaven, I shudder and reject it over and over. All I envision is a simple, crude piece of wood fashioned without great craftsmanship and handed to me.

No, I cannot accept this.

Where is Jesus? I do not want to see Him on the Cross, yet I know it is necessary to remember His unprecedented, unsurpassed, heroic act of sacrificial love for me.

Am I called to do the same for Jesus? *Yes.*

This means I, too, am called to be crucified in some way. Everything I've chased in this world and all of my bodily comforts, including my health, must be nailed to the simple cross made just for me. Resurrection cannot occur without a crucifixion of sorts.

And I don't want to die, yet I am not willing to live haphazardly anymore. I can no longer live for myself or even for another person. I must live for Him alone, but not without first dying. There's no turning back.

So crucify me, Jesus. Make my life and my heart look like Yours.

LIVING WITH LOSSES

The world is parched, Lord, because the land is sick and cries out for You. In some areas, the land is flooded from storms aplenty. Droughts and floods: they are the metaphors for my life. At times I, too, am thirsting for Your touch. These are the desert days of spiritual aridity, of nothingness, of emptiness. At other times I am too consumed with the raging tempests that rob my soul of interior peace, and thus I am too busy with complicated human and worldly issues. In these cases, I need You to rescue me before I drown in them.

Harmony is what I seek, but it evades me. I'm missing something, but what is it? The losses and the grief: at times it's unbearable, and I immerse myself in the drama of pain rather than in the redemption of the Cross.

Can these losses be transformed? Can the sickness afflicting the world and society be healed? They can with only a mere thought from You to will it. They can, but they aren't right now. Why do You permit all of this? What can the sickness teach me about myself, others, and You? Can living in the losses truly lead me into a greater love, a deeper understanding of human suffering?

Lead me, then, to live in the losses and with them so that I might be changed by them.

OBEDIENCE IN SUFFERING

This cruel suffering on the Via Dolorosa, this impenetrable pain I can bear no longer. It is the agony of the unknowing and waiting that slowly kills my spirit. At times I am ready to give up the holy fight altogether and give in to an easier way of living, a more comfortable lifestyle.

When I run from the Cross, I run from You.

And then suddenly, in a flash of grace, my strength and spirit are uplifted as my gaze shifts from self to Heaven. "I look up to the mountain; where does my help come from? My help comes from the Lord."

Oddly, the Cross is my answer. It is my refuge and fortress. Reluctantly at first, I accept it. And then I realize this means I can never look back or return to a lesser way of living and being.

Suffering shifts my attitude from one of rebellion to one of obedience. It produces endurance, perseverance, and patience, but above all, the necessary humble submission to the God of the universe who knows all things and carries me in the palm of His hand.

OUT OF GLOOM AND DARKNESS

"Out of gloom and darkness, the eyes of the blind shall see."
~ *Isaiah 29: 18*

I am blind, Lord, though my physical vision is intact. You have darkened my senses and eclipsed my heart so that I wander – lost, lonely, and looking for You.

I am blind to Your will, though I desperately long for it – to know, serve, and love You always. But this is becoming increasingly difficult as I battle the ravaging disease in my body. Could this darkness mean that You wish for me to acquiesce to my illness? I am afraid of this impending gloom, Lord. I know that You give and take away, but I fear the taking away. I want more of the giving.

But You have called me to be the giver and to permit You to take what You will from me: my health and fertility, my family and friends, our financial security. And I have fought You instead of the enemy in this war. I have resisted the affliction of Your love.

But now the time has come for me to relinquish all into Your hands. I have fought too long, and now my body is weary from the battle. His time to give in – not give up, but to give in, to *yield to You.*

I know I am on the cusp of emerging out of gloom and darkness, but free will is at stake. Am I truly ready to discover what is on the other side of fear?

So take me from what is familiar, and I will follow You on the lost, forgotten roads. Though I know not where You lead me, I know for certain it is out of the gloom and darkness.

PERFECT THROUGH SUFFERING

"For it was fitting that he, for whom and through whom all things exist, in bringing many children to glory, should make the leader to their salvation perfect through suffering." ~ *Hebrews 2: 10*

If I truly desire Heaven above all else, I must be refined in the crucible of suffering. But I cringe at the thought. I do not want *more* anguish, *more* loss, or *more* loneliness. But I *do* want Heaven.

How is it that we can only achieve perfection, everlasting peace, and eternity through the Cross? It cannot be denied, circumnavigated, ignored, or rejected. The Cross stands tall. It beckons me, but I know that the Cross means death.

Do I truly believe in resurrection, or has doubt clouded what little faith I have?

Trust means I relinquish fear of losing all for the sake of all. He holds my hand, and I creep forward with reticence.

Do I believe? Will light follow this inevitable darkness? Is it truly temporary, transitory? Or is it all a farce?

I accept my cross, but I do not immediately abandon myself to the subsequent scourges. This truly seems like punishment. Yes, death is certain. I am dying, withering away.

For a fleeting moment, I question the veracity of the Resurrection. It was true for Jesus, but not for me, right? Where is He in my messy life? I have been abandoned. All is dark, and I was duped.

But I cannot come down from this cross, and the reality hits me hard. I either succumb with hopeful resignation, or I fight willfully. The end of both paths is the same: I will die.

Somewhere in this drama I must consider the possibility of hope and metamorphosis. I ponder it momentarily as a butterfly grazes my face. Ah, the butterfly! I have found my hope in her wings. She took a chance at love and new life. She entered the dark chrysalis, uncertain if she would emerge. And now her graceful, fanciful flight reminds me that I have been given my wings.

I will soon be ready to fly.

REJOICE

Today my youngest daughter is having her sixth surgery (before the age of three), and God's word is reiterating the word "rejoice" to me. I am confounded at the thought of rejoicing in her suffering, but I also realize there is a message of hope in this day. He is asking me to open the door of my heart in trust again.

I want to do this, to quiet my mind and heart, but I am at the ready for the inevitable drama of pediatric surgery. Where is rejoicing in a children's hospital appropriate and acceptable? Does it begin with me? Perhaps. Or rather, yes it does. I can choose to rejoice today, and I will.

We all rejoice when celebrations are in order, but it is a radical act of trust when we rejoice in our afflictions and uncertainties. Today I can enter a spiritual realm of knowing my daughter's life and mine are in God's hands and under His care. When stress arrives, rejoice. Lack of sleep, rejoice. Setbacks and pain, rejoice.

To rejoice is my choice. I am certain of one thing: hidden in the darkest and ugliest of circumstances is beauty and blessing. God surprises us with these to remind us of His love in the thick of our grief, and today is no different.

Today I rejoice.

SEA OF CORRUPTION

Scripture speaks of darkness and light, sometimes in contrary terms, where the night of light somehow supersedes physical, literal darkness. What is the night, and what – Who – is the light?

Jesus, the Light, is always shining, always illuminating, but the world cannot see or comprehend Him. Therefore, the unholy darkness corrupted by sin overshadows the world's ability to see the Light penetrating through every crevice of darkness.

Conversely, many faithful people persevere through their

trials, yet do not feel or see Jesus, the Light, lifting the veil of night from their souls. This holy darkness is like a mother's womb, which encases the soul in goodness and protects it from the damage of unholy darkness. In this case, the Light, though invisible or imperceptible, guides the faithful soul in a hidden but sure way. Trust is what the soul must exhibit.

So light and darkness, in a spiritual sense, may be the same. We consider darkness to be absence of light, which is its pure, scientific definition. But darkness itself can be enlightening to the soul on the deepest possible level. In this abyss, God, the unfathomable Light, dwells within a person. It is said that, if anyone saw this Light, he or she would die of love.

So the Light is always present, though not always perceived. Corruption of both social and personal sin can blind us to the Light when He makes Himself known, and the Light may, for a time, hide Himself in a pure soul so that He may be loved more fervently and perfectly.

Let us not focus on the darkness, then, but on the Light that dwells in the thick of night, who surpasses darkness, who remains a steady presence, despite our inability to see, hear, or feel Him. To the devoted soul, I assure you that He is with you in the most unfortunate of circumstances, and precisely during the moments you feel He has forsaken you is when He has drawn you so near to Him that you are veiled by the protection of darkness. And this shields you from dying of love, which is a severe mercy.

Persevere, and the night you experience – the long, dreadful emptiness and longing for Light – will be fulfilled and is, in fact, being fulfilled in and through you now. Darkness isn't absence of the Light. It the absence of the self, the ego.

SOWING IN TEARS

I've never carried a bodily struggle like this one before:

undiagnosed, invisible, yet real and tormenting in every way imaginable. My bones are no longer merely dry, but they are on fire, seemingly attacked from within.

Tears are my daily bread. Someone once told me that our tears are like holy water, cleansing offerings to the One who suffered beyond all.

Were You thinking of me in this moment, Jesus, when You sweated blood in the Garden of Gethsemane? Did You see me, here and now, barely able to cling to anything at all, except my tears? Yes, I believe You did. And that is why You suffered so much more than I am now – out of an unquenchable, undeniable love for me.

Sow in my tears, then, love for You. Sow beauty in this ugliness. Sow joy when I am overcome by the spiritual attack of despondency. Sow hope when I am near despair. Make something magnificent from these tears, for they are all I have, Jesus, for You.

And I am becoming nothing at all – bodily, emotionally, spiritually empty – so that You may rebuild me to glorify Your name.

THE BED OF THE CROSS

"Jesus sleeps on the bed of the Cross, so that we can wake up."
~ *Fr. Dan Scheidt*[viii]

Have I become drowsy from the anxieties of daily life, burdened by my own cross? Jesus offers Himself on the bed of the Cross so that I can wake up and be healed. "By his wounds we were healed."

Such beautiful irony! Only through the agony of Christ am I granted healing of body and soul. His suffering produced miracles of hope. His death gave me life and continues to do so.

Will I selfishly watch as He sleeps and offers all for me? Yes, I have done this. It's true that I've taken much from Jesus and given Him little in return. But today I am moved by my guilt and His compassion. Today I see Him on the bed of the Cross stretched and poured out for me, and I cannot abandon Him so that I may live as I wish.

When I think of Him there, I long to join Him. But the only way to do this is through my own suffering, my "bed of pain," as Psalm 41 calls it. This means I suffer for love of Him who suffered for me, that I may unite my pain with His to compensate for the lack of love so present in today's world.

THE CUP OF SALVATION

In my youth, I drank freely from my cup and once an adult, I handed it to You empty. I knew only You could fill me, Lord, and so You did – with Your own sacrifice. You handed me back a chalice, a cup of salvation, and bid me to drink.

What does it mean to partake in this cup? For You, it meant inevitable torments leading to physical death. For You, it meant a blood sacrifice – a total gift of Yourself for all. What, then, does it mean for me to take this cup?

I wonder now if it's an invitation. Lately life has become more cumbersome, and I wake every morning wishing for some change to occur outside of myself. But instead it seems You are beckoning me to change from within, to die to my former self and way of life, but I wrestle relentlessly to let go of it all and acquiesce to the spiritual passion to which You have called me.

Is this what it means to draw nearer to You? Love must hold nothing back, and my heart has freely expressed an inimitable desire to be with You in every way. This drinking of the cup of salvation has opened the door for a newfound love, O Jesus. Let me become inebriated with You.

THE LIGHT AT SUNRISE

"The God of Israel spoke; of me the Rock of Israel said, 'One who rules over humankind with justice, who rules in the fear of God, is

like the light at sunrise on a cloudless morning, making the land's
vegetation glisten after rain.'" ~ 2 Samuel 23: 3 – 4

Today is another dreary, dismal day, and I awakened to the
sound of raindrops pattering on the rooftop. I didn't bother to
peek at the morning sky behind our bedroom curtains, because
it was obvious I would not witness a sunrise.

Lord, it seems these summer storms linger for days and weeks
without reprieve. My heart has captured these storms, for they
have symbolized the din in my heart – the once fiery embers of
joy and light now grown bleak and lifeless. Jesus, You have
crucified my heart again, and rightly so, for my weakness and
sin are ever before me. But when, O merciful God, will the
sunrise come again to resurrect all that has grown frail, all that
is lost, or what has become a distant, pale memory?

The light at sunrise, I know, is unnecessary in a literal
sense, for the rain and sun alike serve to fertilize and cultivate
all the crops and flowers. But Your light, O Jesus, has been
extinguished somehow in this weary heart of mine. When can I
expect the Son rise to once again live in me and make me new?

I await the light of the morning – the perfect dawn after an
interminable night – in my soul. I've been watching and
waiting for it as the years pass, with seemingly no change in
my interior life. As I grow more infirm in body and spirit, my
hope is that Your light will rise anew in me – fresh, blinding,
illuminative.

Rise again in me, O Light of the morning, O Sunrise, and
resurrect me to Your everlasting glory.

THE LIGHT OF DARKNESS

"If I say, 'Surely darkness shall hide me, and night shall be my
light' – Darkness is not dark for you, and night shines as the day.
Darkness and light are but one." ~ Psalm 139: 11 – 12

I have been blind to the beauty of Your darkness. Most of my life I've errantly believed that all darkness was filled with hopelessness, nothingness, and eternal death. It seemed void of any fruitfulness or goodness. All seemed empty and unknown in the darkness.

But Your benevolence is so vast that the darkness You choose for me is holy. You hide in the dark crevices of my heart. You sleep there and choose to remain quiet, invisible – as in the Holy Host.

But this darkness conceals mystery, and You are Mystery. In the mystery, You remain unchanged, yet You are constantly beckoning me to grow and move closer to You. Sadly, I often fear what I cannot see, for I don't know where You're leading me or what You will require of me for this journey.

Still, walking in darkness with You is path that requires unfathomable trust. It is the only way for me to find Your light – by trusting that the darkness will lead me there, to where You have and will illuminate my entire being. For now, I wait and walk with You in this dark place until You choose to reveal Your light once again.

THE MORNING STAR

"You will do well to be attentive to it, as to a lamp shining in a dark place, until day dawns and the morning star rises in your hearts." ~ 2 Peter 1:19

How can I see your visage, O Morning Star, for You are hidden from me in the light of day? It is true I am only capable of enjoying the radiance of Your light in the dark of night, and so I wait in the stillness of night for Your brilliance to capture and captivate me.

So often I dread the night. It lingers on, and I can no longer see myself or You with clarity. At first dusk, I am rendered helpless once again at the mystery of night, and my soul is concealed by the withdrawal of Your presence.

The night presents me with interior labor pains and

groaning for the desert darkness in which You have left me. I see nothing. I hear nothing. Worst of all, I feel no comforts or consolations of Your love, which has always been so evident and abundant in the light of day.

Yet, without the night and darkening of my senses and soul, I would never encounter You as Morning Star. I would miss the hope of Your light altogether without the gift of the nightfall. During the day, Your Morning Star remains hidden, so I pray You may hide Yourself in me. Rise in me with the dawn of day, that the brilliance of Your luminescence may be known to others in and through me.

I am just one, small soul in the grand scheme of eternity, but my soul longs for the cycle of dawn and dusk within as without. As it pleases You, let all be made known in the light of day, and all that is hidden in the light be revealed in Your holy darkness. For both dawn and dusk are necessary as they settle upon the earth and in man. The rise and fall of day and night represents the cadence of Your presence, always surrounding and encasing me, but not always felt or experienced.

O invisible Star, rise then in the night of my soul, that while You hide in latency there, I may reflect Your dawn, and when You rise in the night, Your illumination may remain permanently transfixed in my heart.

Infuse me, O Light, with Your incandescence.

THE ONLY REAL SUFFERING

"To the well-ordered soul the only real suffering is sin; all other pain is joy in potency." ~ Brother Jacopone da Todi

True suffering is comprised of all my miseries relating back to sin – those of omission, those of commission, my vices and poor habits, my undeveloped or underdeveloped virtues, and so on. The more I become aware of my true nature and all that coalesces into my nothingness and wretchedness, the greater my suffering will be.

When suffering mingles sweetly with joy, it is a supernatural grace based upon my acceptance and even love of whatever trials and maladies God permits for the refining of my soul.

Irrespective of suffering caused by sin or circumstance, we must remember that the more miserable the sinner, the greater is God's mercy, as was revealed to St. Faustina. May His mercy envelop me, miserable as I am, so that my suffering may be sweetened by the potency of sheer joy.

THE PAIN AND THE POTENTIAL

I'll never forget one isolated, seemingly insignificant part of a college lecture in one of my undergraduate psychology classes: *Pain invites us to change.* My professor continued about how pain triggers the part of our brains that signal our minds and bodies, so that we cannot remain as we are. We must move through the hurt and continue onward toward positive growth.

That segment of the lecture had a lasting impact, at least on me. The Holy Spirit spoke to me that day through this lesson, which made so much sense out of acts and feelings in my past that, up until that point, seemed senseless and meaningless.

Pain invites us to change. In every loss, grievance, irritation, or misunderstanding, there exists the potential for healing, wholeness, restoration, and reconciliation. The potential for greatness is an essential component to pain. God never wastes anything that we are willing to give to Him in hope.

Sometimes chronic pain, be it physical, psychological, emotional, or spiritual, becomes cumbersome and draining. We carry an onus too difficult to bear alone, and the ensuing internalization transforms into depression, anger, and even guilt. During these times, pain seems more an enemy than a welcome visitor. We'd rather live painless lives.

Still, God beckons us. Pain presents an opportunity for us

to rise above it with God's grace. The potential of pain is that it can destroy or restore us. The choice is ours. If we choose restoration, the journey will be difficult, but faith requires risk. The question we must ask ourselves is, "*Am I willing to risk losing all for the sake of gaining all in Christ?*"

THE SHADOW OF THE CROSS

I dwell in Your shadow, O Lord, hidden in Your wounds, beneath Your wings and under Your shadow. All too often I search for the limelight, but You call me back to my only shelter and place of refuge: the Cross.

I dwell in Your shadow, because I am not far from You and yet still not fully united to You in every way. I follow You closely, intentionally, but I am still very much clutching my worldly attachments, too timorous to abandon all in Your favor.

The shadow of the Cross reminds me of the severity and tragedy of that fateful Friday, yet it also pinpoints my own death, bodily and figuratively. My interior death approaches, and Your shadow reminds me of what lies ahead.

But the shadow of the Cross is so much more than death. Death is necessary, yes, but not a pointless one like suicide. The Cross doesn't signify desperation or depravity, not really even destination. The Cross is a turning point for my salvation. It is not the end, but the beginning, of my life. So I dwell always in its shadow to cling to its sweet victory over sin and death.

THE UGLINESS OF OUR CIRCUMSTANCES

"There are those in every age in whom the suffering of Christ is manifest, almost visible, the beauty of his love shining through the ugliness of their circumstances." ~ Caryll Houselander[ix]

To those who carry visible crosses, life is an uncomfortable confrontation for others who meet them. Because of my daughter Sarah's craniofacial condition, people immediately see her cross. It's written on her face: the harsh features (buggy and droopy eyes, large and misshapen head, small mouth, and jagged teeth), but also the emotional torment that accompanies a person who is so visibly set apart by physical appearance. In an instant, people see all of the layers of pain, and they often become paralyzed with fear, unable to speak. But their silence tells me everything.

I know what their silence means, because I've had to confront my own discomfort with Sarah's suffering, which has also become my cross. That jarring reality, in which we must face ourselves, reveals much. We do not want to suffer. We hate watching someone else in pain. Seeing a person who defies secular beauty reminds us of the ugliness of our circumstances.

You see, suffering is ugly, but it can also be handled with finesse. Human anguish tears at our hearts so that we suffer along with those in pain. We wish it would stop, so that our own lives would not need to be shaken in order for us to wake up from our spiritual slumber.

Deformities, accidents, diseases, diagnoses – these all draw us back to the reality of our mortality and our need for God. In this way, ugliness is a gift, because we become needy, like children, dependent on God alone. Suffering prepares us for the joy of Heaven.

THE VALLEY OF DARKNESS

"Day unto day pours forth speech and night unto night whispers knowledge." ~Psalm 19:3

The day – the dawn, the spring – is when and how God reveals His story in my life. It unfurls delicately like spring's first crocus, and I, the sojourner, the pilgrim, welcome the gift of today as God sprinkles my heart with showers of cleansing hope.

This is my story that unfolds by day, but it is not exclusive to me. It is the universal story of humanity in all of its daunting glory. We all shed blood and tears together. We all rejoice and laugh in the same language, for the heart speaks joy that resounds in and elevates the soul in the wake of day.

Day is significant, because it represents the temporal reality of *now*. Now is all we truly ever have, and it just as quickly slips from our grasp as we attempt to cage it.

The night is sure to arrive, yet we seldom welcome it with the same enthusiasm as we do the light of day that offers clarity and certainty. The night shadows our senses and intellect. The night blinds us to the potential predators lurking and looming about.

Yet we reside safely in the shadow of His wings at night, safely under the shepherd's careful watch. We may sleep, and so may He, but either way, the slumber bears fruit in our life's work. Slumber reveals our legacy, both individual and collective.

At night the message of our developing story takes shape. Daybreak builds the foundation through the unfinished manuscript of our lives, but nightfall showcases the masterpiece of its completion.

The story never truly ends, but the message – the indelible legacy – lends itself from time to time as punctuation that breaks the monotony of our story. The message awaits the night when all is quiet and still, so that those who receive it may enter into contemplation.

WHAT GOD SAYS IN THE DARKNESS

"What I say to you in the darkness, speak in the light; what you hear whispered, proclaim on the housetops." ~ Matthew 10: 27

Could it be that my affliction has a message, not just for me, but a universal message? Perhaps the darkness of suffering and unknowing is a preparation for what is to come.

The world ignores God's whisper and runs from His darkness, but I am intrigued to know its purpose and meaning. I know it's true that God uses all things for good to those who are called according to His purpose. Therefore, my anguish has immense value and merit.

All of our sufferings are valuable. Though we live in secret pain, God wants the invisible message to be made known to all.

We are His voice.

The world does not want to hear that suffering is necessary for sanctification, but you and I know otherwise.

My pain has a purpose. Remember this often, especially when you feel that God is severely punishing you. One day, you will emerge in the light as a witness to His unfailing love.

WHAT MY TEARS ARE FOR

I cry, if not aloud, then interiorly. My weeping is not always for myself. In fact, my sorrowful heart is laden with the burdens of others – sometimes burdens too heavy for my fragile heart.

My tears are for the lonely
Who live in darkness and
Long for love.

My tears are for the grieving
Whose loss has left a hole
Too great to fill.

My tears are for the lost
Who travel without knowing
The way to Heaven.

My tears are for the forgotten
Who feel forsaken and alone
In their suffering.

My tears are for the lukewarm
Whose apathy has eroded their ability
To love and be loved.
My tears are for the ills and sicknesses
Afflicting the world
For the widow and orphan,
The childless mother,
The frustrated,
Addicted,
Depressed, and
Godless.

And my tears are collected in the reservoir of Your mercy as an offering of love. My tears are not in vain.

WHEN WORDS ARE FEW AND TEARS ARE MANY

Words aren't always necessary, despite popular belief to the contrary. We fill our mouths with useless and often cruel (or at the very least crude and lewd) words that either have no purpose or even cause harm.

Yes, there are plenty of occasions for words to cease. It is prudent to be mindful of our language and speech, yet there are moments when we long for words – spoken and heard – to bring comfort to us. But there are none.

In the drought of language often comes a flood of tears, which then become a silent (yet visible) lamentation. Tears at times are our daily bread, both nourishing and cleansing the soul. They are what we offer as prayer to God when nothing else matters and nothing else suffices.

Tears reflect the love in our hearts. The fact that we are able to feel and our hearts have not become hardened pours forth sweetness (even in the midst of our grief) upon our souls. Tears, unlike words, are never lost on God. He collects them and cradles them in His hands, then uses them to rain upon the earth and bring forth new life.

CHAPTER SIX

Temptation & Pruning

A FRUITFUL TREE

"Along each bank of the river every kind of fruit tree will grow; their leaves will not wither, nor will their fruit fail. Every month they will bear fresh fruit because the waters of the river flow out from the sanctuary. Their fruit is used for food, and their leaves for healing."
~ Ezekiel 47: 12

We bought two Bartlett pear trees three years ago as saplings. They were tall but fairly paltry, as one might expect for a young tree. I wondered how – if – they would survive the impending winter, replete with ice storms, subzero temperatures, and heavy snowfalls. Every so often I would peer out of our west-facing family room window in an effort to check on them.

They were still standing tall.

No high winds, heavy rains, blizzards, or ice would become the enemies of our new pear trees. Astounded, I admired their tenacity, seemingly rooted in rich, fertile soil. They were grounded, as I wanted to be spiritually. I sought to be like these little trees in character and behavior, which wasn't easy.

But bearing fruit, I thought, would be another story yet to be determined. I could hardly imagine picking a ripe pear and eating its juicy flesh one fine fall day. But the day did, in fact, arrive in late summer as I was perusing the yield of our vegetable garden with some disdain, shooing away the brown hare that had made his home among the butternut squash vines.

There it was: a tiny pear so small I could hardly see it with certainty. So I drew nearer and noticed not one, but four small pieces of fruit dangling from the scrawny branches of one pear tree. Could it be that, despite the hardships our little trees endured, they could still bear fruit for us to finally enjoy?

After three years, this came to pass. And one autumn afternoon I plucked those pears and cut them up, one for each of our family members. They tasted sweeter than the nectar of honey, reminding me of the Old Testament. They were the best pears of the season.

And here I was, dreading the first snowfall, yet pondering the life lesson I gleaned from watching our trees grow. I pray often that my life may "bear fruit that will remain," but I know this must be cultivated through the crucible of adversity. The fruit that comes forth is patience, kindness, faithfulness, gentleness, self-control, etc. But they only develop gradually and for as long as I remain rooted in my faith, clinging to Jesus when the dangerous storms attempt to separate me from the True Vine.

Bearing fruit entails attachment to the root – the Source – of our life. Anything other than that will assuredly yield rotten, useless fruit.

A THORN IN THE FLESH

"That I might not become too elated, a thorn in the flesh was given to me, an angel of Satan, to beat me, to keep me from being too elated. Three times I begged the Lord about this, that it might leave me, but he said to me, 'My grace is sufficient for you, for power is made perfect in weakness.' I will rather boast most gladly of my weaknesses, in order that the power of Christ may dwell with me."
~ 2 Corinthians 12: 7 – 10

I was born as a thorn in the flesh of my mother: unruly, fiery, stubborn, and difficult. I wailed and moaned throughout my childhood, not yet disciplined in matters of sacrifice and suffering.

I was given a thorn in the flesh when I grew into adulthood, but not yet a mother: "a gift," the Lord told me, "of my love for you." It was likened to the pearl of great price. *A pearl?* I questioned with incredulity. *How can a thorn become a pearl?* I did not yet realize the sweetness of suffering and how the depths of love are a piercing pain when sacrificed fully for the sake of the other, for the sake of all.

I accepted the thorn in my flesh, and it supplanted all other earthly goodness. The thorn, though intensely painful, did not harm me. It became a reminder of the ultimate price that I must offer – my life, my soul – because of the One who paid the ultimate price for my sake.

I returned the thorn in my flesh as I approached the end of my fleshly, pre-converted existence. The Lord removed it with tenderness, and I was left with a gaping wound that scarred quickly. It served as a battle scar to attest to the love of a crucified heart.

From one who was born as a thorn to one who carried it throughout life, I was blessed by the fragrance of the rose – a gift upon death, a gift of victory – and the fruit of suffering's sweetness.

From a thorn to a rose…that is what I became.

AN UNLIKELY PRUNING

"'I am the true vine and my Father is the vine grower. He takes away every branch in me that does not bear fruit, and everyone that does he prunes so that it bears more fruit." ~John 15:1-2

O True Vine, You have planted me as a mere seed, and I was sown long ago. I've waited for many years with the groaning agony of a restless heart, and now the time has finally arrived for me to bear the fruit of the vine – Your vine, Your handiwork.

I flourish for a time, basking in the wealth of spring and

summer. I do not think of the harvest or consider the impending arrival of winter. Now is the time for my waiting to temporarily end as the choice fruit continues to overflow on my branches, nearly crushing it with its weight. The time has finally come for me to bear witness to Your glory through the flowering and bountiful selection of what I have borne to honor You.

But I know this moment will quickly pass, for nothing remains steady and constant except You, the True and Eternal Vine. I reluctantly accept my fate – the painful pruning of these luscious branches I have longed for. As You clip away the verdant leaves and thick foliage, I am stripped to only a mere trunk of a plant.

In my public humiliation, I sulk for a fleeting moment but then recall that my roots are strong, because they remain connected to You. I must be pruned seasonally, so that You alone may be glorified and that all the ugliness and disease of my sin may be swiftly discarded and my branches might eventually regenerate more exuberantly and more numerous than before.

I am pruned and left with nothing but a memory of who I once was and who I still long to become. It may be that several years pass before I once again bloom, but I know that when I do, I will be ever-ready to praise You for the gift of my pruning – the hidden blessing of temporary pain.

BE SHREWD AS SERPENTS AND SIMPLE AS DOVES

"Behold, I am sending you like sheep in the midst of wolves; so be shrewd as serpents and simple as doves." ~ Matthew 10: 16

The cunning of the serpent and the guilelessness of the dove - how are we to be like both of them concurrently? One represents evil, and the other purity and holiness.

If we walk as sheep among wolves, we must adopt the

mindset of vigilance and diligence: vigilance to never become complacent among those who wish to harm us or defile God and diligence in the necessity of perseverance for evangelizing to souls who are lost and confused in the midst of today's moral relativism.

We must never presume safety from peril, and yet we must also relentlessly and confidently cling to the promise of salvation. To reach the wounded souls of the world, we must – in some ways – become like them in order to meet them where they are. This is the cunning of the serpent. Yet at the same time, we must remain rooted in the Good Shepherd, who commissioned us as sheep among the wolves and so – as sheep and doves – we must remain simple and pure of heart.

This poverty of spirit leaves us empty of self and worldliness, yet available and open to God filling us up with Himself, so that we can love those He sends to us.

BEING TESTED

"Because he himself was tested through what he suffered, he is able to help those who are being tested." – Hebrews 2: 18

Could it be that the incessant trials of my life are kisses from Heaven? Do You baptize me with grace every day as I struggle with interior darkness?

You test me, Lord, and the discipline feels like punishment. Your chastisements are not yet welcomed and have not yet become sweet to my soul. I often feel as if You have set my intellect and senses on fire to destroy all that I know and feel, and yet my will, though darkened by Your shadow, remains fervent in staying the course.

If I abandoned You and this unwanted path You have laid before me, I would immediately plunge from a holy darkness – where You uphold me by Your grace – into an unholy one, thrust into despair.

I cannot despair. Though my body is broken and my heart

torn, I recall Your promises: "I am with you always." "Do not be afraid." But I fear my increasing weakness in the weight of my sorrow. Will You not show me Your kindness, and in Your mercy, refresh my soul? Jesus, I trust in You.

CONQUER THE FURY OF DESIRE

Human desire can take over our reason in irrational and wayward directions. God, of course, gave us a heart to love and feel all sorts of grand emotions, but passion can grip us and control our ability to make decisions with prudence and temperance. Passion, while alluring or intriguing, can lead us to sin through volatile fits of anger or sins of the flesh and even in desiring wealth or prestige.

Lest we think we are exempt from such dramatic temptations, it would be wise to examine ourselves more closely. Different temptations may arise in varying times of our lives and seemingly unexpectedly. Desire becomes fury when it swirls into a vast whirlwind, which becomes chaotic and erratic. God is not a god of chaos, but is the God of order.

For some, desire seems harmless and even adventurous. But our passions must be tempered with the fire of the Holy Spirit, who calms the raging flames and draws us back to Him, our source of authentic desire, which is to love.

If we seek His kingdom and all His righteousness, He provides satisfaction for those recalcitrant longings of the flesh, and He does this by healing and strengthening our resolve through grace. Temptation, though potentially deadly, is our opportunity to abdicate our desires and, once again, plead to know and love God's will in all things. Then our hearts are united to his, and our desires become a thirsting for holiness, beauty, and love. When we desire Him with an urgency and longing, He has conquered our temporal desires by pursuing us with love, the antidote to earthly desire.

FALSE PEACE

We live in an age in which people do not believe in Satan, evil, or even sin. Therefore, they remain cloaked in a false sense of peace, deluding themselves. I find myself recalling the phrase, "Watch and wait! Your enemy the devil prowls about like a thief in the night." (See 1 Peter 5: 8.)

God does not want us to be fraught with anxiety over this, but to instead be vigilant. Vigilance requires a heart at rest in the Spirit of God while remaining aware and awake for evil's potential attack.

Let us rest in the Spirit of God; we do not carry a false peace – we who know we are engaged in a war between good and evil. To a world that negates and nullifies the reality of evil's existence, we appear to be fools. We appear to be creating an unnecessary and nonexistent division, which is the source and perpetuation of their false sense of security.

Our lives are never meant to be lived in isolation and desolation. The enemy strikes us at one of two ends: to fear him and his wrath relentlessly or to deny his existence at all. One is an unnecessary fear (which is really a lack of trust in God's ultimate reign over evil), and the other is a false peace.

To avoid either delusion, we must immerse ourselves in God's mercy, which graces us at the level of the "peace that surpasses all understanding." (See Philippians 4: 7.) Rest in Him. Dwell in Him. Seek Him, but remain sober and vigilant. Recognize God but also the absence of God and overt wickedness. Where God is rejected, denied, or blasphemed, you must flee into His arms, where true peace will flood your heart.

FEAR NOT!

Scripture tells us more than anything else, "Do not be afraid." Fear is dichotomous to faith. When our faith is weak, we do not trust God's ever-present, unfailing love and care, so we respond in fear. I've come to see more evidently how Satan uses fear to prey on all of us in different ways. We each have our weak and wounded areas, and the devil knows this well. So he attacks our emotions and lies to us. We then are afraid and do not believe in God's prevailing promises for our welfare. This is especially the case in our Information Age when so much is filled with apathy, fascination with the macabre, and narcissism. It is difficult to conceive the truth that God is Love, and perfect love casts out all fear.

Love, then, is the antidote to our paralyzing fears. Love heals the wound, enters the sick heart, and makes it well with warmth and vitality. We must permit God to enter our wound of fear, which requires faith so confident in His mercy and benevolence that it supersedes the enemy's lies and our timid response to struggles and strife.

Love begins with a simple *yes*, so that we give full reign to God, that He may do with us as He pleases, and we trust Him in the midst of grave difficulties, certain that He is cultivating everlasting spiritual fruits through them.

Trust is not always immediately felt when our fear runs deeply, but we begin by asking God to shower and engulf us in His love, then persevere in the waiting.

FROM FASTING TO FEASTING

In this desert, I may not be privy to the choicest foods and bodily comforts. It's true that I am deprived of what is familiar and preferred in every facet of my life. I've been stripped to the core, and this pruning is painful, but I trust You, Father, to make me new – into Your masterpiece. In this desert I'm fasting as You once did. The deprivation of the senses reveals the deprecation of my soul.

In essence, all frivolities and extraneous pleasures must necessarily be extracted from my life in order that I see myself more completely and honestly, reflected in Your light. It is Your light that illuminates the darkness where distraction once filled the void in my heart. Your light unveils the decades of filth that You invite me to remove through Reconciliation and renunciation.

I am ready, Lord. Yes, I am ready. The fasting has worn me, and I am bone weary. I know the feasting will come in Your time and way, and it will not be a banquet of choice fruits and sweet wine, but rather it will be a divine feast of Your flesh and blood. You are the food upon which I draw my strength. You are my sustenance. I await this Eternal Feast. I await You.

GOD LOVES A CHEERFUL GIVER

"Each must do as already determined, without sadness or compulsion, for God loves a cheerful giver." ~ 2 Corinthians 9:7

I don't intend to be a hypocrite, but I always end up one, anyway. Are all of us duplicitous at some time or another? I wonder if experiencing this reality is the first step toward humility.

There are times when I give out of obligation rather than genuine generosity. I pray, smile, and carry my cross, because it's what I'm supposed to do. But I long to one day give when it hurts, even though my heart truly wishes to be generous today. One day I hope and pray that my will and heart may be one in cheerful giving – that the feeling and the doing may coexist in harmony.

For now, I permit God to break me. The interior pruning nearly resembles bones shattering, because my heart, mind, and body cry out in desperation at the excruciation of it all. I know this crumbling of my old shell is necessary, but it still hurts. And in the midst of it, my inclination is to fight back rather than to gracefully – cheerfully – yield to it, to God.

That is what causes my duplicity. The will continues to act out of fidelity to God's will, but my senses act out in a recalcitrant rebellion. I have not yet become a cheerful giver, but I do desire to one day surrender all in saintly wisdom – to press into the wounds of Christ and dwell there eternally. One day my hope is not that this earthly suffering will cease altogether, but that it will be glorified, so that I may bear all with gratitude, joy, and love.

GOLD IN THE FURNACE

"Chastised a little, they shall be greatly blessed, because God tried them and found them worthy of himself. As gold in the furnace, he proved them, and as sacrificial offerings he took them to himself."
~ *Wisdom 3: 5 – 6*

Long have I waited for You, Jesus. My life is too frantic – at least within my soul – a life I never would have chosen to live. But You placed me here, in the crucible of suffering, with two children who need love above all else, and at last my life is not my own. I live for You through my daily duties, though at times I do so reluctantly and begrudgingly.

You are proving me in the furnace of affliction, as gold is tested in fire, so that I may exit Earth and enter Heaven as a worthy servant. I know this refinement is necessary, but it hurts so immensely. I cannot bear it some days, but my hope is in the outcome of this pruning – that I might be lovelier after You have chastised me a little and purified me. I want to be a beautiful flower and fruitful vine. I long to bloom for Your kingdom.

Keep me, then, in these flames, engulfed by Your love. The heat overwhelms me, but I know that when You consume me and I become nothing, then the fire will be a delight, a sweet chastisement of love.

LACK OF ROOTS

Whenever roots are destroyed, everything else fades into oblivion. I think of house plants, since I have a particular fondness for them. There have been occasions when I will notice large branches falling off my plants, or perhaps the leaves wilt to an alarming degree. I become discouraged by what I see, thinking my plants have met their doom. Then, over time, with tender and proper care, they somehow revive, and I'm made aware that it was because of their strong roots.

Roots are those lifelines we can't see, so we're inclined to evaluate ourselves and others based on what is immediately evident – physique, clothing, material possessions, or charm. Likewise, there are those we judge as somehow inferior to us based on their appearance; they are unkempt, uncouth, and perhaps disheveled or disorganized. Who knows the heart of the shabby and chic alike? We know the answer but still dismiss it.

Roots are those hidden strengths that perhaps no person can perceive upon observation, but God sees all. Roots uphold us when we begin to wane in strength or wither from the elements of a hard life. Roots retain the life-source necessary to revitalize our drooping spirits.

So we cannot know a plant's or a person's ability to persevere merely by looking at the exterior. Some are beautiful but are not solidly rooted in rich soil. Some appear to be shriveling, yet will come back, vibrant as ever, after a period of pruning and rest.

To be rooted is to allow God to plant us in His heart, where we grow steadily over time. The longer we remain connected to Him, the deeper and more impenetrable our roots become. This is what it means to remain in Jesus, so that He will remain in us. We can then go and bear fruit that will last.

LIVING IN THE DESERT

How many times have I grumbled when You have rescued me? It seems that a call to greatness requires intense trials as preparation for something more, something better. But too often I'd rather remain in my comfortable and familiar environment of slavery to sin.

The Israelites remind me so much of myself: they hated

their state of enslavement in Egypt, yet when God delivered them by Moses's hands, they groused about the desert. Sin – slavery – often appears more enticing when we are living in the desert. The desert is a place where we are stripped of earthly pleasures, bereft of bodily comforts, and severely tested in a spiritual sense. Desert living is not pleasant or desirable, but it is necessary in order that we reach the Promised Land as new creations – people of conversion who are no longer shackled by sin.

I've been living in the desert for quite some time now, and I'm constantly aware of my need for You. Each day I am desperate for You, Lord, but I also gripe about these long, lonely, interminable, and agonizing days of seeming nothingness. Have I made any progress at all in my interior life?

Most of the time, my old way of living tempts me to go back and abandon this call to desert living. Though I was spiritually and emotionally infantile back then, life seemed so much easier – more fun – than it is here in the desert.

And, like the Israelites, I wonder, "How long will this last? Can I trust that a Promised Land even exists?" To stay the course, year after year, when all seems barren, truthfully tries my faith in God's promises. And what exactly is the Promised Land?

Many believe it is Heaven, and I will not dispute this clear analogy. But I happen to believe the Promised Land also represents our individual calls to mission and purpose. The commissioning occurs when we abandon our old, sinful ways of living and choose to follow Jesus – in faith – into the desert. However long we remain there is at His discretion, but we walk steadily forward, certain that one day we will rather unexpectedly stumble upon the Promised Land, where our call to action meets community.

At long last, I will discover my life's purpose unfolding with resounding clarity and beauty. It will be my Heaven on

Earth indeed.

PASSING THROUGH

"Life is the agent for trials and tribulations." ~ Fr. Polycarp[x]

What do I anticipate when life falls short of my expectations? My reaction of constant disappointment is due to failure on my part to both acknowledge and embrace the mess, the struggle, the ugliness.

I must embrace the struggle.

We are all fighting a battle, whether or not we see this viewpoint, because our very birth into this world started the war to conquer our souls. Yet we'd like to believe that life should be full of pleasure and free of pain. Suffering is to be eschewed at all costs, so we numb ourselves with various forms of escapism. We distract ourselves with busyness.

Then life becomes a true nightmare, because we've fled the true struggle that tries our character and proves who we really are at the core.

God wants us to live the dream, but the dream is not perfected or achieved without loss, failure, and frustration. That is why the fight – within ourselves, against the world's biting criticism, or based on our circumstances – must be so that we gain eternity.

Earth is but our transitory home and we its guests. We must not concern ourselves with things of the world, but instead we should rise above the battle and frequently shift our gaze heavenward. Then we will realize the meaning of entering the mess with the intention of conquest, for Heaven is our destination.

PRAY, BUT DO NOT WANDER

How often do I discipline myself with a distinct time, sacred space, and open heart for encountering You, yet my mind and heart wander into dull and distant thinking? These days, everything seems to distract me, and I cannot afford distraction, for time is not a commodity at my disposal.

Teach me to pray without filling my mind with empty and endless thoughts of busyness. Where, O God, can I find You but here – within my heart – and the tabernacles of the world? Could it be that You might make my heart a tabernacle where You wait, hidden and expectant, for my visit? What I long for above all is to rest and abide in You, despite the invariable surprises that fall upon my life. Is it possible to contain unfaltering peace within a tumultuous body or life?

May there be a day when Your presence will fuse the chaos outside myself to the desert longing within. I do wander, Lord, because I continue to seek. Perhaps You are beckoning me to stillness and solitude, that I may discover Your indwelling in me rather than outside of me.

For as long as I recall, I've asked that my heart might become a tabernacle, a sanctuary, a refuge for You. I want my heart to house You – but not contain You, for You cannot be restrained. I want my heart to offer rest, safety, respite, and encase You with all I have and all I am – as You have done for me. I wish to love You more and more until my heart no longer wanders but finds a permanent home in You and You in me.

Above all, may Your peace abide in me, so that I may go on speaking truth without fear. A wandering heart is restless, but a heart that has found a home is at rest in You.

RESERVOIR OF SIN

"Sin is a reservoir of insolence." ~ Sirach 10: 13

I've created this reservoir, which has become dank and musty over time. It is filled with the filth of my sin, a pride that outsources itself unknowingly. The reservoir feeds my bondage to sin, yet I often do not recognize the danger of living in the reservoir.

My heart is ready to drain this water, which has only fed

the tangled brush, debris, and weeds in my life. No true life-giving water exists in this reservoir of hubris. It is here where my anger grows tall, receiving its ugly nourishment from the muck and thick, gooey substance. Pride has become stagnant, and I sense this, so I run to Confession. There I beg for forgiveness, and I am set free at last.

But to drain muck takes many years of hard work. Pride is not vanquished all at once. I work diligently to remove the filth, and at the same time plant flowers of virtue as the reservoir of pride lessens and fresh spring water – the Living Water – replenishes what was lost.

All is never lost, even in the reservoir of pride, because You are ever-present, earnestly awaiting my sanctification. I take Your hand and get to work each new day, knowing it will take a lifetime to be rid of my sins.

SPIRIT OF SLAVERY OR ADOPTION?

"For those who are led by the Spirit of God are children of God. For you did not receive a spirit of slavery to fall back into fear, but you received a spirit of adoption, through which we cry, 'Abba, Father!'" ~ Romans 8: 14 – 15

God has set before us life or death, the blessing and the curse, slavery or adoption. Through the gift of free will, we choose the path to follow each day. Slavery and the curse lead to death. Adoption and the blessing lead to life. (Perhaps slavery yields the curse, and adoption the blessing.)

There are two kinds of slavery: slavery to sin or slaves of Jesus. Both are drastically divergent, but they are both a type of slavery. Slavery to sin is bondage and oppression. We are shackled and imprisoned with this type, but slavery to Jesus happens when we choose live as adopted sons and daughters of God. We no longer belong to ourselves but to Him. Through this slavery, we are set free from sin and oppression.

Slavery to Jesus is a choice we make as we deepen our

spiritual walk. The interpretation of the word "slave" disturbs most of us, but to the spiritually aware, its connotation is clear and desirable. Yes, the word "slave" conjures images of subjugation, but when we choose to belong to Jesus, we trust that He will free us and care for every detail of our lives. This is what it means to live as an adopted child of God.

TETHERING FREEDOM TO TRUTH

"Make us truly free, by tethering freedom to truth and ordering freedom to goodness." ~ Cardinal Timothy Dolan

We celebrate our liberty, yet freedom is so often disdained for a fluffy, superficial ideology, such as "love wins". What is love, anyway? What is freedom? If God is Love, then Love certainly didn't win the day same-sex marriage became federal law in the United States. And to equate romance or warm emotions to love and freedom – or, as they say, freedom to love and marry whom we choose – then our modern concept of liberty is also gravely errant in origin.

How do we tether freedom to truth? Only in truth – that objective moral order ordained by God – can freedom be accurately understood and authentically lived. Freedom is found in disciplining ourselves to a higher order than our sensory pleasures and pursuits. Freedom is standing in between holiness and evil – knowingly – and choosing the right, the good, and the true. But only insofar as we are rooted in God can we unreservedly choose what is righteous and honorable. Freedom, therefore, is found in God alone, for He is righteousness and truth.

True freedom cannot be separated from truth; this is why it must always be tethered to truth. Truth liberates the soul to love honestly and to seek sanctity with sincerity.

THE CONSUMING FIRE AND EVERLASTING FLAMES

Lord, shall I request to be saved both from the consuming fire and everlasting flames? It is clear that the everlasting flames connote eternal damnation, but Your Spirit is all-consuming fire.

Now I realize all-consuming fire may temporarily feel like I am doomed to hell, because the purgative state of spiritual refinement hurts, and I realize my wretchedness with resounding clarity.

But Your consuming fire vastly differs from the everlasting flames, because Your fire is gentle and burns me into an image that reflects You more purely if I surrender to Your fire. But the everlasting flames destroy instead of make new. You renew me, but the flames of Hell would torment me, should I be damned.

I know by evidence of Your mercy that Your Spirit will love me with totality through the consuming fire, so if I walk the path of light and truth, I will not be damned. Consume me, then, O Holy Spirit, that I may be saved by Your pure fire from the everlasting flames.

THE DOOR OF MY LIPS

"Set a guard, Lord, before my mouth, keep watch over the door of my lips." ~Psalm 141:3

The door of my lips is the gate that determines what enters and what exits my mouth. Do I entertain filth and foulness, folly and frivolity through my speech, or what I eat and drink? Or do I discern prudently, temperately, what is pure, practical, and peaceful, allowing beauty to be spoken?

What passes the door of my lips surely determines the content of my interior life. So often I mindlessly consume food and drink out of mere pleasure rather than for nourishment. I do not guard what passes the gate of my lips, and therefore I do not wisely ascertain what should leave my mouth, either.

I consider the idle chatter and banter of our day. So many of us speak indiscriminately and without thought. We speak unnecessarily, and I, too, am gravely guilty of this. More often than not, I do not guard my speech – or rather, I do not seek counsel from You in protecting the vessel within (my heart), so that silence may typically prevail over imprudent and thoughtless babble.

I am seldom silent, Lord, except during this time with You, and even then my thoughts are not entirely quiet. How is it possible to feel completely lonely when I needlessly talk, whether in my heart or through the spoken word?

You have enlightened me to a new and rare truth today, Lord, a forgotten truth that seems to exist only in the distant past – well before the onset of fast and frenzied technology and information. The truth is that speech is often unnecessary for me. Silence is the more charitable response to others. I must learn to listen with deliberation and empathy rather than awaiting the moment I can hastily dump my thoughts and feelings onto someone else. Silence is my teacher, Lord, but how undisciplined and untrained yet is my tongue!

Be, therefore, the guardian of my tongue, dear Lord, for I require a gatekeeper to keep watch at the door of my lips. Teach me to listen with charity, especially when it is an affliction and aggrieves me to remain quiet. In turn, help me to speak with careful consideration and always out of love.

THE FRUIT OF PRAYER

At times the act of praying becomes a mere obligation or perhaps drudgery. We may set aside both time and space to enter into the heart of God, but we are met with a certain, stark awareness of our spiritual poverty. All that is undesirable – negative emotions, facing our nakedness, and our ugliness (sin) – is cause enough for us to flee. But if we persevere through the temptation to escape the reality of our nothingness in the presence of the One who is all, our lives will bear fruit that will last.

And what is this fruit, conceived in the heart? We bear witness, much like St. John the Baptist, to what is and is to come, through the development and maturation of our interior lives. We neither embellish nor deny what is. We are merely reflections of what is to come, that is, the Word-made-Flesh, the God-Man, the Christ Child.

In this sense, all of us are mothers and fathers, because we have the potential to bear Christ, not literally, but mystically. The Holy Spirit imparts to us the seed of faith, and, through the mysteries of our souls and the perseverance of daily, disciplined prayer, that seed is cultivated and eventually becomes Jesus, who is birthed through our life's mission and purpose. Let us not neglect to recall often that all we have and all we are is a direct result of this seed, and the fruit to which we grant life belongs to God alone.

THE PARCHED LAND WILL EXULT

"The wilderness and the parched land will exult; the steppe will rejoice and bloom. Like the crocus, it shall bloom abundantly and rejoice with joyful song." ~ Isaiah 35: 1 – 2

Is this what it means to hope: that the desert of my heart, now barren and dry, will one day bloom with exuberant flowers? Where are the flowers, O Lord? Even a desert flower does not unfurl in this heart right now. Perhaps I am that desert flower, much like a winter rose: an oxymoron, a paradox, a contradiction.

Your Cross was a contradiction, yet Your Cross was victorious over eternal fire. A dry, castaway segment of wood became the utmost symbol of Love Incarnate. Perhaps, too, the crude and rough edges of my heart will smooth and soften through Your love.

Time seems to be my enemy these days. It either slows to a

halt, or it is so rapid that I cannot maintain its pace. Of course it is not time that changes, but I. It is what my life, my days are filled with, often not of my own volition.

So the desert longing remains, regardless of space and time. It is a steady ache for You, for renewal and deliverance. My heart has become a contemplative memorial of the Israelites in exile for forty years: the waiting, the suffering, the struggle. It all appeared for naught, but the faith of Moses (ah, how I wish I had the faith of Moses) kept them on a sure way to You.

Like the stubborn Israelites, I want to run away from the interminable desert. I want answers, solutions, resolutions, clarity. Could it be that if only I kept forging ahead in the nothingness, the darkness, and the uncertainty that I will be led to a place of fruitfulness and abundance?

THE WARRIOR'S CROWN

"Truly the Lord is our shield, the Holy One of Israel, our king!"
~ *Psalm 89: 19*

When we enter the battlefield of life, we have little, if any, armor to equip us for what may come. Sheer will and determination push past the initial resistance we face from the enemy. As time progresses, we pick up the shield and sharpen our swords, but most of our time is spent fighting against the devil, the flesh, and the world, and all the while our heads remain unadorned.

Sometimes we notice this lack of head gear, and we panic. If the enemy strikes at our heads, will we survive? In our minds exist the most intense battle of all, and the enemy is well aware of this. Instead of fearing our exposed heads, we must choose to trust in God's protection and provision.

In a sense, we become warriors in this life, for we all face different (but equally trying) times of war and struggle. If we cling to God, our strength, we will surely persevere, even in the midst of the most overwhelming and ghastly of moments. He will never lead us to where He will not see us through.

In the end, when the battle is over, and the war for our souls has been won, we receive the victor's crown. Though we lived an earthly lifetime with no helmet, we are given this gift upon death as a share in the victory of Jesus. We are His soldiers, His warriors, and we know through the final symbol of victory that death and evil did not conquer. Our crown is a symbol of our thanksgiving and His glory.

THE WIND OF TEMPTATION

"Let our flame burn strongly, that the wind of temptation may increase the fire, rather than put it out." ~ St. Augustine of Hippo

Temptation surges through my intellect, my senses, and even my will so unexpectedly and unheeded. I am shocked and taken aback, yet instantly humbled by the reminder of my raw humanness. All attitudes of superiority vanish in the throes of intense temptation.

Thankfully, temptation instantly challenges me to run toward You without reservation or second thought. I cling to You, wrapping Your arms around me tightly, because I do not trust myself when left to face the wiles of the enemy alone. But I trust You.

And temptation increases my trust in You. Like everything I face, temptation is another opportunity for me to exercise my free will. I can deny You and succumb to my sensory pleasures, or I can run to You, begging You for the grace to withstand it.

And You will grant me the grace to rebuke temptation if I ask for it. You will never deny me this. I may deny You a thousand times, but Your mercy will instantly swoop in to rescue me at the slightest movement toward You instead of away from You.

When I choose You instead of myself, temptation fans the

flame of my devotion and charity. Virtue burns more brightly, and my strength is renewed in Your presence. This is why You permit horrendous temptations to befall us at times. Am I awake, or have I become drowsy with apathy?

Pay attention, dear soul, for you know not when the hour will strike when your time on Earth will end. Stay awake. Remain vigilant. Thank God for temptations and become ever more dependent on Him to be your all-in-all. In this way you will grow in humility and never forget your fallibility while at the same time realizing God's infinite goodness. May you increase in gratitude for the potential gift that temptation presents you.

THE WORDS OF MY MOUTH

"On the day I cried out, you answered; you strengthened my spirit. All the kings of earth will praise you, Lord, when they hear the words of your mouth." ~Psalm 138: 3 – 4

In my youth, I often spoke out of turn and of useless folly. Words were merely a commodity to me. I dispensed them liberally and without careful thought, for my heart was undisciplined and insolent. I cannot truthfully declare that I've fully outgrown these petulant ways of foolishness, but I recognize now the gravity of my words – whether written or spoken.

Too often in our technological age, I see people tossing around words because of fierce emotions – through text messaging, social media, and digital communication. So much is lost, and so many unnecessary misunderstandings ensue as a result of our imprudence and intemperance of thought and speech.

What has become of words? These days they are rarely treasured or offered as blessings. What about the words from my mouth? Do I speak truth, defend it, and use my words to encourage and uplift rather than denigrate and malign?

This is the reason I turn to Your Eternal Word, for it centers and humbles me as I engage in both interior and exterior combat. Your word reminds me of so much I have forgotten and draws me to the wellsprings of clarity, honest self-appraisal, and fecundity of spirit, so that Your Word may be born in my words.

Lord, make me barren of speech in these silent moments, that one day Your word may be planted and sprouted in my mouth. I desire to proclaim Your praise and speak charitably, so that the flower of my speech may bear the eloquence and beauty of Your will.

TO LIVE OUTSIDE MYSELF

"To live by faith is to live outside myself." ~ Fr. Thomas Dominic Rover

To live outside myself is to refuse permission for my body to collapse, though it is weary, weak, achy, and mysteriously infirm. The Spirit must overcome my flesh day after day, and I have never understood this more clearly than I do now.

To live outside myself is to forget myself in all my narcissistic tendencies for the sake of the other: my brother, my neighbors, husband, children, parents, in-laws, friends, and yes, especially my enemies. It is a law of love that supplants the law of restitution.

To live outside myself means I am unreservedly available to God, regardless of convenience to my schedule or my plans for the day. It is an ever-present, ever-ready openness to waiting, to action or to active waiting.

When I live outside myself, I no longer am "I" but "we." I become transformed so intimately by Him whom my heart loves that the cohesion of our wills occurs, and we somehow become united. My desire is indistinguishable from His desire, and so my thoughts, attitudes, and behaviors are fluidly thought, felt, and acted upon outside of myself.

I must learn to live in this dimension of "other," never seeking personal gain or comfort and forsaking my egocentric persuasion in order that I may more fully engage love through encounter.

To live outside myself is to die, to permit God to crucify me of my wantonness, so that I may be resurrected in His love.

TRIED AND TESTED IN FIRE

"Your promise is proved by fire." ~ *Psalm 119: 140*

Somehow I've believed – at least in the subconscious corners of thought – that Your promise would be fulfilled in me gracefully, effortlessly, and swiftly. I'm not sure why I thought this, because nothing in my life that's been worthwhile has come easily. Effort, diligence, and frustration have been themes whenever I've striven for what I truly believed was Your call, Your will. Perseverance, however, only recently came into play.

You see, Lord, I know now that, even though my life has been one great interior battle after the next, I never truly understood the importance of staying the course through exhaustion, rejection, discouragement, and waiting. Effort doesn't reap fruit immediately, though the world says it should. The greatness within any of us must be tried through Your fire. Otherwise, it is just mediocrity.

I believe in Your promise and that it is being fulfilled through this pruning, however painful and chaotic it feels. I know You honor a soul who doesn't give up hope and keeps moving forward in Your will and grace.

UNCIRCUMSIZED IN HEART

"You stiff-necked people, uncircumcised in heart and ears, you always oppose the Holy Spirit; you are just like your ancestors." ~*Acts 7:51*

Our modern world seems to be uncircumcised in heart. We surround ourselves with a protective, but unnecessary, layer of distraction that detracts from the spiritual and emotional transparency we must possess in order to flourish in our interior lives.

Our hearts, too, are uncircumcised when we remain as we were at birth – unchanged. The layers that encircle our hearts have, in fact, hardened them. We become calloused. We are not open to the workings and the ways of God when we are uncircumcised in heart.

Conversely, we are permanently transformed when we permit God to strip us of that familiar coping mechanism, that layer of protection, around our hearts that has truly never served a useful purpose. When we are circumcised in heart, God may cut away at parts of us that have blinded us to truth and love. This spiritual circumcision is painful at first and may leave a scar, but the scar serves as a reminder that we are changed. We are no longer who – or what – we were at birth.

Circumcision of heart leads us to a newfound vulnerability. We leave behind the familiar and embrace a life lived in and for Christ. The pain of pruning results in exuberance and exultant living.

CHAPTER SEVEN

Finding Peace & Unity

A SEVERE PERSECUTION

Anger snowballs into rage within me, and then the storm of fury takes over my spirit. This kind of interior disturbance nearly always produces some sort of sinful exterior manifestation – the same incitement that led to Stephen's stoning and Saul's persecution of Christians.

At times we are the ones inflicting the severe chastisement to others, while at other times we are on the receiving end of the persecution. When we receive judgment and the stoning of our hearts, how much more, then, should we respond to others with a severe mercy instead of harsh bitterness?

More often than not, my anger does not stem from someone else's provocation. Anger resides in the pit of my belly, like a sleeping monster that only requires a slight nudge in order to boldly awaken. That nudge can be what others say or do to me, or it can be triggered by circumstance.

But the truth is my anger is simply my own sin, and it is a compounded sin at that, for it begins as a wound to my ego from some petty slight and then swells into an uncontrollable pit of darkness that can easily and often overcome me. This becomes my severe persecution when I allow my sinful anger to fester without sacramental healing. The wound then becomes vulnerable to infection. I am shackled by my sin and cannot escape it, so I turn it towards others who have somehow become unassuming victims of my bitterness.

Must I remain caged in my interior persecution? I am like Saul before his splendor of metanoia. Must I, then, kill others in spirit because my own spirit has died due to my sin of carrying anger rather than releasing it to God?

Severe persecution only ends when I make the first step toward conversion, which leads me to sacramental healing. Severe persecution begins and ends with me. I am both a victim and a perpetrator, but I can approach the altar of mercy with humility and find the Father of mercy earnestly awaiting my arrival with open arms. My affliction is no longer inflicted upon others when I offer God my wounds, and He touches them with His grace, so that I may be made new.

Anger may incite this pattern of destruction in me, but in the end, I can opt to immerse myself in Mercy and thus become a severe mercy to myself and others.

A VOICE THAT SPEAKS OF PEACE

"I will listen for what God, the Lord, has to say; surely he will speak of peace to his people and to his faithful. May they not turn to foolishness!" ~ Psalm 85: 9

A voice that speaks of peace –
Quiet,
Calm,
Gentle
Balm -
A whisper in the wind.

A voice that speaks of peace –
Strong,
Sure,
Steady,
Secure –
A lion reclining with the lamb.

A voice that speaks of peace –
Unafraid,

Obedient,

Zealous,

Thoughtful –

A poet and philosopher, an orator of God.

A voice that speaks of peace –

Shatters,

Divides,

Separates,

Sorts -

The wheat from the chaff must be selected.

A voice that speaks of peace –

A voice that shouts Truth

Without uttering a word or single syllable

Is a voice of God,

A disciple

Who lives the parables and walks with Jesus.

We are the voice that speaks of peace.

We whisper or smile,

Frown or command,

But we do all at the Spirit's prompting –

No more, no less.

BE AT PEACE

In the stillness of this morning, I am immersed in peace, yet my heart feels so conflicted with the uncertainties of my life. Today is a day in which I want solutions and resolutions. I need conclusions and am tired of every aspect of life leaving another open door or unresolved concern.

But God calls me into this stillness, saying to me as He did the wind and sea, "Quiet! Be still!" And then, "Why are you terrified, O you of little faith?" My small, frail faith has grown lackluster on days like these where I'd rather not live in the midst of the mysteries or Mystery Himself. Why is it that I must remain in this dark tomb of waiting? Still, I wait...and I watch in the stillness of this dreary, rainy morning.

Being at peace is what I truly crave, but it often eludes me as does the butterfly or hummingbird outside my window. I may capture them for a moment, but they quietly and unexpectedly flutter away again, and I am left – once again – in the watching and waiting.

Today I will practice the art of being still in the movements of solitude offered to me. I will pray, then, to be at peace with the unknown and rest in a known God.

DWELL IN ENDURING PEACE

"Had you walked in the way of God, you would have dwelt in enduring peace." ~ Baruch 3: 13

It seems that those of us who choose to take the often trying ways of Christianity experience greater suffering and are tested more than those who are not apparently following the ways of Christ. Why is it that the wicked seem to prosper while the faithful struggle?

The wicked may enjoy worldly gains, but those who "walk in the way of God dwell in enduring peace." Our confidence resides in His providence and grace that sustain us and draw us nearer to Him. We are granted supernatural gifts that have no worldly value and yet are eternally priceless.

"The peace that surpasses all understanding" (see Philippians 4:7) is our reward in times of great trials. He washes and bathes us in this peace, so that we live among and within it as long as we continue to trust and walk in His ways.

In the end, what matters most is whether we have kept our eyes and hearts fixed on Heaven rather than on all that is fleeting and fades away on Earth. Then everlasting peace will greet us as our heavenly reward.

FINDING PASTURE

I often ponder St. Faustina's vision of Heaven, Hell, and Purgatory, but the one I vividly picture more than the rest is her image of Heaven. To me, it is when we find pasture and gaze upon the lazy meadow.

In my mind's eye, I am walking along an unknown path of great loss and significant suffering. It is a path in the thick of the woods, and, while beautiful, it is enigmatic and at times dark. The green trees of all varieties surround me, but the path itself is simple: dirt nestled underneath the earth's floor of decaying leaves, rocks, and branches.

Suddenly, in an unexpected moment, the path clears to a beautiful meadow. It is not visible from the forest's trail, but once I set foot there, I am completely lost and enraptured in its splendor. The meadow is encased by trees, but it is vast and full of every colorful wildflower imaginable.

The meadow is the verdant pasture, where my soul remains forever reposed. I stand in the meadow – alone, so it seems – and my entire being is elevated to the clear skies and bright sunshine above me. A gentle breeze cools and calms as it sweeps past, grazing my neck and tousling tendrils of my hair. The meadow is tranquil and conducive to rest, to endless hours or perhaps years of restorative sleep.

How I pine for that pasture, which is Heaven. Upon first glance, I instantly forget about the thorny path of suffering that led me to this majestic meadow. Every part of that path was worth an eternity of peace, joy, and perfection. The pasture is where I can perpetually praise, glorify, and thank God for His goodness and love.

And to reach the pasture requires perseverance and trust. Without these, I would have long ago abandoned the path that appeared to lead nowhere.

GATHERING OR SCATTERING?

"Whoever is not with me is against me, and whoever does not

gather with me, scatters." ~ Luke 11: 23

Roaches scatter and hide when light reveals their mischief. Moles scatter and hide when their tunnels are disturbed as the spring weather softens the ground. What is done in the darkness will eventually be seen in the light. If we scatter, we do so out of a true guilt and shame that result from our sinful living. Scattering creates division, too, because everyone runs in different directions out of frantic fear of being caught and facing the consequences of our behaviors.

Gathering, though, is an act of unity, because we are bringing together those who have scattered. We come together as one mind and heart – to rejoice, to mourn, to listen, to celebrate, to worship. This is why it's so critical that our Church be *catholic*, that is, universal. Its universality is a form of unity, because we worship together under one doctrine of faith.

Let us gather today – the lost and aimless, those scattered by shame and sin. If we restore unity, we restore love through Him who heals.

IN SILENCE AND PEACE

"I have stilled my soul." ~ Psalm 131: 2a

Noise taunts me everywhere. Even in my exterior environment, when all is quiet and calm, the interior chatter remains. It grows louder as my surroundings remind me of peace.

Peace eludes me. It is a spiritual fruit for which I have desperately prayed, but I am immersed in chaos. It is the internal chaos that stifles any possibility of peace. It chains and shackles my soul.

But the unrest is an unwelcome visitor. I never desired to be so conflicted and restless, yet my wandering spirit somehow got the best of me. Now I am wounded, jaded, and wary of change.

May peace rest in me. In the silence, I discover the invitation for peace, and the Spirit grants it to me on occasion. Today is one such occasion of rest devoid of responsibility.

Rest in Me. Abide in Me.

I sleep in Your presence, for Your slumber in my heart delights me, and I find You there, within me all along.

PEACE BE WITH YOU

"The precondition for peace is the dismantling of the dictatorship of relativism." ~ Pope Benedict XVI

How ironic that peace requires a sword and that to obtain and maintain the "peace that surpasses all understanding," we must take up arms in some way. We do not have a human enemy, of course, and we know the war is a spiritual one, a new and holy crusade. But it is a holy war against the principalities and powers of darkness that manifests itself in the cultural milieu of apathy and ambivalence – relativism.

How odd, then, that such neutral (or seemingly neutral) perspectives and philosophies are truthfully antipathies to peace. No one can enter the narrow gate through apathy. No one possesses the peace of Heaven by remaining neutral or lukewarm. It is precisely that our hearts are set ablaze to stand for something mighty, to discover the meaning of Jesus's words, "Peace be with you," that necessarily moves us to battle against indifference and cold hearts.

The world is full of bodies encasing hearts of stone, but peace is not a neutral offer extended to us. It is not an invitation to live a quiet and reclusive life devoid of strife and struggle. On the contrary, peace demands that we love, and to love often means we shake things up and rock the boat a bit. "Peace be with you" is the announcing of our call, the onset of our mission as disciples of Christ.

To be at peace and to spread the peace of the resurrected

Christ is to be a champion, a warrior of love. No, we cannot remain indifferent to the blood that is shed from abortion, self-harm, hypocrisy, greed, euthanasia, capital punishment, and now the modern martyrdom of Christians everywhere. We cannot stand idly by for the sake of a false peace.

True peace rises in us so that we stand for justice, demand and command it through charity. It does not mean we return violent acts for other violent acts, but it means we strike the core of relativism that has infested and infected our society with laissez faire attitudes towards others.

Peace shelters us in the scars of Jesus's wounds. His scars remind us of our own self-sacrifice, freely extended to slay the deep poverty of lukewarm hearts. Peace arms us with clarity and wisdom, love in truth, and to boldly confront heresy and sin. Peace anoints us in this mission, so that we can bring the peace of Christ to those who are hurting.

RESTORING ORDER

"Suffering restores order." ~Jacques Benigne-Bossuet[xi]

God is a God of order, not chaos. The enemy thrives in chaos and disarray; thus, confusion and disorder are his tools to distract us away from tranquility, which exists when all things come together effortlessly through grace. If sin brings about immense turmoil within, we can be sure this self-imposed suffering is chaotic. However, suffering has many dimensions, and one of its higher purposes is to restore order in our lives.

Consider a person who lives recklessly and without forethought, exhibiting the vice of daring. He loves parties and imbibing to excess, but one day, in a drunken stupor, he falls from a window and becomes paralyzed. The miracle, the grace, is that he has not died in a state of mortal sin, but the natural consequence is that he must suffer.

In this case, he could choose to allow his suffering to become a crutch, so that he plays the role of a victim. He could become bitter and blame his paralysis on life's tragedies. But there is something greater, something more, that is presented to him – an opportunity for order to be restored in and through his suffering. This is ultimately the goal of redemptive suffering: that we permit God to use every mistake, every ounce of pain, and every wound for His glory and our sanctification.

Suffering is not the end, as we know, but the beginning, of our hope. When we suffer and choose that God may use it in any way He wills, we are transformed by grace, through hope, into joy.

The joy is not so much from the suffering itself, but from the use of it, its purpose that surpasses our transitory pain. We must always fix our gaze to the Cross and recall its glory, the fulfillment of generations who anticipated the moment of their salvation. When our aches and grumblings are given to God, we compensate for the lack of suffering elsewhere. We participate in the Paschal Mystery and thus in the glory of the Resurrection.

STORING UP INNER RICHES

All this while I've concerned myself with what is too little: food, time, money, fun, sleep, etc. It's as if I doomed myself with this thinking, because I was concerned only with my lack – or apparent lack – of temporal needs and wants. My soul became wrecked as a result, consumed with worry and anxiety, fearful of what might happen if I lost everything.

There's no doubt that losing my home, my health, or my family would devastate me like nothing else up to this point. But if I still could claim my faith, moreover, trust in God's Providence, then my heart would be full and at rest.

That's really what any of us yearns for, isn't it? To have a heart at rest, one that is content and undisturbed with life's unexpected and often unpleasant circumstances, is what we wish we could possess and maintain. What if we stored up riches in Heaven, despite our life's apparent poverty? Our hearts would reside elsewhere, as would our thoughts, and we would keep our focus on what is in store for us in eternity.

My life may always be one that is hidden and unknown to the world. I may never become a phenomenon in this life, yet my heart, set on Heaven, will be satisfied and even overjoyed with the promise and blessings of eternity.

SUMMIT OF PEACE

"Confess the power of God, whose majesty protects Israel, whose power is in the sky." ~Psalm 68: 35

My whole life has been one long-winded war, battle after battle against the enemy, my sinful nature, and the world's deceptions. Why is it so difficult to acquire – and then remain in – peace? The summit of peace is the peak of the mountain that kisses the sky. I imagine the heavens opening up the skies when one reaches the height of that long, dusty climb.

The summit of peace seems unattainable in this life, but I know this is yet another impediment to my sanctification, another tactic of war from the enemy. But so few people seem to be at rest, in a place of security and safety, assurance and confidence in You. The mass populace appears instead to be heavy-hearted and massively plagued by busyness, illness, and complex relationships.

I do not wish to join the majority. I long for solitude, structure, freedom, prayer, and contemplation. Is it possible to reach the monastery of peace within my tumultuous heart? O Lord, I desire that sanctuary of the unbounded skies. The chains of sin and worldliness shackle me where I am today, but I know You free me from them in the grace of the Sacrament of Mercy.

Carry me to the pinnacle of peace, Father, for I am but a helpless child nestled in Your arms. I cannot make this climb alone.

THE ABSENT ONES

I have been absent from the most significant of events, the Mass. At one point in my life, I took it for granted and emotionally "checked out" altogether. In a sense, I resembled Thomas, because I wasn't present or available to the Risen One. I had rescinded my once-open heart and retracted it into the safety of myself, not realizing that Jesus wanted my woundedness and brokenness.

Where are all the doubting Thomases of the world? Have they, like I once did, retreated from the One whose scars reminded them of their own seeping sores of the heart? I wonder why we run from Jesus when we face Him without barriers or facades. In that stark and jarring honesty, we become afraid – not of Jesus, but of our wretchedness. And instead of allowing our shame to become our gift to Jesus, we recoil in horror at His blinding light. We recoil from ourselves reflected in Him.

But Jesus beckons us, "Peace be with you." There is always a message of peace hidden in our darkness and interior chaos. We must sift through our ugliness to find Him residing there, waiting for us, ready to heal us. "Peace."

THE BOND OF PEACE

"I, then, a prisoner for the Lord, urge you to live in a manner worthy of the call you have received, with all humility and gentleness, with patience, bearing with one another through love, striving to preserve the unity of the spirit through the bond of peace."
~ *Ephesians 4: 1 – 3*

If we truly knew how to love one another as we ought, we would dwell in peace – not necessarily void of conflict, but in a common striving for Heaven. Since Heaven is our shared hope, we would overlook petty grievances, forgive faults, and seek out commonalities among our Christian denominations.

Peace for the sake of avoiding conflict is not true peace. The fruit of the Spirit nestles within each of us as we faithfully persevere through trials and difficulties. It's true that the world can be in tumult all around us, yet our hearts remain undisturbed, resting in His peace.

This is the bond that is forged between Holy Spirit and humanity, but it is only derived from authentic love, that is to say, self-denial, self-abasement, emptying of self, self-sacrifice, etc. All of love is based on the virtue of humility, which we should earnestly seek and pray for daily, so that we may essentially become agents of God's peace in the midst of a world filled with no direction, a world void of serenity.

THE FIRST STAGE OF WISDOM

"The fear of the Lord is the beginning of wisdom."
~*Psalm 111: 10*

I have long prayed for wisdom, because I am so often lost and directionless each time I face a decision – about how to parent or prudently use money or simply using my time for holy and intentional purposes. Wisdom seems such a lofty virtue, unattainable to someone with so much ignorance about the ways of sanctity. Yes, I seem to be stuck in the locale of eternal frustration, yet I ask God for the eyes of my heart to be enlightened. However, they are infrequently unveiled by fleeting revelations of wisdom and then they return to a state of waiting and unknowing.

Today I realize that the first stage of wisdom is a holy fear of God – not a trembling terror, but a fondness and tender love for Him. Love always draws me away from myself and toward the other. Love dissolves my hesitancy, malice, frustration, and fear. To fear the Lord is to approach Him in love, which is a pure state of humble submission, yet an incredible confidence in and desire for His mercy.

This is the first stage of wisdom: to discover and maintain that ever-elusive peace, I must first enter into Love each day and remain in Him without retreating. This is a confident, rather than incomplete, love, and so it is wise to immerse myself in the One who is Wisdom. Love is the source of all, so that God may be all in all in me.

THE SEAL OF UNITY

"The blood of St. Josaphat even today, as it was three hundred years ago, is a very special pledge of peace, the seal of unity." ~ Pope Pius XI

Sometimes people mistake unity for tolerance or coexistence, but authentic unity can never be separated from the acknowledgment of an objective Truth. Instead, unity may exist in very violent situations or when divisions occur, which seems like an oxymoron.

But God uses these sorts of enigmas to remind us that His thoughts are above our thoughts, and His ways are above our ways. He wants unity to be a natural, rather than only supernatural, principle, which begins at the individual level. We must personally strive for interior, rather than exterior, peace.

This is the seed of unity (interior peace), which is cultivated through the development of virtues. Unity can only flourish in society when its individual members have definitively grown in their respective interior development.

As with St. Josaphat, unity may require martyrdom. What we do and how we live (and die) determines the perpetuation of the Kingdom of God on Earth. We long for wholeness that only God can fill, so we are bonded with His seal of unity.

CHAPTER EIGHT

Faith, Hope, & Charity

AWAKE FROM SLEEP

"It is the hour now for you to awake from sleep."
~ Romans 13: 11a

We have become drowsy and indifferent toward the interior development of virtue. Our apathy extends to a lack of concern for others. Somehow we've become quite content with holing up inside our homes and shielding ourselves (both literally and figuratively) from potential suffering through encountering Jesus and people in pain. In turn, our souls have fallen asleep, too comfortable to keep watch. Vigilance is too much effort for a drowsy soul.

But we are exhorted to wake up from this spiritual inertia and wait with earnest expectation. The hour has come. The hour is now. Acedia will not survive the times ahead that only serve to test our character. What are we truly made of? It is grit that is tempered through the fire of divine love, which becomes fortitude. Persistence changes into perseverance. Waiting transforms into patience.

And it is the refinement of such virtue that will not only wake us up from a long slumber, but will also keep us awake. Virtue insists upon interior stamina and self-denial. It never accepts mediocrity, but instead it thrives on spiritual excellence. And this excellence only comes into existence through trials and changes, challenges and sensory fasting. The soul must supersede the self. "I" must melt into "you," other. Then the soul will arise within us and take hold of our laziness and ambivalence. We will rise with the Son on the last day.

DO NOT LOSE HOPE

These days mark incredible confusion. People I have trusted – often with very personal aspects of my spiritual travails – have left their call and abandoned God in favor of happiness.

Happiness: I've grown rather disgusted and disgruntled with the word. I'm not sure I'll ever be happy in this life. Maybe "reasonably happy in this life and supremely happy in the next" is my true hope for happiness. Yet it seems to me that the modern concept of happiness is incomplete and superficial. It is based largely on emotion and moral relativism – "What's right for me" or "What makes me happy."

What does that mean, anyway – "What makes me happy?" I mean, I could do whatever I want right now, and I might feel good for a fleeting moment, but is that really happiness? It seems the masses are pursuing happiness when they don't really know what it is or how to find it. It's a concept loosely based on a false sense of freedom.

As more and more faithful fall away, I am tempted to lose hope and get swept away by their deception. It makes me question truth and the God I know and love, but only because I thought these were true followers of Christ – honest believers, witnesses, and even shepherds of the Church.

But I cannot lose hope, nor can I turn back or choose a new path. God has assured me that this road is steady and certain, and He guides my steps, but how quickly and easily I could fall into the enemy's snares! I must maintain focus on God alone, His Church, Word and Sacrament, rather than following those who stray from these.

FAITH ENTERS BY LISTENING

The air I breathe permeates my surroundings with tension. It is palpable as I inhale, then exhale with exhaustion and panic. The tension mounts, and I desperately attempt to resist the sudden urge to talk my way through it, distracting myself by initiating or engaging in idle chatter.

My faith weakens with each word I speak without intention or consideration of consequence, because faith only grows through the invitation of solitude: listening.

This is active, deliberate listening, a sort of heart language or emotive sense toward Heaven. I wait for Your prompt. At times I am impatient or hasty. I want to move forward with my day and get on with the business I've planned.

Yet I've found in my life that You often choose to speak to me at the most inconvenient, inopportune moments: while I'm driving the car or the girls are screaming, in the shower, or in the garden. I want to dismiss it out of frustration, but there it is, the familiar beckoning.

Tap, tap, tap. You knock on my heart to wake me from the drowsiness of daily life. *Tap, tap, tap.* Am I listening? Will I respond?

Faith invites me to respond to Your call, whether it is convenient or inconvenient. It is always growing or receding, waxing or waning. What will I decide?

I answer Your invitation, sometimes wearily, but never with regret. I open my arms and state with stouthearted certainty, "Here I am, Lord. What is Your invitation today?"

These are the difficult but fruitful moments of faith: it expands within all of us when we respond to You affirmatively, and then it is multiplied to extend far beyond our limited scope.

FAITH GROWS IN SILENCING OUR HEARTS

Too many of us spend our time talking or engaging in mental chatter through our meandering thoughts. Listening is likely one of the most difficult aspects of communication, yet it is also the most important. When we lose our way, our foothold, or our sight on God, it's often due to our inability to listen to Him.

Faith enters our hearts when we listen to God's voice. We cannot merely hear Him, because words fall deaf without a change of attitude, which is a heart change. Listening pierces our hearts so that God's Word comes alive and enters our way of being. Faith grows, then, when we listen.

Listening requires discipline, or the charism of self-control. We must set aside a sacred time and space every day that is conducive to listening. God often speaks through subtleties, like a whisper, because He wants us to truly be drawn to Him and seek Him wholeheartedly.

Perhaps God will speak to you in ways other than words. It could be in a flower or bird or some other symbol found in nature. Maybe you hear a song lyric and are reminded that God is with you. But a heart that is not open or is always distracted will not perceive God in the ordinary, natural circumstances.

Be attentive. Be alert. Vigilance means you are always ready for God to speak to you and act in you, but you wait for His directive. Wait with a patient love, but always keep the ear of your heart open to receive Him.

HOLY INSPIRATIONS

I have my heart set on sights too grand and lofty for human possibility, so I second-guess the origins of such desire – the devil, the flesh, the world, or – God? Am I seeking selfish ambition for the sake of my own glory, or am I sincerely attempting to do my part by responding to God's call in order to bring about His greatest glory?

The perpetual pull between Heaven and Earth is exhausting. Earth seems to be more practical and possible. I am literally "grounded" when I operate my reason using logic and clarity of thought. Yet pragmatism often gets in the way of what is possible with God – His holy inspirations that supplant what is clear and logical.

Naturally, God uses my ability to reason (my intellect) for a higher purpose, by way of human nature. For one who has esteemed pragmatism to a fault, it may just be my mind that detracts from the other, deeper side of me – that which imagines Heaven and longs for it one day.

The imagination can also draw me away from God when it drifts into dreams of worldly gain and pleasure. But God uses my imagination, too, to draw me back to Him in some odd wedding of my intellect (possibility) and imagination (impossibility). One balances the other so that I find God present and active in both. This only occurs if I am remaining in Him, if my soul is in a state of grace, and I seek Him with a pure and sincere heart.

Divine inspirations, while sublime and sometimes enigmatic, come to fruition with faith (believing God's promises), hope (waiting for the fulfillment of those promises) and charity (actively working for God's service, loving Him for His sake, nothing more or less).

Charity is the birth, the fruition of what appears ridiculous or unlikely through human reason alone. Charity is what makes everything possible through the assistance of divine grace. It seems that God often chooses the impossible to bring fulfillment to His plans, precisely so that we can deduce no human hand or influence in how something came about.

We must learn, through loving and living all that is of God, to see His hand move in the ordinary possibilities of every day, as well as the extraordinary impossibilities.

HOPE DOES NOT DISAPPOINT

"Hope does not disappoint, because the love of God has been poured out into our hearts through the Holy Spirit that has been given to us." ~ Romans 5: 5

In all my life, the one virtue that has remained steadfast, however weakened it became at times, was hope. I always longed for something – Someone – more than this life could offer me, Someone bigger than I and greater still than this universe and all galaxies combined. This yearning left me always anticipating God's promises for my welfare rather than woe (Jeremiah 29:11), knowing that every circumstance in my life would be used for my greater good if I remained in God's favor (Romans 8:28).

Yes, God's Word gave me hope, but so, too, did His flesh and blood, which nourished and fortified me to hunger and thirst for righteousness of His kingdom. This hope often grew within me exponentially, and a newfound zeal sprang forth so that I then began to hunger for the salvation of all souls, especially those in most need of mercy.

You see, hope may become fragile in times of desolation, but for the faithful, baptized Christian, it never completely vanishes. Hope seals our confidence that God is a God of wonders and a God of His word. We believe in His constancy, because His Word is Truth and He is Truth.

Therefore, hope does not disappoint, no matter the seeming contradictions that linger. In the face of trial and adversity, hope springs eternal; that is, our hope should become greater still, for we know, love, and serve the Triune God who never fails us and will not lead us to ruin.

Then hope without faltering. Hope in the fruit of such virtue, so that you may also grow in faith and love, the siblings of hope.

HOPE, EVEN AGAINST HOPE

When all else fails, I turn to hope, because despondency and discouragement are my natural, temperamental inclinations. Hope somehow finds me when I have lost myself and am drowning in a sea of nothingness.

Just when all seems lost, and I am on the verge of giving up, hope breaks through, if only momentarily. It is as if hope – enflamed in my heart and infused in my soul at Baptism – sometimes acts as a quiet, unnoticeable ember that is feeble and flickers subtly, almost extinguished. It burns gently at times when I feel hope has left me altogether, and then suddenly I feel a surge of hope – something new, renewed, exuberant – like a burst of flames grown stronger from the cooling embers.

To hope against hope sometimes means I don't know if I still have any hope remaining in me. It means God sometimes rests quietly in me, or even sleeps, and then He awakens everything I believed was forever eradicated.

Awaken hope in me today, Lord, and may I never be without prevailing confidence in Your love. May I hope against hope.

PEACE BEGINS WITH FAITH

My anxieties rouse troubling thoughts and even more disturbing emotions that distract me from an interior solitude – a state of perpetual peace, which is likened to a clandestine oasis in the soul.

At times I recognize this calm that does not waver in the midst or onset of crisis or catastrophe. It seems enigmatic and ethereal to me, but it truly is You dwelling in me, O Peace and Stillness of my soul. Why, then, am I sometimes so intensely restless and at other times, the storms within are quieted by Your presence?

Do I truly possess faith the size of a mustard seed, or is my faith still locked in infancy? I wonder how I can profess exteriorly the delights of faith and even speak boldly, with unwavering confidence, of difficult truths of faith, yet I so infrequently maintain a state of peace within.

How small is my faith in reality when I lose that gift of tranquility. Regardless of life's circumstances, no matter the illness or unexpected disasters and debacles that invariably strike, the peace You have given me is to remain steadfast. No one and nothing has the power to vanquish this "peace that surpasses all understanding." Yet how readily I relinquish it in my weakness.

I am weary, Lord. Be my peace. I am lonely, Lord. Wrap me in Your peace. I am sinful and wretched. I have nothing pure and of virtue to offer You, so grant me rest and refreshment in Your peace.

O Light, O Way, Truth and Life, You are the source of peace in my heart. Increase my faith, however slight today, that I may reside with You, in You and for You without disturbance.

PERFECT LOVE CASTS OUT FEAR

"Perfect love drives out fear." ~ 1 John 4: 18

What can I purchase with fear? The short answer is that I purchase nothing of value with fear. Fear leads me to a self-imposed anguish, because I am trapped inside the *"what ifs"* that fill my mind.

Fear paralyzes me to inaction when God is beckoning me to take a risk like never before. Fear tells me to stay put where it is safe and familiar.

Fear purchases slavery – slavery of sin and anger. I am a captive to fear when I succumb to it. I am not truly free. Instead, I limit myself and do not give God permission to do great things to me and through me.

Fear is the antithesis to love, yet perfect love casts out all fear. Today I am given a choice, just like every day: to fear or to love. What I choose determines consequences of slavery or freedom. Love will release me from captivity, while fear keeps me chained in torment. Fear leads me to acedia, but love leads me to fortitude.

Which path will I choose today?

RICH IN WHAT MATTERS TO GOD

"Thus will it be for the one who stores up treasure for himself but is not rich in what matters to God." ~ Luke 12: 21

I have two girls with special needs, and there are some days I am tempted to put them in the same category as typical kids, because I hear so often about the importance of athleticism and academic achievement. My perspective on what matters most in their development differs from many moms, however, because I consider the condition of their souls and their formation in the Faith.

What matters most to God when we die: a person who has straight A's and high post-secondary accolades, or one who loves well? If we do not love, we have nothing. In essence, we are spiritually bankrupt without virtue.

Because I know and see many children with cognitive impairments, I am more firm in this belief than ever before. I see their hearts so full of love, and I know they matter, simply because they exist – not for what achievements or accomplishments they have made.

What is rich to God is a soul well-schooled in faith, hope, and charity, as well as temperance, prudence, fortitude, and justice. I would even dare to say that love alone is what matters above all in the eve of our lives, as St. John of the Cross so aptly stated.

THE FIRE OF DIVINE CHARITY

"No sadness befalls charity, only joy: Charity makes the heart expansive and generous, not double or narrow. The soul who is pierced by this tender arrow does not show one thing with her face and tongue when she has another in her heart." ~ St. Catherine of Siena

I have been ashamed at my lack of charity. Only divine charity can intervene where there is such a dearth of goodness in me. Day after day, I attempt to tackle the constant hardships placed before me – new and ongoing – but I fail time and again.

I fail, but You never fail. How is it I have come so far in my life, yet I've never asked – begged, even – for the gift of divine charity? All this time I have wasted, desperately trying to handle everything on my own and yet my heart is filled with turmoil. I am covered in sadness, discouragement, and despondency rather than in divine charity, which leads me to joy in all things.

If only my heart were no longer duplicitous! If only I knew how to discipline myself to speak when there is charity in my heart, then life would offer me more peace and less confusion.

But You see my poverty of spirit, and I know You can do all things in me if I only ask for this divine charity. Grant me, then, a heart ablaze with the love from Heaven, for earthly love has failed in all regards. I long for a heart that gives without restriction or condition, a generosity that is an extension of Your Most Sacred Heart.

May the fires of Your divine charity refine my heart, my lazy and limited scope of humanity and what it means to serve others. Then one day perhaps You will grant me a spiritual heart transplant so that I, along with the angels and saints, may participate in this divine charity.

THE HEART IS A SYMBOL OF LOVE

I must not know what love truly entails, for my heart is always wounded, always bleeding, always breaking. My heart is heavy with grief and full of sorrow and suffering. Is this love?

Where, then, is the joy that transcends the black hole of grief? It is depleted. Instead, I am replete with a hollowness that is cold and silent. I am encased by my sins. They taunt me, lest I forget my nothingness, my incredible lack of virtue, or lest pride tell me differently.

I hear You whisper, "You are precious to Me. You are my beloved daughter with whom I am well pleased," but I am bereft and left with confusion. My reflex is to hide in shame and fear, to wallow in the din of sinful darkness, lest Your light blind me.

But I need to be blinded by Your illumination, O Love. If

not, I truly am nothing. I have nothing without You. Your mercy cloaks me in heavenly peace, and I cry tears of pain, rejection, betrayal, heartache, and even of spiritual attack. They are shed as an offering to You, the only gift I have. May my tears become pure as holy water and my eyes the font of the Living Water of life and love.

Could it be true that my heart – as battered and torn as it is – still remains a symbol of love, of Your love? Yes, for the old has passed away and the new has arrived. You make me a new creation time and again through the sacraments of healing. Behold, all is refreshed and enlivened by Your touch of grace and gentle embrace.

Consume me, then, by the flames of love that destroy what is infirm by its white heat, and then by that same heat of Your Spirit, enflame my heart. Set my entire being ablaze with the quiet, yet persistent, embers of Love.

Then may my heart and my life no longer be a symbol of love, but instead the representation of Your flesh, which is Love Incarnate. May the blood of Your heart mingle with mine.

THROUGH FAITH AND PATIENCE

"We earnestly desire each of you to demonstrate the same eagerness for the fulfillment of hope until the end, so that you may not become sluggish, but imitators of those who, through faith and patience, are inheriting the promises." ~ Hebrews 6: 11 – 12

I've never been a patient person. In fact, since childhood, I've been quite the opposite – fussy, demanding, short-tempered, and easily irritated. Patience, or long suffering, is a virtue for which we all strive, yet it comes more naturally to some than others.

To suffer by waiting can drag on ad infinitum, yet doing so by faith – that is, believing in God fulfilling His promises – we grow in virtue, particularly perseverance. Faith and patience, then, go hand-in-hand. One tends to increase the other and draw us closer to the other. The foundation of patience must be faith, because without it, we grow slack in zeal and fall into unbelief or doubt. When we doubt, we may attempt to control everything or put matters into our own hands, thus slipping back to impatience.

Lack of patience seems to be a matter of control stemming from fear. When I am fearful of a particular situation's outcome, I lose self-control by tightening the reigns and becoming overbearing. We do not want to wait for much of anything, and we usually don't have to. Modern life offers many conveniences, so that we can hurry along and move to the next task with the same mentality of rushing.

This kind of intemperance is not only rooted in one's temperament, but it is also fed by anxiety and fear. When we live in a constant state of flurry and hustle, we become internally jittery. We have lost our peace. And somehow we become, at the very least, accustomed to this interior condition, if not comfortable with it. If we pause long enough to quiet ourselves or seek a moment of solace, our discontent surfaces, and we tend to divert ourselves from honest appraisal because of the reality of our restlessness.

Patience, however, produces the fruit of forbearance. The word itself implies that suffering is present and involved, usually because we bear something – a hurt, injustice, or some personal loss – that, instead of reacting in anger, we offer to Jesus as prayer. For those who are prone to impatience, this is no simple feat, but over time, our restless hearts are tempered in the fire of long-suffering, and they are quieted, still.

Faith is what drives us to be patient, because we realize our waiting is not in vain. The waiting itself is potentially fruitful if we are not assailing ourselves with all sorts of distractions in the meantime.

To pause, stop, or wait is contrary to the societal perspective of busyness and is considered a waste of precious time that we could otherwise fill. But God waits for us and seeks us in these breaks. He dwells in the silence of waiting.

WAIT WITH ENDURANCE

"But if we hope for what we do not see, we wait with endurance."
~ *Romans 8: 25*

Faith, hope, and charity are like beloved siblings who have grown closer over time. Branching from the same parents, they overlap in personality, yet remain very distinct from each other. They are unique in substance, but they share the same beginnings.

Charity is the oldest sibling, so faith and hope grow up admiring and emanating her traits, often looking to her for wisdom and guidance. Charity excels in heroic love to the point of always denying herself for the sake of what's best for another.

Faith is the one who believes in all revealed Truth without seeing or even fully comprehending all she has been taught. Faith knows that Mystery is beyond her; humility is her pearl, and she believes, because she loves Him who created all and revealed the divine mysteries to her.

Hope is the child who waits for answered prayers, the second coming, a revelation, or consolation. Hope is the youngest sister. She believes what she does not see due to Faith's influence, and she waits with endurance out of the heart of Charity, that is, love. She loves Him who promised joy and peace, so she waits expectantly for this fulfillment.

Hope prevents us from drowning in despair. We wait, not with discouragement or boredom, but eagerly and earnestly. We wait with endurance.

WE WHO HOPE

If there's one virtue that I clasp when my life is in shambles and I am being attacked on all sides, it is hope. I have come near to despairing many times, and at this point in my life, everything is uncertain and messy. Every aspect of my daily life is shredded, so that I may fix my gaze on Heaven rather than on myself.

Hope cloaks and enshrouds me. It is the blanket under which I seek refuge from the madness that I cannot unravel by myself. My inner and outer world is mass chaos, except I cannot flee from myself. Myself I must face with honesty, integrity, and a sincere desire to change.

Hope catapults us into the realm of growth, for pain invites us to hope in Someone greater and for something beyond the mess of now. Pain points us in the direction of change, and hope always waits for us at this crossroad.

Hope extends a candle newly lit into our hands as a reminder that His light permeates the darkest crevices of our being. Let us cling to hope, and may it never falter, especially when all seems lost and fragmented in and around us.

WHAT IS SOWN IN THE HEART

One seed can sprout into miraculous yield, perhaps twenty or even one hundredfold. One seed planted by Your loving hands, then nurtured by the sun and rain, is all it takes to plant an entire garden of virtue in my heart.

Today I feel that my heart has become overgrown with weeds. The brambles and thorns have taken over my heart that was once vast and amenable to new growth and new life. I have been careless, Lord, in tending the garden of my heart.

So plant Your word and sacrament in me. Though I am often conflicted, frustrated and full of sin, I know You can make me new again. One day You will sow patience, humility, and charity within – as You always have – but one day those seeds will fall upon rich, rather than rocky or sandy, soil.

The harvest will then be abundant. I have hope in this. I am confident not in myself, because I am fallible, as is evident with the brush and brambles in my heart. But my confidence is in

Your mercy, because mercy is the rich soil that dissolves all toxins from my soul. It is on the land of mercy where the garden of virtue will, at last, flourish within me.

CHAPTER NINE

Solitude, Silence, & Mystery

A HIDDEN MERCY

Why should You hide Yourself, Lord, on the road to Emmaus? Why is it You hide, too, in the form of simple bread and wine? Is it that You hide, or perhaps is it that the eyes of my heart have been darkened by seeking complexity, much as the Jewish people of Your time believed their messiah would reign as an ostentatious king?

I know the further I look for You, the nearer You actually dwell. You desire that my heart becomes empty, simple, and poor so that I may see with clarity what has always been before me: Your indwelling. You walk with me on this odyssey of life, yet I fail again and again to recognize Your presence next to me, near me, within me. Instead, I desperately grasp for everyone and everything else, duped into the delusion of finding You anywhere but where You truly are – hidden, invisible, disguised.

You are my hidden mercy, Jesus, for You desire that I seek You not in the exterior busyness of my milieu, but rather in the crevices of my heart. Your wellspring of mercy overflows somewhere too deep within me to acknowledge and name, a place beneath my consciousness. When I stop seeking, I find Your hidden mercy with me. I discover Your unveiling as the travelers on Emmaus finally recognized You.

You are walking with me, despite my inability to see or even believe this truth. You converse with me in simple ways, so I must throw off this cloak of complexity that I wear and risk inner exposure so that You may transform me into Love.

A SACRED VEIL

Some believe that all secrets are concealing some type of sin or, at the very least, deceive us. There are truths to these assumptions, because two old adages (one from AA, the other one from Scripture, respectively) are "You're only as sick as your secrets" and "What is done in the darkness will be revealed in light." Sickness and sin are bred in secret in order that the sinner remains in the dank dungeon of denial.

Other secrets are entrusted by God. Consider the Fatima visionaries. The Lord gave them information that was to be concealed at least for a while and then revealed at a designated time.

All of us have secretive moments and encounters with God. In Song of Songs, these are described as trysts with a lover. The deeper our love for God becomes, the more our hearts are able and willing to receive His trust through a type of sacrosanct relationship that only lovers share.

Not all secrets are sinful. God's secrets are a gift, an act of trust and total love. In fact, the self-giving acts we offer to God are also fruitful, but hidden and private, acts of profound love. In a sense, the human heart is cloaked in holiness through this clandestine love affair with God.

Modesty, too, is an exterior manifestation of this hidden – but very real – love between God and person. We conceal our bodies, and women veil their heads, because they are holy and meant to be ensconced in darkness in order to reveal the light.

The tabernacle, too, is veiled by a lace curtain or some type of cloth that hides the Blessed Sacrament, or rather, protects and shelters it, from unnecessary exposure and plain sight, requiring us see with the eyes of faith.

Secrets are the ways God chooses to summon us for pursuit. We tend to believe God is always seeking us, which is true, but He equally desires to be sought. This catch-and-chase rhythm is what captures a love interest, and God longs to be our sole love interest. We must seek Him, then, in the invisible recesses where He opts to hide – in the Blessed Sacrament, in a whisper, in our hearts. In this way His darkness reveals sweet and pure light, which illumines our souls to receive Him in the most intimate, personal love possible.

Seek Him, dear soul, and He will be found.

AUTUMN RAIN

"As they pass through the Bitter Valley, they find spring water to drink; the early rain covers it with blessings." ~ Psalms 84: 7

We've enjoyed the bounty of summer, so let the autumn rain cleanse the earth and make it ready for the rest of winter. Let us prepare our hearts for the blessings that await us with this rain. It is a renewal, a baptism of hope, and newness of being.

Autumn signifies harvest, but it is also a season of preparation. We may dread the winter because of the harsh and bitter winds, chilling frost, icy blasts, and snowstorms. Winter makes all seem dead, so we retreat in our inner warmth until it passes and we await the thaw.

The autumn rain reminds us that abundance doesn't last forever, and scarcity is needed for a hearty spiritual life. Scarcity tests our willingness to persevere through adversity, so the autumn rain showers us with a remembrance of the sobering season of winter as it nears.

We thank You for the abundance and the scarcity, O Giver of all. We welcome the hidden blessings of this autumn rain. Prepare us to enter into all You have in store for us.

BY PATHS UNKNOWN

"I will lead the blind on a way they do not know; by paths they do not know I will guide them." ~Isaiah 42:16a

"By paths unknown I will guide them." Your Word haunts me this day, because it seems I've been walking on unseen, unveiled paths for a long time. I wonder where I am headed and if I am going in the right direction. Since I cannot see what is before me, I never truly know for certain if what I am doing or where I am focusing is in accord with Your will. How will I know?

Perhaps in this life the invisible paths reveal my need to trust in You rather than in myself or others, to grip your hand firmly and not let go so that I may not falter by allowing You to lead. But so often I feel lost, cold, and abandoned on this dark road. It seems to be a forsaken path, and I receive no indication that it is a righteous one. Still, I keep moving forward, trying desperately to cling to You.

At times I do not feel or see Your presence. How do I know You are there and that I have not gone astray? I've discovered that trusting You – the sort of wholehearted, unreserved abandon into Your heart – means that I must also deny my supposed right to any certitude in this life. Certitude does not signify truth and right paths when it comes to my journey toward sanctification. Certitude is clinging to Your Word and Sacrament, because there I know Truth exists. But since I am not the Truth, the Way, and the Life as You are, I must trust that by faithfully following Your Word and staying close to the sacraments, then I am indeed on the right path.

But I may still feel lost, and this is okay. My journey to Heaven is not contingent upon my feelings or even my thoughts. It's a confident reliance that, even when You lead me into darkness, You guide my steps and protect me from evil. You are my ever-present, ever-ready help, and the darkness will not consume me, for You are a light unto my path and a lamp unto my feet.

BY WAITING AND BY CALM

"By waiting and by calm you shall be saved; in quiet and in trust shall be your strength." ~ Isaiah 30: 15

My strength wears more thinly with each passing day, and I

am bone weary. Even my spirit has run dry with exhaustion. I have been forced into a painful state of waiting: waiting for what, I do not know, but waiting nonetheless. I cannot move forward with any plans I've made or for any purpose. I am stuck here in this place of waiting.

Waiting is a constant struggle for me, because I always want to be doing something, staying busy and active. Waiting, however, forces one into an inert state, a condition that is conducive to resting and being.

Do we know how to simply *be* anymore? The pervasive flurry of activity overwhelms even those who are drawn to quiet and calm. To rest in God is what He asks of you and me: to simply wait for His presence and be still with Him, expecting nothing and perhaps offering Him little or nothing, but just *being*.

By waiting and by calm we are saved. This is shown even in modern science. Rest produces homeostatic levels of hormones in our bodies, so that they remain in or return to harmonious balance. The Lord's wisdom is clear: to combat stress and sickness, we must be tempered by periods of rest and relaxation in Him.

HIDDEN SWEETNESS

He hides Himself, dear soul, that you may seek Him and find Him sleeping, resting in your heart. Jesus doesn't ask us to love Him casually. Love requires difficult sacrifices and entails an expedition of self-denial. Jesus wants our love to be sincere, so don't despair if you do not see, hear, or feel Him for a time. He hides in you in order to abide in you. It is precisely because He loves you that He chooses to conceal Himself at times, so do not weep or grow mournful. The risen Jesus wakes from His slumber to reveal to you that He remains in you.

But when He sleeps, be content. During periods of waiting for Him to love you, show your love for Him through fidelity to prayer. You will learn to base your love for God on your actions rather than emotions in this way, so your faith deepens and matures. It is sweet that Jesus loves us so much as to hide in the depths of our souls – in recesses and crevices of ourselves about which we are only remotely aware or entirely unaware.

The more your love for Jesus grows, the more periods of spiritual aridity you may undergo. He is latent but present. Do not dissolve your faith, for this is true: He never leaves you or abandons you, despite your temptation to believe otherwise.

It's true that we may not feel Him or experience the warmth of His love. At times life will seem cold, unpleasant, and callous, but He remains in you. Abide in Him. Rest as He rests. Awake when He awakes. Then your heart will become more closely bonded with His as His will becomes your will, His longings yours. All He possesses He will then grant you.

HOPE IN SILENCE

"It is good to hope in silence for the Lord's deliverance."
~ *Lamentations 3: 26*

Silence bears the seed of fruitfulness, prosperity, and growth. Silence requires intense discipline, because it appears to be hollow. Indeed, silence can be hollow if we do not purposefully encounter You and others.

Silence is my classroom. I learn more from listening to You as our hearts beat in unison than from all of the great theological or philosophical discoveries of the modern era.

Therefore, I hope in silence. I wait in quiet wonder, knowing that sometimes Your Spirit stirs subtly and almost unknowingly, while sometimes You rest in my soul altogether. But I can always expect You to reside in my inner chamber, where I long ago made You a welcome guest. And so hope resides in me and in silence, because You dwell in my heart, where my innermost secrets are carefully kept.

When You act, I will be ready, because hoping in silence is

an active, contemplative waiting. It requires constant reflection about You and with You, then an unspoken understanding between us that You will fulfill Your promises in and through me. Your kingdom awaits in the silence of hope.

HOUSE OF SILENCE

Lord, make my heart a house of silence, where You and I meet and in which we both live. You then become my indwelling and my heart, a tabernacle. For so many years I have protected my heart from inevitable afflictions based on previous betrayals. The wounds never healed and were only compounded by my sin and the next toxic relationship. But today is different. Today I desire healing, though I know I must face the wounds of my past before silence and serenity become permanently transfixed in my heart and soul.

But if my heart becomes a house of silence, I know you will rest and reside there. I long to be Your shelter, Your refuge, Your resting place.

Teach me, Lord, to listen in the quiet of my heart and thus to become empty of the exterior noise and interior chatter of my idle thoughts. Once empty, fill me with silence – not a futile silence, but a silence that is fruitful. Then, at last, my heart will be ready to greet You at its door, and the welcome will be so sweet that You and I shall never part.

The door of my heart will eventually disappear, so that no threshold can contain You as You pass through and in me at Your will. What a happy silence to participate in Your mystery at last and offer You a steady and secure shelter of fruitfulness.

Make my heart a refuge of silence for You and for the world. Amen.

LIVING IN THE MYSTERY

"In him we have redemption by his blood, the forgiveness of transgressions, in accord with the riches of his grace that he lavished upon us. In all wisdom and insight, he has made known to us the

mystery of his will in accord with his favor that he set forth in him as
a plan for the fullness of times, to sum up all things in Christ, in
heaven and on earth." ~ Ephesians 1: 7 – 10

The times when life is darkest and I struggle most are when
You are acting miraculously. This is living in the mystery. I am
unaware of goodness within – only without. I can see Your
distant light shine in nature's sweet song, fragrance, or kiss. I
catch a glimmer of Your majesty by witnessing acts of mercy
from one to another. I see Your movements so evidently in the
intricacies of someone else's life, and I praise and thank You
for reminding me that You are still very much alive, active,
and loving.

It is so easy for me to fall into the pit set to ensnare me, a
hole of blackness that will swallow me in one fall or slip. I see
Your wonders elsewhere, but I do not see them in the
blackness that clouds my own life. I do not see goodness in
these daily struggles, both interior and exterior, but I continue
to move forward in faith, simply accepting the truth that, yes,
You are present in this mystery of darkness.

One day I shall live in light again.

RIVERS IN THE WASTELAND

"In the wilderness I make a way, in the wasteland, rivers."
~ Isaiah 43: 19b

I've come to realize that my soul is where God makes a river
and breathes new life into me, because my entire being is a
wasteland. There's a three-step process by which I understand
myself in greater depth and also see God with greater
gratitude. I am full of weakness, wretchedness, and
nothingness, while He is full of unconditional love, immensity,
and infinity.

In the beginning of the purgative stage, one sees his soul in
terms of weakness. Perhaps he sees (for the first time) his

inclination for laziness, slack in zeal, ambition, acedia, propensity for comfort, etc. In essence, he knows the reality that he, in and of himself, is a weak creature, infirm in spirit and possibly physical stature or strength. At first, he may become discouraged, both from lack of humility and lack of fear of the Lord. He is still in his spiritual infancy and expects that he will accomplish good on his own rather than by grace.

In the second stage, the illuminative stage, a person sees his wretchedness. This may coincide with entering the dark night of the soul during the purgative stage, in which God chooses to cloud the will, intellect, and senses. The soul in this state feels utterly abandoned by God and may be tempted toward despair. Hope and fidelity through perseverance must be fostered and nurtured as the person now sees his weaknesses but also vices or deeply entrenched sinful patterns of behavior or habits. He knows he can do nothing of his own accord but is not yet empty of himself. He is well on his way if he perseveres in hope.

In the third stage, the soul is emptied of itself and begins to love its poverty and emptiness. This nothingness is not necessarily a void; rather, it's a space inside of oneself God may fill with virtue and even Himself. One in this place has long accepted and embraced his humanity, realizing his need for God in complete dependence on Him to achieve virtue or practice charity. His desire to please and love God operates in his will to choose the right and the good, not for avoidance of punishment, but for its own sake.

Nothingness becomes a prime place for life to flourish. No longer a wasteland or desert, God's essence comingles with the essence of our nature. Only He raises up what was lost and dead within us so that we may bloom through charity. This is the gift of the wasteland and is the driving force behind how and why God makes us prosper by way of spiritual aridity. This, then, is our hope.

SLUMBER OF LOVE

When God Is Silent, a brilliant spiritual gem by Luis Martinez[xii], speaks at length about the times in our lives when we do not see, feel, or hear Jesus. He is seemingly absent, so our temptation is to abandon Him, or at the very least, to doubt.

Martinez begins with a reflection on the Gospel story where Jesus is asleep on a boat with the apostles present, and a storm erupts. Frightened, the apostles wake Jesus, who tells them not to be afraid and then calms the storm. Martinez explains the mystical symbolism to mean that there are times for all of us when Jesus isn't absent or distant from us – He is merely sleeping.

Jesus sleeps in the hearts of His beloved disciples. Sleeping in us connotes a particular level of closeness between us and Him, a familiarity grown into comfortable fondness. He sleeps in us to rest, to abide deeply within the places of ourselves of which we are unaware. It is in those depths where Jesus asks us to allow Him some respite. This is, in fact, a very beautiful opportunity for us to prepare a place for Him who had nowhere to rest His head – from the manger to the Cross.

This slumber is an opportunity for us to love Jesus, even and especially when He chooses to remain inactive, preferring the solitude of our hearts' sanctuaries to being roused from slumber. Do not wake Jesus, dear soul. I know you are fearful that His love has left you. You feel alone and forsaken when life's tempests arise. Be assured that, though He sleeps, He is very much present within you, and you are safe where He abides.

Learn from Jesus' slumber of love so that you will retreat often to the "cell of your heart," as St. Alphonsus Liguori describes. Seek solace in Jesus, but do not rouse Him. If you permit Him to sleep, when He wakes, He will be pleased with how well you have loved Him during the periods of quiet and waiting. Then your reward will be great, because love is always multiplied exponentially in a soul that loves well.

THE ABSENCE OF TIME

While I was walking my dog one brisk December evening, I lamented to no one in particular, "My time no longer exists." And, as soon as the thought flitted through my consciousness, it occurred to me that this was, in fact, an incredible grace of the moment. It's true that *my* time has changed into *God's* time. No longer do I have endless hours at my disposal to ponder, pray, or peruse my books. Life is not about me at all, which is why the time I have allotted to me (*chronos*) is at God's disposal now (*chairos*).

Days are filled with the flurry of endless activity, but most of the time my hands, heart, and head are full of children's clothing, diapers, dishes, or goofy and catchy tunes. When I speak, it's to inform or correct one of our little ones rather than to debate some abstract notion of philosophy. Even my thoughts are consumed with *the other* rather than what pleases *me*, and, while my ego is bruised by this, my soul has significantly matured.

All of life and love involves sacrifice – endless tokens of self-giving, altruistic, and benevolent in nature. The rhythm of one's interior life necessarily mimics the outward expression of "giving until it hurts." One's heart resides closely to one's behaviors and attitudes. Therefore, since what was once "my" time is not entirely "God's" time, I may be weary at the day's end, but my life – however fleeting – is fruitful and fulfilled.

THE EMMAUS QUESTION

"Peace be with you… Why are you troubled? And why do questions arise in your hearts?" ~ Luke 24: 36 & 38

Today Jesus asks us two questions, which were originally posed to His followers after He journeyed to Emmaus: "Why are you troubled? And why do questions arise in your hearts?" These are poignant and pertinent to most of us, who never seem to flee from stress and worry. There's always something or someone pushing us back to a state of fear, and we capitulate to it.

But Jesus brings us to ask ourselves why we're upset or why we worry over many unanswered questions or prayers. If we look at ourselves honestly, perhaps we'll catch a glimpse of what's really nagging at us. For some of us, worry erupts easily and often through small and petty occurrences that build up over time. Others of us worry about the big picture but not so much the details.

Jesus asks us these questions as a reminder that He is always with us, always walking alongside us, even and especially when we don't recognize Him there. Our faith must be such that we lean on Jesus more fervently during the times we can't see or feel Him near. Sometimes our own busyness clouds our ability to see Him, and other times He chooses to be hidden in and among us. But to a heart that loves well, He will still be the focus of devotion, whether He is visible or hidden, felt closely or seemingly distant.

Our faith, our love, hinges on these questions. We must learn to love Him in the mystery, the darkness, and the times of elation or celebration. We must love for love's sake, nothing more or less. This lesson is vital in order for peace to reign in our hearts, because our unreasonable expectations gently wither into oblivion, and we are left with a sort of spiritual nakedness that suggests to God, "Here I am. There's nothing holding me back from You, and I am not ashamed to be exposed."

THE ONE THING NECESSARY

In our modern age, we falsely interpret busyness as productive work. Somehow we glean a sense of accomplishment when our hands and minds are kept active, not realizing that our frenzy is actually acedia, the devil's means of distracting us away from the one thing necessary: Jesus.

How do we return to Jesus? To begin, we must discipline

ourselves for opportunities of silence. When these pauses happen throughout our day (or maybe we schedule them if life is too hectic), we choose to enter into that space with an open heart that is ready to receive Jesus. Silence begets solitude, which begets prayer, and prayer is our holy dialogue with the one Person necessary.

Silence is not empty or wasted space and time if we fill it with love, the essence of God Himself. In this way, it becomes rich and fertile soil, where God's seeds are watered and bloom within us. Take time for the one thing necessary, and your heart will be at rest. Choose to love, and what exhausts you will become what energizes you.

THE PILGRIM WAY

"Listen to my prayer, Lord, hear my cry; do not be deaf to my weeping! For I am with you like a foreigner, a refugee, like my ancestors." ~Psalm 39: 13

My life is fleeting, Lord, like the flicker of a flame that is so quickly extinguished with a gentle puff of air. So, too, am I like the dust, for I once was formed from dust by Your hand and, once again, I will return to dust.

I am but a pilgrim on this land, wandering but not aimlessly, for I know my end goal is Heaven. I wander in search of You, the One whom my heart loves, and it indeed takes me an entire lifetime to reach You.

With calloused hands and weary feet, I travel – sometimes geographically, but always interiorly, charting the terrain of my soul.

Where are You, my Beloved? My heart is one on the pilgrim's way, for it is there that I travel, experience torrential storms, seek You, and ultimately arrive at my destination, for Heaven is my home.

Along the pilgrim's way, I feast upon You, my food for the journey. Your Body and Blood sustain and fortify my body for the road ahead. As a pilgrim, I've abandoned my earthly pleasures and comforts for the sake of my Heavenly home. I seek Heaven now, no longer temporal acclaim and wealth or posterity.

My life is but a breath, for by Your breath, You willed me into being and one day my breath will be extinguished into oblivion. On that day, my pilgrimage will end, for that is the moment my breath will join the breath of Your Spirit for eternity.

THE ROAD TO DAMASCUS

"They heard the voice but could see no one." ~Acts 9:7

Saul spent his life pre-conversion in an inundation of chaos and slanderous speaking, which led to the death of many people's lives as well as their spirits. In turn, Saul's conscience had been dulled by his sinful actions. Something drastic was necessary to draw greatness from him.

When Saul fell blind, he received interior enlightenment. For many years, he had been sinning in the light of day. Because he was graced by the Light of the world, his sinful persecution was all the more grievous to Jesus. Saul lived in the light, yet chose works of darkness. This is why Jesus struck him blind. Saul's exterior vision had to be temporarily extracted, so that he could more clearly identify his wrongdoing, repent, and thus truly choose the Light over darkness.

How often does God use darkness to draw us nearer to Him? We are often distracted by the splendor of His light and, at times, it is altogether too much for us to bear. But when He removes Himself – His presence as revealed in consolations – for a time we are harshly thrown into a frenzied panic as the darkness envelops us, much like the dramatic way in which Saul was thrown from his horse.

We erroneously assume this darkness is a punishment

when it is, in fact, a grace. The darkness, over time, blankets us. It serves to warm our hearts – hearts that were once cold and sterile but have now thawed and increased with newfound charity.

The darkness is our mentor, for it offers us much to learn about ourselves without the night of our senses. We continue dwelling in comfort, familiarity, and sin. Complacency becomes the fruit of our vision.

But when God elects to withdraw us from the world, we are thus drawn inward. In the abyss of our hearts, we meet Him, and He gently admonishes us for a time, until we are refined in His fire of love.

The flame of God burns and yet also reveals Truth. We see ourselves more honestly, and after a while, we are prepared to embark on our mission. This is the gift and beauty of the nightfall of our senses and souls.

We are made new. We no longer see, but we can hear God with resounding clarity. Our chastisement proved us, and we can no longer deny Him whom our hearts love. We can no longer revel in raucous and uncensored barbarity.

We are changed. We are new creations. In the darkness, we have discovered all in God's purifying light. His flame of Spirit burns in our souls, and we go forth as witnesses to attest to His light and love. We are transformed from Sauls into Pauls.

THE SECRETS OF HIS PROVIDENCE

Most of us, when we pray, expect grand things to happen...lights, a shooting star, a rose appearing in winter, or other unusual manifestations that somehow prove to be an answer to our supplications. Sometimes God does speak to us through extraordinary signs, but most of the time, miracles are hidden, so that we will continue to seek Him with all our minds, hearts, and souls.

Consider everyday miracles – the birth of a baby, a small tree surviving a great storm, or a fragile bird's nest in a tall tree unscathed. But there's one exemplary miracle that we often overlook: the consecrated Host, Jesus physically and sublimely present in a small wafer, available to us anytime.

God provides for us the "manna from Heaven" in the form of Himself, plus other extra kisses and hugs from Heaven every day. He chooses to do some of these in secret, so that we will not become complacent or fall into acedia. He wants our wholehearted devotion and ardor, so we must constantly look for God in all the clandestine ways He is present every day.

Every time we are tempted to believe something is mere happenstance or even serendipitous, remember that all are aspects of God's great providence. Every detail is fine-tuned, so that we will intimately encounter God's love for us. He touches us in personal "God-incidents" to remind us that He remains both at our side and within us.

So do not grow lonely or slack in zeal, dear soul. Remember your despondency is the enemy's guise of distracting you from finding the One you seek, the One you love. When you notice the veil of despair is lifted, you will see everything with fresh eyes, and nothing will be overlooked. Do not seek signs and wonders, which are mere sacramentals, but instead seek God Himself, and you will not be disappointed.

He will reveal Himself in small or perhaps invisible ways, but your soul will alight when it recognizes Him who it loves. Seek God and His kingdom above all else, and all these things will be given to you besides.

THE WINGS OF THE DAWN

"If I take the wings of dawn and dwell beyond the sea, even there your hand guides me, your right hand holds me fast."
~ Psalm 139: 9 – 10

I saw a little sparrow take flight the other day, and I wondered if he knew what a gift he had in flying - to fly away carefree, and to soar above worries and cares and even danger. Though

I am incapable of flying in a literal sense, I am much like that little sparrow: poor, plain, and rather unnoticed by the populace.

But it is the sparrow's song that draws notice. Where is my song then? It has long ago dried up, along with my spirit. I hear the little song sparrow as day breaks, and I wonder how I, too, might be able to join him as on the wings of the dawn.

Dawn reminds me of the newness of today and that all things are possible once again. The wings of the dawn are how I am uplifted and renewed in hope, even as I suffer unceasingly. They signify Your love and Your Sacred Heart, where You carry me to hide and rest when I am bone weary.

Then one day I will rediscover my own song and join the little songbirds with joyful praise and thanksgiving for the new day, a chance to start over and find myself in You. Take me away, then, on the wings of the dawn.

WATCHING AND WAITING

"In the morning you hear me; in the morning I will plead before you and wait." ~ Psalm 5: 4

Sometimes I wonder if this stagnancy will ever end. Day after day, my life seems to be on hold in nearly every area, and my interior disposition wants to give up out of frustration and desperation. But You whisper to my heart, "Watch and wait." As day breaks, I continue my perseverant waiting, though the stillness – the seeming nothingness – pervades.

Watching and waiting are agonizing. They seem to involve inaction, though I know that watching is not necessarily a passive state. If I watch, what am I looking for? At times I wonder if what awaits me is something so subtle I may miss it entirely if I become too distracted. And why do I wait? I wait in expectation for You to act, of course. I do not move into action until You signal that "now is the time."

Am I a soldier trained for war? With this connotation, it

appears to be the case, yet I know the battle is with the fallen angels who seek to devour me. May I be faithful to this time of watching and waiting, rather than fall victim to the enemy who wishes to snatch me from the God who knows all and plans everything for my life according to His perfect timing.

CHAPTER TEN

Growing In Humility

A MAJESTIC VINE

"Thus it became a vine, produced branches, and put forth shoots. It was transplanted to a fertile field by abundant waters to produce branches, to bear fruit, to become a majestic vine." ~Ezekiel 17:6, 8

How do I become a vine that flourishes and bears choice, ripe fruit rather than one that withers over time? How, Lord, do I become a majestic vine – one of many created things that reflects Your glory and beauty? If I am to be exemplary, I must only be rooted in You, but more than that, I must be a branch – a fragment – of You, the True Vine. In my essence, I must not only emulate You but be part of Your Body.

If I am majestic rather than mediocre, very little is required of me, except trust, simplicity, humility, and total detachment from the soil of the world. My only real requirement is to remain intimately focused on and connected to You. When I choose to pursue the distractions of my false gods, I wither and fade.

I must be lowly. I cannot bear pretention, for then my fate would be to perish. If I remain lowly, I can withstand the inevitable tempests and dodge the predators of my soul.

I do seek to be a true reflection of You, my True Vine. I long to be majestic – not of my own right, but as an authentic representation of You. Your majesty transforms me into someone exquisite.

ALLOWING GOD TO LEAD

For those of us who are natural-born leaders, allowing someone else to lead us, including God, feels awkward. Being led is a humiliating act, because we relinquish control in favor of movements that no longer resemble familiarity or predictability in our minds.

There is a psychological component to being led, much like in dance steps: subtle, but present. Our minds must be alert and yet entirely devoid of knowing what will happen next. In dancing with God, I hold His hands as He leads the next step. At first it feels uncomfortable, and my feet stumble and fumble. But once I surrender the knowing, my movements become graceful as I glide in tandem with Him.

The surrendering I experience is an act of the will. I must consciously choose to let go: of fear, frustration, and failure. When I do, I am transformed. I am profoundly aware of my littleness and God's greatness. Even more, my gaze is fixed on Him rather than on myself. I become lost in His eyes. This is the first stage of learning to trust God without reservation: allowing Him to lead me in the dance of life with its smooth movements and sometimes syncopated rhythm.

CLOTHED IN HUMAN WEAKNESS

What a beautiful concept, and, even more, a reality, that Jesus was clothed in our weakness so that, by our weaknesses, we might be glorified in and through Him. Never has this happened in all of history, except through the gift-sacrifice of this tiny God-Child. And we, the sinful carriers of human weakness, are the recipients of His blessing from the unblemished Lamb who takes away our sins. By this very singular thought, our hearts necessarily fill with gratitude and humility. How could we otherwise consider such a gift?

Jesus Himself is our gift, and we come to love Him more perfectly by emulating Him. Thus, if He who is spotless is clothed in human weakness, so must we become empty of the world's frivolities and follies. We must abandon all that is not of God so as to embrace the fullness of heavenly bliss. Our bodies were made to honor Him, so we should abase ourselves by denying ourselves excessive pleasures. We come to know the emptiness of poverty – and the joy it can provide – when we deny ourselves of every comfort and desire.

We come to know Jesus when the excess is swept away, and nothing remains but our own human weakness. It is then that Jesus clothes Himself with us. He takes our nakedness and clothes Himself with it. This is love, and because of this love, we are to do the same: to go out into the world and take upon our hearts the human weaknesses that need to be changed through prayer, our spiritual charisms, and our time.

NOTHING HIDDEN

"There is nothing hidden except to be made visible; nothing is secret except to come to light." ~ Mark 4: 22

Though my senses and intellect have been overshadowed by Your love for some time now, I know that all of this darkness serves but one purpose: to *be* revealed so as to reveal Your goodness. Truly, even this holy darkness is a kind of light, my own luminary that leads me in ways I do not yet fully comprehend. But, as Your little child, I take Your hand in trust and follow Your lead. I know You direct me to greater things than this place of waiting in the unknown.

Anything unknown or hidden is only dark to me as a created being with limited abilities. It is impossible for me to know Your vastness, to grasp everything there is to know about every subject or topic. But there is no darkness in You, and in Your light, we see. Even what I perceive as darkness is really Your blinding light.

Today You remind me that all things concealed by You serve a grander purpose of enlightening my soul. Even secret acts of sin that hide in the shadows of unholy darkness will come to light someday. In Your light, nothing is hidden. We must all face the truth about ourselves and all matters concerning eternity.

Though You perhaps hide from me for a time, I cannot do the same with You. I may run away or ignore the tapping of Your Holy Spirit on my heart, but all is visible to You. What humility is needed for me to expose my inner chamber willingly and gleefully! I must be robed in this virtue in order to honestly disclose who I am to others, but firstly to myself. Then I will be clothed in the light of Your love, and all will be revealed at the proper time.

OBEDIENCE AND SACRIFICE

"Obedience is better than sacrifice." ~ 1 Samuel 15: 22

When we submit ourselves to either an earthly authority (e.g., a boss, a parent, an elder, a priest, etc.) or to the only heavenly authority (God), we are yielding self-will to God's desire for humility in our hearts. Obedience is always pleasing to God, because it involves an interior act of humility, which may come by way of humiliation.

Sacrifice, however, is any exterior deed we determine will somehow reflect our interior disposition. Many of us make sacrifices out of habit or duty rather than genuine love for God. We fast or donate money to charity. We attend Mass on Sundays and Holy Days, because "we're supposed to." Obligation doesn't indicate *desire* on the part of the one obliging. Duty is honorable in the sense that it grounds us and keeps us connected to our humanity, but it is only a spiritual oblation if it is done from the heart of humility.

Obedience, then, can include sacrifice. For many of us who struggle with self-love (pride), dying to that selfishness is truly a sacrifice, because we may rather live for ourselves. It seems that obedience and sacrifice are both pleasing to God when they stem from an authenticity of heart that can only be derived from both humility and charity.

When we love, we look beyond our narrow vision of self and into the eyes of another. When we first love God above all, everything else becomes arbitrary, so we are indeed delighted to honor Him through sacrifice, humiliations, and constant obedience. A heart that loves knows that all circumstances are potentially leading him back to God, if only he surrenders his will time and again.

OF DUST AND EARTH

The simple elements comprise my complex organs and bodily systems. It is from the prosaic things of the earth that You create exquisite works of Your hands. But no work has surpassed that of humanity, because we are a reflection of Your eternal image. Our souls are a composite of Your grandeur, Your word, Your flesh and blood, Your spirit.

From One who has no beginning or end, we are created to begin and end and begin again. Our infinity is realized after our fleshly, earthly end. Our eternity begins after our mortality ceases. You who are infinite molded me – of dust and earth, of water and blood. The crude and rudimentary elements shall be the basis for my humility, because I am not superior to the ground on which I walk or the water I ingest.

I am merely human, of dust, to dust, from dust. But I am Your masterpiece, the work of Your hands. You molded and fashioned me for this life. Now form me for eternal life with You.

OUT OF THE NOTHINGNESS

How is greatness born? Some might say from greatness itself, that it is inherent somehow or that it graces particular people. But You, Lord, know that true greatness springs forth from nothingness. Only when there is nothing can You be magnified. From nothing to something great is how others recognize Your hand in all good things.

What a gift in this type of creation. When I create, it is from a blank slate or page. Only when I start from nothing can I begin to develop anything, which I hope will become a masterpiece in its own right. Greatness in nature, too, sprouts from small seeds. Every tree and flower, however tall it may tower, once had humble beginnings as the tiniest of seeds, perhaps some so small and delicate that the human eye can barely behold it.

Humans, too, are Your finest work. We were created from dust – that is, remnants of what once existed but disintegrated. We were – we are – nothing, which is precisely why we have the potential to become *something*, even someone great rather than mediocre. And You want this for all of us – greatness. But You know (and we gradually learn) that, in order for us to become great, we must consider our nothingness, which requires humility. Even more, we must desire to be so small that the only good others may see in us is You.

This is what it takes for true greatness, not the self-made variety of pomp and arrogant ambition. When we are feeble or merely incapable of greatness, yet rely upon God to do the impossible, indeed He does. And His masterpiece in us far exceeds our dreams and expectations.

SIN AND GRACE

"Where sin increased, grace overflowed all the more."
~ *Romans 5: 20*

When we think of our sins, we must immediately shift our minds to the reality of grace. Without both, we fall short in grasping a very critical spiritual truth. If we focus entirely on sin, we despair, yet if we only consider God's mercy without justice, we likely will fall into presumption.

The balance of sin and grace is what makes us the created and God the Creator; we the redeemed, and God the Redeemer; we the sanctified and God the Sanctifier. We must always remember our lowliness, and, in fact, be grateful for it.

It is our nothingness that draws us back to God's wellspring of grace time and again. It is precisely because we are nothing that we need God for everything.

He is all. He must become *more* to us than our sin. Grace, then, is that undeserved gift that encases us when we look to Heaven with a sincere attitude of repentance. We may fall thirty times a day, but may our eyes never shift their gaze from our Father, who waits for us to return to Him thirty times more.

We cannot believe that grace is deserved, but we must always know it is a true blessing of God's love for us. When we sin, He receives us in grace – in love – if we return to Him.

So we must never allow sin to deter us from grace, yet we must also never sin with the *expectation* of redemption. The eyes of our hearts must keep both under careful watch, and we who are vigilant will vie for God's love all the more at the hour of our death, where, hopefully, our sin is finally conquered once and for all by grace.

SLAVES OF RIGHTEOUSNESS

"Freed from sin, you have become slaves of righteousness."
~ *Romans 6: 18*

If Jesus freed us from sin, how is it possible that we are still slaves? Oh sweet soul, do not consider slavery to Jesus as bondage and suffocation; it is quite the contrary. Slavery to Jesus is a holy submission bound by humility and manifested through His grace.

When we come to realize what we truly are – nothing – and who He truly is – everything – we naturally and necessarily arrive at a place of slavery to Him. It is a hunger to do all and be all for Him, for God to do with us as He wishes. This is what it means to be a slave of Jesus.

We are slaves of love, then. Love is the driving virtue behind our desire for nothing less than total capture by God. It is more than merely belonging to God by choice; slavery is when we hand over ourselves to Him fully and freely, knowing we deserve punishment, yet receiving mercy through His eternal goodness.

We know we deserve nothing, but we have been redeemed to the One who created all living things. Jesus is no cruel master, which is why we *willingly* submit ourselves to His service as we spiritually mature. Even more, we *enslave* ourselves to Him, which is a more extreme commitment of trust in Him.

Enslavement to Jesus is pure bliss, because we know He will lead us to Heaven with all that He perfectly and permissively wills for us on Earth.

SWEETNESS MINGLED WITH TEARS

When a soul is constantly burdened, not by sin but by love, it becomes both heavy with love and light with joy. Downtrodden though it may be from time to time (for love produces a painful effect in the soul), God's grace elevates it to a particular sweetness. This sweetness is a consequence of one who has learned to live in the wound of love, to hide inside Jesus' Sacred Wounds and to contentedly dwell amidst suffering.

There is sweetness in suffering, and even tears produce a bittersweet effect on both the body and soul. For the body, tears are a release of tension, a sort of invisible sign that one has let go and permitted a waterfall of sorrow to graze his or her face with unbridled freedom. To the soul, tears are tokens of love to the One who shed countless tears – tears of blood – for our sake. Tears cleanse us and remind us of our weakness, our inability to do what is good without God, and even our incapacities or bodily infirmities.

Tears, when tasted, are bittersweet and warm. The salt mingles with the warmth of this watery substance. To the soul who loves well, tears are expressions of both sorrow and joy, of a broken heart and of gratitude – often at the same time. The salt is a spiritual preservative, while the water is a symbol of life.

Suffering can and does embitter some souls, but to a humble and contrite soul, suffering *heals*. Suffering deepens one's resolve to persevere in fidelity to God and to love Him all the more. It is a trying test of one's character, yet in the darkest and weakest of souls, the grace given in tears sows love. And love, once it breaks through the invisible barriers around the heart, liberates the soul to both suffer and give freely, unrestrained.

Sweetness in suffering, then, is manifested by our tears, which water the earth to form new life – elsewhere and within us.

THE BLESSING AND THE CURSE

All of life is twofold – on the one hand, a blessing, and on the other hand, a curse. Our natural talents, our temperaments, and our spiritual charisms all have the potential for greatness or for destruction. This is why we should never boast, except in the Lord, because *everything is grace*, as St. Therese of Lisieux once famously wrote. If this is true, and we live in such a way as to reflect the power of such a statement, then even our weaknesses, setbacks, and mistakes can be redeemed to glorify God. Indeed, our weaknesses more fully reveal God, because any goodness stemming from them is a clear indicator of God's grace. Our capabilities then become less evident.

In this way, we live the beautiful act of humility proclaimed by St. John the Baptist: *He must increase; I must decrease*. It seems that God has made it so that any giftedness or blessing or accomplishment might have a darker counterpart so as to keep us dependent upon Him and devoted to glorifying Him alone. Then we grow in humility as we acknowledge this truth: everything we experience is an opportunity for us to grow in holiness. Even the blessings we enjoy are often accompanied by heavier crosses – not so much for us to become doubtful or discouraged – but instead for us to become people of perseverance and courage. Our strength comes from the Lord.

The weaker we become, the more we decrease. We become smaller. In turn, our prayer is that Jesus' presence will be more manifested, that others will see Him in our lives, and yes, in our struggle, that we may glorify and honor Him through and in our weaknesses. This is the blessing and the curse.

THE FOUNDATION OF THE WORLD

"You loved me before the foundation of the world."
~ John 17: 24b

I sit here shamefully assuming that Your love for me is as my love for You – limited, conditional, shallow, and weak. How is it possible that Your love for me is so personal and intimate that it existed before You created Heaven and Earth?

All of creation praises You but also groans in great suffering because of sin. Yet before Your word breathed life into the cosmos, Your heart was set ablaze for love of me.

Me? I am but a shadow, a passing specter. I am only one, small, hidden person among countless masses of people throughout the ages. But You plucked me out of the populace to remind me that You've counted all the hairs on my head.

You know me far more intimately than I know myself. Life for me is but a passing gust of wind that withers and fades, but Your love for me withstands time. Your love for me is why You are the Alpha and the Omega: it had no beginning and will never end.

THE HIDDEN GRACE OF FLOWERS

I walk into the meadow and meet You there. Putting Your arm around my shoulder, You say, "Look at the flowers, my beautiful daughter. You are worth more to me than all of them." I look more closely and notice the delicate splendor of every petal, leaf, and stem. Each flower, though it does not utter a word, reflects Your glory in magnificent and extraordinary ways.

"Watch the flower, my daughter," You continue as I offer a slight nod. "It possesses nothing materially, yet it wants for nothing. You must become a little daisy or rose. Be like the flower: possessing nothing, yet having all."

In my invisible affliction – my wound of the heart – I think I finally understand. I watch the flowers and long to be in their company. For far too long I have complicated my life, and the unintended consequence is misery. But the flower is simply a flower. It grows where it is planted and trusts its Maker to provide the necessary water and sunshine.

The flower does not needlessly toil as I do. Perhaps all I strive to achieve is merely vainglory, yet the hidden grace in this moment, in this flower, is that humility – above all – grants me access to this meadow. Humility forces me to acknowledge the truth about my nothingness and to finally, after countless years of needless wrestling, yield to it unabashedly.

I am finally free like this flower, planted in rich soil but eternally free. The flower has taught me everything without speaking at all. In order to possess all, I must first want for nothing and be completely empty.

THE HUMILITY OF SILENCE

When all is said and done, hearts are injured and relationships strained. Sometimes – oftentimes – speaking freely not only displays a lack of self-control but also a lack of charity. There's a reason why we are warned in Scripture to "guard the door of our lips." It is because our lips are the gateway to sin through pride. Thoughtless, careless speech forms a target and draws battle lines. The victims are the ones in our way while we are verbally spewing. Speaking in such a way also provokes the sin of anger, another manifestation of pride.

I once had a friend tell me, "Not everything needs to be said." This was following an incident where I did not exhibit prudence over my thoughts and speech. Careless as I was, I hurt my friend by "honestly" expressing every thought and emotion.

Sometimes we are called to speak up and speak out, at times radically or boldly, but never at the expense of wounding a person or group of people. We must ask ourselves, as is taught in 12-step programs, is it true, helpful, important, necessary, and kind (T.H.I.N.K.)? The discourse must fit all five categories before one speaks, and then only following prayer.

Silence, or keeping our mouths shut, is humbling in two ways: first, it tempers the body's senses and emotions; second, it tempers the will. At times keeping quiet will consequentially involve persecution or judgment. This is especially true if one is refraining from defending oneself. Hence, humiliation to the person who knows and bears the truth (but who is willing to turn the other cheek) results in an opportunity for that person to grow in humility.

Silence bears on its wings humility. Look at Jesus as He began His journey to Calvary. He spoke very little and accepted all without resistance. His silence profoundly spoke of humility, which is why so many onlookers believed Him and repented. We, too, should be ambassadors of humility, so that others will see the fruit of our silence and thus draw nearer to God through our actions.

THE SPIRIT OF TRUTH

Pilate once asked, "What is truth?" and it seems there are many among us today who ask the same question. We who were baptized in the name of the Triune God were given truth as grace to be expanded in our hearts. The Spirit of truth dwells there and facilitates the development of our conscience.

Many walk among us who have not been baptized. Still

others have dulled consciences from listening to and adopting the secular reference point of postmodern relativism. The world tells us that objective truth is a fallacy, and if we accept any sort of objective truth, then we are intolerant, bigoted, misogynistic, and so on. Subjectivity guides most of us, as does existentialism and humanism: what do I feel, and what do I experience? Then *that* is truth. *That* is reality.

The error in this thinking is that both feelings and experience are fickle and easily influenced by exterior conditions. Feelings and experience cannot be the basis for our truth. No, truth must be derived from somewhere and Someone outside of my limited scope. Truth is unfaltering, steady, and certain, a light that guides me to interior tranquility when my feelings and experience inevitably fail me.

If I truly desire peace in my heart and in the world, then I must humbly and graciously invite the Guest of Truth to dwell within me, to guide and correct me. I must be willing to accept admonishment without shame, to recognize my need for the other. Anything but this wrecks my potential for serenity. The more I pursue my wavering, subjective truth – which is not truth in actuality – the less peace rests upon my soul.

Spirit of Truth, I eagerly implore You, then, to reside in me. Teach me Truth, the lucidity that will lead me when all around me turns to chaos and calamity. I know You will never lead me astray, for You are my voice of Truth.

THE SPIRITUAL FRONTIER

Life has a way of proving us along its twists and turns, the unexpected and expected milestones and our quest to find meaning. This quest becomes a spiritual conquest, insofar as it is the drive that propels us toward our heavenly home. The spiritual frontier is that vast wasteland of our hearts, once we enter the desert with Jesus and become empty and powerless before Him who embraced all in divine condescension.

This wasteland is not dead, but on the contrary, it is a land full of possibility, presenting us with a future of hope. You see, when we enter that interior spiritual frontier, we realize that God can do anything and create all from our nothingness. We must be willing for Him to "make a way in the desert" of our souls, so that He will bring forth fragrant and colorful blooms and streams of water where the land is parched.

All frontiers are seemingly empty and useless at first glance. We, too, may be inclined to believe this about ourselves. But Jesus waits for us in the wasteland. He knows that the frontier within us is endless and presents Him with all we have and are. We may bring Him nothing, but it is precisely our nothingness that He desires from us.

Only nothing can become something, which is everything. Only nothing can be fruitful if that nothing is "I" and that everything is "God."

TO BECOME BLIND

"[The blind men] would follow Jesus on the road to Jerusalem, on the road that would lead him to his passion, to the cross. They took the road that so many others refused…" ~ Jaime Garcia[xiii]

We all desire to be illuminated and enlightened. Somehow in the developed world, knowledge has become equated with power. It is a god of sorts that has replaced our need for a true Deity, a personal God. Academia encourages our pursuit to know more through science and reason. This is, of course, a good and right use of our faculties, except when it overrides our ability and desire to know God above all else.

What if we were to become interiorly blind? I imagine we'd become keenly aware of our need for Jesus, because we'd realize our poverty. To acknowledge our lack would only make our desperation for Jesus more palpable. Perhaps this is the cure for the god of human knowledge: that we become blind and thus poor, so that we may see and know the One who gave us the capability of learning and knowing.

If we pray for this interior blindness, we know we have nothing at all to offer Jesus, except our poverty. Then our hearts become sincere as we seek to know ourselves more honestly. In that stark confrontation with ourselves, we no longer present a façade of haughtiness about our intellectual accomplishments. We instead present our unpretentiousness and littleness. Because we have nothing and have gained nothing of our own accord, we are no longer afraid to be ourselves and live authentically.

Only if we first become blind can our hearts be healed of darkness. Jesus enters our dark places as the Light, and our interior sight is again restored.

WITHOUT COST

"Without cost you have received; without cost you are to give."
~ *Matthew 10: 8b*

How am I to know what to give and to what extent? My body screams for me to slow down because of the incessant pressures and demands of daily living. It's a silent scream, though – to stop, for me to give up, and to just sleep a while. Still, I defy my body. I get up and begin anew each day. Is this what it means for Your Spirit to overcome my flesh?

Does my life truly appear to others as if it is all put together neatly in a shiny box? Today I feel as if I will collapse any moment, but then who would be here to rescue me? The truth is I am terrified of crumbling to the ground in a heap of surrender, because I have no one to care for me, except You.

Would You send the angels to comfort and assist me, as You sent Raphael to Tobias? Or would I just remain a visible mess – alone, afraid – finally an obvious declaration of what I have been carrying inside for many months, years even? Despite this, You still call me to give more. *More?* What do I have left? I should sell all that I have and give it away. I should toil and labor more, but I am drowning in the misery of my heartache and bodily suffering.

What does it mean for someone like me – wretchedly stained with guilt and the filth of my sins – to give without cost? I already bear ongoing shame, humiliation, and guilt for all that others have done for me and our family. My biggest fear today is that they will all scatter and abandon me, though I know I cannot repay them. Are the interior scourges enough to repay those who have cleaned my house, babysat for free, donated money, and organized an entire fundraiser? It seems this would be inadequate still, or is that the foolish pride telling me it does not suffice, because no one knows?

No one can see my offerings for them, which is the only real payment of gratitude I have to give right now. What more am I to give, Lord? I am truly empty, so I have and am nothing without You. You are my portion and cup. To experience this level of poverty is excruciating. It is humiliating, yet how many more people suffer in this way, or worse? I cannot bear to ignore the silent cries in their eyes, hidden behind their smiles. I cannot forget or forsake them in their agony, because I know well their secret pain.

How, then, do I give to those suffering and in terrible torment? This is the only way I know how to give without cost, for I know the gifts offered to me will run dry eventually. It is to be present to people in their loneliness and pain, to suffer with and for them. This is how I will give relentlessly and willingly every day.

CHAPTER ELEVEN

Simplicity & Evangelical Poverty

A WITHERED HAND

"Jesus said to the man, 'Stretch out your hand.' He stretched it out, and his hand was restored." ~ Mark 3: 5

My daughter, Sarah, was born with fused fingers, so that her hands appeared to be like little mittens with smooth skin concealing the bones and ligaments of each finger. I've often pondered the beauty and remarkable significance of hands since we've had Sarah, so this gospel reading struck me – about a man with a withered hand.

Consider what a withered hand symbolizes: years of toil and hard labor, much use and handiwork, perhaps to provide for a family. Maybe the man's hands were withered from a disease, like rheumatoid arthritis, so his fingers appeared mangled and of no use anymore. We can surmise he was also in pain, if not physically, then most assuredly on an emotional level because of the certain mockery and belittling from his peers. If all who were diseased or disabled were also categorized as sinful, then surely this man experienced ostracizing and maligning.

Our hands signify our lives and sometimes reveal a particular story. We look at our fingerprints and they, like our DNA, are unique only to us, one person. Some hands have scars. I know mine do. In fact, my left hand bears a scar I will never forget from high school chemistry class when some nitric acid spilled on it and ate away a portion of my skin.

Withered hands denote a kind of poverty, too. The humility of such withered hands is that they perhaps can no longer serve their purpose of creating, kneading, bathing, etc. The man with the withered hands needed Jesus in order for his work and dignity to be restored. And Jesus, indeed, took pity on him to heal him of both his physical infirmity and emotional shame.

Shame, then, is at the root of all need for healing. We all carry shame, not only because of our sins, but also for our natural weaknesses, our bodily wear and tear, etc. But Jesus is reminding us through this healing of two things: one is that we must love our humanity and all it entails, including our flaws. Two is that our flaws remind us of our dependency on God and that He truly desires that we are made whole – if not physically, then certainly spiritually.

Jesus can never be outdone in mercy, and we must, in faith, cling to His promise of healing and restoration throughout our sicknesses and darkness.

ALL GOLD IS A LITTLE SAND

"Therefore I prayed, and prudence was given me; I pleaded and the spirit of Wisdom came to me. I preferred her to scepter and throne, and deemed riches nothing in comparison with her, nor did I liken any priceless gem to her; because all gold, in view of her, is a bit of sand, and before her, silver is to be accounted mire."
~ *Wisdom 7: 7 – 9*

The world and all its riches are but dust in Your eyes, O God, yet I have nearly made wealth and its acquisition an idol like the golden calf. Man has made precious metals into desired possessions, and we view them in light of their extrinsic value to us rather than for their intrinsic beauty.

But I am humbled by the reminder that all gold is a little grain of sand to You, because money, wealth, riches, and possessions mean nothing to the One who created the world, universe, and galaxies beyond my human imagination. I, then, am but dust, ash, and sand. All of life is fleeting, yet You remain the same. And now I see for the first time that You are my treasure, and Heaven is full of the desires of the human heart at last fulfilled: peace, joy, hope, love, etc. All of these virtues are my gold, and through wisdom I am growing closer to obtaining a rudimentary practice of them.

So set my eyes on matters of the heart and away from cultural and societal success, for my gold is You who dwell in my soul, more precious than any created being to me.

BLESSINGS OF SUCCESS

"You have granted him his heart's desire; you did not refuse the request of his lips." ~ *Psalm 21: 3*

The world tells me to grow up and become someone important after attending a prestigious postsecondary institution. Intelligence, education, and positions that require both are the first steps toward worldly success. And after I have achieved these, I must earn a viable living – beyond that, even an excessive wage – and begin to acquire all of the symbols of my status and wealth, including fancy cars, lavish homes, luxurious furnishings, and extravagant vacations.

Are these the blessings of success of which the psalmist speaks? Perhaps, but it is doubtful, and this is because God desires my fidelity over secular accomplishments and accolades. In the spiritual life, success equates mastering the virtues, but if we attempt this mastery, we are guaranteed hardships. Mastery of anything, be it sacred or secular, cannot be obtained without hard work, sacrifice, and above all, perseverance.

Perseverance is that virtue that drives us to continue pressing on, despite numerous impediments or setbacks along the way. Perseverance proves our character by encouraging us to never give up – to hold fast to our hope, faith, our dignity, or whatever virtue is threatened.

The only true measure of success is that which leads us to Heaven. If I live my life with the true end in mind – Heaven – will my actions, decisions, and attitudes reflect the world's measure or God's measure? I don't have to be or do anything spectacular or substantial in order to enjoy the riches of Heaven. I just have to be faithful – to all that is presented to me this day, to rising above what the world tells me is important, to believing in God's love in the midst of mystery and tragedy.

My value and self-worth must be derived from my identity as a Christian, and if I truly consider myself a follower of Jesus, I must remember that my life will involve its own journey to Calvary, its own passion, death, and resurrection.

It is the resurrection that is my hope and promise of blessing. Whether that blessing occurs in my life on earth or in eternal life is only known to God. But I open my heart again today, seeking the path of abandonment, humiliation, and renunciation, for that is what will lead me closer to the heart of Jesus and will offer me true success.

GRIT AND GRACE

Life has a way of revealing our true character, especially during times of scarcity. For me, the virtue of evangelical poverty has emerged, and I realize that, in order to live in such a way, I must possess a combination of both grit and grace.

Grit comes from my character, or rather, the development of tenacity that only arrives by God's goodness and grace. Grit is that inner fire that rises up when I am facing a new challenge or living in the midst of ongoing adversity. Grit keeps my faith alive by sheer will when all is dark, and nothing but shadows remain.

Grace, of course, is the unearned gift I receive from God every day. It is the outpouring of His Spirit into my being. Without grace, I would have long ago perished. Grace has become like water to me: a wellspring of love that keeps me alive, flourishing, and remaining on a steady and sure path.

Grit and grace together equal a powerhouse. They provide the only way for me to persevere, never give up, or relinquish the truth and faith I have in a righteous and benevolent God. Grit and grace are the backbone to why I keep going on.

LOVE'S AND POVERTY'S BEGINNINGS

All good things must return to their source, that is, God, from whence they came. Love's source is God Himself, for He is Love. And He bestows the first and greatest commandment through His very being. We must love God first and above all, returning to Him daily in holy conversation. We need Him in order to love ourselves rightly and then love those closest to us, our family members.

This is not so easily accomplished, especially since we tend to get the worst of those who live with us. The glimpses of their best sides are few and fleeting. Instead, spouses hear griping and grousing, see sickness afflict them through flus and colds, observe their stress levels and notice the less-than-stellar moments.

Parents must tolerate whiny, disobedient, and perhaps coddled children who haven't napped well or who are hungry or ill. While the world may see our smiles and hear our cheerful greetings, they are seldom privy to the challenges of our daily lives and homes.

But this is where true poverty of heart is best revealed – in our homes. A cry from a child may indicate a desire for attention and affection, though it displeases a mother's ears. A frazzled wife may signify to her husband that she is depleted and has nothing left to give that day. A quiet husband may be toiling in his heart, as well as in his work, struggling with all of the burdens he carries.

Our homes are where poverty – the empty holes and spaces in our hearts – must meet love, which fills those crevices with renewed strength and hope. Love draws us out of ourselves and into another's world through their lens. We are able to do this by grace through Him who is Love, and we receive this grace when we return to our daily prayer.

Love never runs dry if its source is God. It's certain that we will experience more bad days, weeks, months, and even years, but our emptiness can always be filled with love, with God. When we are tempted to lash out at the grumbling spouse or indigent child, perhaps we should respond with a dose of love – a hug, a prayer, a listening ear – instead. Then our homes will be filled more frequently with love than emptied in poverty of spirit.

MY POVERTY AND PAIN

"You who seek God, take heart!" ~ Psalm 69: 33

Pain and poverty go hand-in-hand, often because pain renders us weak, depleted, and incapable of maintaining our normal, daily lives. Pain screams at us, "Stop!" But we often ignore its warning until it becomes so excruciating that we become incapacitated altogether.

Pain is our teacher, but it is also our friend. When the road of life is riddled with dust and dirt, pain reminds us of our poverty. You see, when we are vibrant and healthy, we may deceptively adopt the lie that everything we've accomplished is due to our own strength or intelligence. But pain, as our companion, gently redirects our attention to the Other – the One who is our all and our strength.

When we accept our poverty, that is, our emptiness and raw humanity, we are more apt to depend on Jesus all the more. What do we have left if we're simply a muddled, messy heap of brokenness? Jesus wants our brokenness and asks us to surrender it to Him daily. He doesn't reject what is flawed about us; in fact, He loves our weaknesses, if only we would offer them to Him as gifts.

It's interesting to think that pain can lead us closer to Heaven, but consider this point: do you need Jesus more when you're full of energy, or when you're sick? Your poverty, or emptiness of spirit, necessarily draws you to Him, because you know it is impossible to make it through the day without His grace.

Thank pain for accompanying you today, and bless it. Ask it to become part of Jesus, and hold its hand until it's ready to depart. Then, in your restored health, you will thank God all the more.

POSSESSING ALL IN A NEW WAY

St. John of the Cross reminds us that we must seek to possess nothing in order to possess all, to be nothing in order to be all, to have nothing in order to have all. The key to spiritual fulfillment is to desire to be poor – empty – so that God may fill us with His riches.

Scripture tells us similarly, "I know your tribulation and poverty, but you are rich" (Revelation 2: 9). Are we rich in what matters? The scope of eternity puts into perspective that our lives matter little when we constantly pursue the things of this world. To desire poverty is quite a radical paradigm shift, but a necessary one indeed.

It is not economical poverty to which we are called (though some are), but rather evangelical poverty, which is poverty of spirit. I am poor only when I have been drained of complexities in intellect and even will. Poverty is deeply interconnected with the virtue of simplicity. We must also carry the faith of a child in our hearts, and this can only occur through an emptying of self.

When we are called to this type of poverty, it is usually because God wishes to bless us with a very important mission in this life, though it may seem contrary in the process. Often we must be stripped interiorly, so that God may be able to work freely in and through us in order to do great things in our lives.

POVERTY AND OBEDIENCE

Today I realize the reality of my being. Today I've finally come to love my emptiness, my nothingness. In the past, I often glorified myself, because I adopted the lies of the enemy, the "if/thens" or "what ifs." I neglected the beauty of here and now, which is where You meet me.

Obedience is nothing more than acquiescing to my innate condition of spiritual poverty. If I am nothing without You, then it is precisely my poverty that You desire, so that Your very self might fill that void in me. You want me to have everything – which You are – but I cannot possess You unless I first submit to my emptiness.

Sometimes I fear the void, as if it were a chasm to Hell, but the truth is that I fear what I cannot see. In succumbing to this dark hole, I offer an act of trust in You, because I am weak, infirm, and incapable of greatness without adhering my lack to Your all.

In fact, I've tried to overcompensate for my fallibility by accepting the erroneous deceptions of the devil. Each time I have tried to make myself a queen, I've surrendered myself to the desert temptation rather than to Reality, to You. I often vacillate between creating an idol of myself and turning to You, the One True God, but both are inspired by my misery.

When I suffer, it's because I realize I am not all I made myself out to be. I am not worthy. I possess nothing of inherent value. So Satan uses my human frailties as bait to either tempt me toward pride (the overcompensation of my lack through making myself great) or despair (neglecting to turn to Your mercy in my misery).

The truth is that I am poor and have no particular talent or ability that sets me apart from the rest of humanity, yet that is what I bring to You now as an act of faith in obedience. When I turn to You with my painful void, You fill me with Yourself and bestow every good grace and gift I could never create on my own.

So I thank You for my poverty, Lord, because it constantly draws me back to You when I begin to stray. Your love is my all.

THE ART OF BEING POOR

"The art of being poor is to trust God for everything, to demand nothing – and to be grateful for all that is given." ~ St. John Chrysostom

Some of us are born into circumstantial or generational poverty; we do not choose to be poor, but it is all we've ever known. To live with few material items makes man's heart abundantly rich, for he values people above all things. But others of us were born into a life of wealth. They have been surrounded by luxurious commodities and modern conveniences, never truly realizing their excess. They perhaps seek more – greed, not need. They perhaps desire every good thing, every new device and shiny piece of equipment or furniture.

None of this is new knowledge, but let's consider for a moment what life for all of humanity would be like if we learned the art of being poor. Art is an expression of beauty. It is rife with creativity and flourishes with vibrant, novel descriptions, demonstrations, or illustrations of that which elevates the soul to Heaven.

What if all of us – rich and poor alike – were to embrace this type of art rather than gripe and grouse about our lot in life? To choose a spiritual richness above material consumption or to accept the deficit in which we already live – and then transform it into art? That is truly virtuous and perhaps even heroic.

The art of being poor, then, becomes our unique gift to God. Each of us has varying ways of manifesting creative genius, so our poverty of spirit becomes an act of great love that combines a masterpiece, a tapestry of human hearts, that pleases God very much.

What if my art were to express the poverty of my circumstances and soul rather than vainglory or other vices, such as lust? If my talent is used as an art of being poor, then it may lack secular luster, and yet it displays a miraculous, marvelous beauty that can only be viewed through the lens of one who is empty of self and full of the riches of the Kingdom of Heaven.

Poverty reflects simplicity of living, of being, of doing, of wanting nothing and lacking nothing, yet possessing everything. For Christ is all in all, and He remains the sovereign entity Who demands all we have been given in this life. He is the only King Who rules without tyranny and instead with gentle and guiding love.

Are we willing to deny Him what He asks of us? Let us begin today to empty ourselves of useless fillers and distractions of heart, and in the space that remains, may we create our art as a beautiful gift of thanksgiving to the One Who gave us all for the sake of all.

THE COST OF DISCIPLESHIP

Nearly everyone knows it's a difficult decision to follow Jesus wholeheartedly. Many of us want to be comfortable, or nominal, Christians so that we can maintain our cozy and even pleasurable lifestyles. How many of us pause long enough to consider the weight of time and intentional discipleship?

Intention requires thought and motivated action. Instead of mindlessly acquiescing to our culture, we leave everything behind – figuratively, spiritually, and sometimes literally to heed the call of authentic discipleship. Yes, this call bears a weight that may appear undesirable, but it is the price of self-denial and self-sacrifice that costs us so much – essentially all.

As St. John of the Cross aptly and sagaciously stated, "To

become what we are, we must possess nothing." Essentially we must lose all (self) to become all (Jesus). We must go by an unfamiliar and uncomfortable path, devoid of pleasures and earthly comforts, in order to arrive at our destination (Heaven).

True discipleship isn't pomp or Pharisaism. It is a reflection of our everyday attitudes and decisions, which are sometimes weak and sinful, but are holy at other times, but always a striving for the good and noble. We aim for truth and we stumble at times, but we keep moving ahead, hand-in-hand with Jesus.

THE GIFT OF THE MIND

Many of us are given the gift of a sharp intellect, quick wit, an articulate tongue, and a well-formed conscience. Some, however, do not have access to sound reasoning or natural pragmatism. Among us are those inclined toward academia and intelligentsia, but there are those who are more simple-minded and drawn to the wisdom and beauty of simplicity that the intellectuals overlook in their complex thinking.

Both intellect and simple-mindedness are gifts, yet only the former is truly upheld as honorable in modern society. Yet we have a God who sees the human heart – our will, intentions, and motivations – and pierces our hearts with His just and merciful chastisement. Only in a heavenly Deity could the sharp-minded folks be humbled in an instant while the simple-minded are exalted.

We must be cognizant of these dangers, which are the dangers of pride, presumption, and pretense that often accompany an intelligent thinker. Our ability to debate, analyze, philosophize, or soliloquize is truly a heavenly gift and even a charism if we use our thinking to advance God's Kingdom on Earth. But we all eventually lose our minds, if not to dementia, then certainly to death.

The complexity of intelligence can convolute our ability to

appreciate or even notice beauty in a supernatural sense, too. Let us humble ourselves in gratitude, both for the gift of the mind, as well as for those whose thinking simplifies everything so that the Divine might be revealed through their lives.

THE GRASS OF THE FIELD

"If God so clothes the grass of the field, which grows today and is thrown into the oven tomorrow, will he not much more provide for you, O you of little faith?" ~ Matthew 6: 30

Life is not meant to be ostentatious and frivolous. Life is meant to be lived simply, joyfully, and gracefully. Far too often the enticements of grandeur, pomp, and wealth lure us away from the poignant lesson in Matthew 6: that the beauty in life is discovered in our natural surroundings and within our souls.

Consider the flowers, birds, trees, and grass: they glorify God in their splendor, yet contain nothing in and of themselves. The more frenzied life becomes, the more I long to be like them, carefree yet deliberate, always trusting that God will provide for their needs.

It's difficult to believe this when one does not feel God's presence or see and hear Him clearly on a regular basis. The temptation then is that God has abandoned us when He, in fact, cares intimately and personally about each of us.

God glorifies Himself through His creation, from the small blade of grass to the flamboyant peacock. And in us. We, too, are the reflections of our Creator when we opt for simplicity and humility. In a sense, self-degradation so that He may shine in and through us to the world is what makes us beautiful reflections of Him.

THE GREAT AND THE SMALL

"For the Ruler of all shows no partiality, nor does he fear greatness, because he himself made the great as well as the small, and provides for all alike." ~ Wisdom 6: 7

If God shows no partiality to the rich or poor, humble or proud, famous or unknown, then let me be smallest of the small, for the littler I am, the greater God is in and through me. I am content being small, though sometimes I am tempted to join the wealthy and well-renowned. I do not disdain them, but I do feel nostalgia for who I once was, which contradicts who I am today.

The greater I sought my life to be, the less room there was for God. I didn't need Him in the same capacity that I do today because of my weaknesses and bodily infirmities. Today I seek Him more wholeheartedly, because I realize my nothingness. And with gratitude I extend my hands and heart – empty but eager – so that God has room to love me.

When I am full of self, there is no room for God, which is true impoverishment. I'd rather be among the lowly, for there is wisdom in this type of humiliation – not false humility that draws attention, but a hidden poverty of spirit known only to God and me. He rests in that space in my heart, and I am content for Him to do so, for when I am weak, He is my strength within.

THE NEED FOR EVANGELICAL POVERTY

"Because we live amidst a 'materialism which craves possessions,' we simply forget other people…Poverty reminds us of 'the needs and sufferings of the weakest' (St. John Paul II)."
~ *Fr. James Sullivan*

Our family attended a craniofacial retreat in Orange County, California, a while back. Every time I stepped outside of our hotel, I felt as if I were living in the Twilight Zone. My surroundings were aesthetically pleasing, but it all seemed so unnatural, plastic, and phony. Just a simple trip to the high-end shopping mall across the street from where we were staying opened my eyes – but more importantly, my heart – to the reality that exterior beauty, material wealth, and luxury are the gods of this epoch. How empty were the faces of the "perfect people" we saw. How vacant and haunting were their gazes.

In most cases, people entirely ignored our typically cheerful Sarah, who greeted everyone with equal enthusiasm. But many even gawked at her and two of our friends with Apert Syndrome. My heart broke with every stare and glance I caught from others. How ironic that we invaded this bubble of cosmetic surgery centers and designer retailers with our distorted faces, ordinary clothes, and plain language!

The lust for luxury was palpable, and yet we proudly walked among the wealthy, comfortable, and beautiful people. I hope we jolted them awake, if only for a moment in time. This observation left me restless and wondering how our culture has regressed so far from the morals and values of Christianity. But even more than that, I realized the grace of evangelical poverty – that stripping of self, the emptying of my spirit in favor of the Holy Spirit's sweet invasion – is nearly null and invisible, at least where we stayed.

But the grace remained very much alive in my heart – a renewed fervor and ardor for my nothingness and emptiness, and thus for the immensity of God's love and mercy. Instead of expensive gifts, I longed for – even mourned over – the simplicity of rural, Midwest living, where my mornings are cloaked in silent perusal of God's wonders in nature and the Psalms, where my neighbors know my family and reach out to care for us, and where the lack of pretension of the simple folk remind me that the value of a stranger's smile – much like Sarah's sweet hellos – are far greater than anything a Maserati or Aston Martin could offer me.

THE RICHES OF WISDOM

"In his riches, man lacks wisdom." ~ *Psalm 49: 21*

In her simplicity, wisdom roots out all trivial distractions from our lives. Our concupiscence draws us toward all that glitters, but we know the truth about glitz and glamor. We know it deceives and pulls us away from our eternal destination.

The psychological and spiritual clutter often builds up in us over time, based on the amount of physical or environmental clutter in our lives. The more we accumulate, the more we must maintain, and we all know that things break, wear, and decay over time. Must our souls decay along with our possessions?

Wisdom, then, seeks simplicity. A simple life is not merely one devoid of chaos (though that is an essential beginning), but it is one filled with the treasures of Heaven. It is a life built on virtue and showered with spiritual fruits. Wisdom seeks such things.

Or rather, she does not seek things in terms of material wealth or property. These she uses for the good of her family and community. Rather, wisdom is the path to a holy, interior life, which is then reflected in one's lifestyle and home.

THE SPARROW'S SONG

"Look at the birds in the sky; they do not sow or reap, they gather nothing into barns, yet your heavenly Father feeds them. Are not you more important than they?" ~Matthew 6: 26

Why does the sparrow sing with such gusto, as if always rejoicing and never fretting? The sparrow is a plain and simple creature, certainly overlooked and often underwhelming to us. We notice the flamboyant colors of tropical birds or even the sideshow of a peacock's feathers in an array of colors and movement.

We forget the little sparrow, small and meek, a mousy brown and having no particularly defining characteristics. But the song of the sparrow is melodious, light, and even effervescent. The sparrow always exudes praise and gratitude at his meager life of living off the land. The sparrow's song is unwavering, for he delights both in the surrounding creation and his creator.

We are to be like the sparrows, because Jesus reminds us that He cares for them and every detail of their lives, just as He cares for us. Though we are worth more than many sparrows, we often seek to be more like the parrots and peacocks – entertaining, conspicuous, and vibrant.

Let us imitate the sparrow's humble submission, simplicity, joy, and eagerness to praise God in all ways and in all circumstances. Then the sparrow's song becomes our song – a prayer of thanksgiving lifted up even in our trials and sorrows.

THE WEALTH OF GENEROSITY

"For in a severe test of affliction, the abundance of their joy and their profound poverty overflowed in a wealth of generosity on their part." ~ *2 Corinthians 8: 2*

How can I be rich if I give away all that I own and, even more, all that I am? This extreme poverty is not only unappealing, but it is also truly ghastly and abhorrent to my sensibility and flesh. While the world harkens to the cries of material acquisition, You whisper softly, *Give more, and you will be more.*

God doesn't promise that we will be wealthy in monetary gain when we give the meager offerings of two coins or even if we donate thousands of dollars to a worthy cause. The replacement of temporal goods doesn't necessarily follow, but rather, it's the deepening of our character and development of virtues that often result from acts of charity.

The wealth of generosity is measured by the spiritual fruitfulness of our lives. We do not gain more, but we become more as we empty ourselves and voluntarily relinquish all to God's provident care. This, indeed, is the heart of stewardship: trust. We trust in the God who gives and takes away.

UNBURDENED BY USELESS BAGGAGE

Consider what we carry in our hearts: many burdens that torment our psyche and spirit. What is the origin of such burdens? It is only this: attachment. So we must ask ourselves, then: What is the antidote to releasing our attachments to possessions, people, and even our talents or accomplishments? We must become detached from all, except God, through the practice of holy indifference.

Holy indifference begins with an act of the will, in which we choose to be content with whatever happens in a particular circumstance or to something we own and even whether we lose a friendship through any means other than our sin. As we grow in this spiritual principle, our hearts are changed – gradually but steadily – and the fruit that dwells there is peace.

To one who practices holy indifference well, the virtues of simplicity and evangelical poverty become more attractive and plausible to live. We may begin by purging our homes and offices of "useless baggage," which is all that we accumulate over time. But the true test is whether we still remain attached in our hearts.

The only attachment we should have is dependence on God. When we are unfettered by the destruction or lack of material things, we're likely to know the liberty that holy indifference affords us. Likewise, if we live in simplicity, we're also more likely to be generous if times become more prosperous for us.

WISDOM OF THE SIMPLE

Why am I lured by the wisdom of the simple? They speak so plainly and yet profoundly, and I am rendered speechless, in awe of the gift they possess. It seems the simple have very little clutter in their lives, especially in their hearts. Because of this, they naturally express and exude truth in small but powerful ways. Only in their presence do I realize how complicated I've made my life, that I lack the virtue of simplicity and yet long for it.

My thoughts and emotions are nearly always a tangled array of complexity. This is obvious even in the way I write: I search for the fancy or frivolous word rather than the conspicuous one, and so I get swept away in rhetoric at times rather than simple truths.

Those who possess the virtue of simplicity are not merely simpletons. They aren't necessarily ignorant or intellectually deficient, though they may be. But what matters in all of this is that their hearts are pure and unblemished. They are open always to beauty and rest in the gift of an uncomplicated life. They value the small, overlooked gifts hidden in each new day's sunrise, flower, or song.

CHAPTER TWELVE

Encouragement in Doubt

A GOOD MEASURE

"Give and gifts will be given to you; a good measure, packed together, shaken down and overflowing, will be poured into your lap. For the measure with which you measure will in turn be measured out to you." ~ Luke 6: 38

We know that every good gift comes from God, but do we ensure that every gift from us comes back to glorify God, even indirectly? Our gifts are not always proportionate to our interior gratitude, but we can change that today.

Somehow gratitude makes my heart sing just a bit louder and expands my capacity to love and give. I cannot give what I don't have, so I may retreat within myself at times and become miserly with my talents, time, and treasure.

But gratitude changes everything, so that we somehow transform into magnanimous people. This metamorphosis may seem random, but we know its source is God. All we have to give in the beginning is something so meager it is nearly unapparent.

This initial gift opens our hearts to desire to give more and more away to others and ultimately to God. True generosity is not measured at all. It is a sort of state of being in which I no longer focus on my need or lack but instead rely upon God's goodness and promise of a "good measure" as my reward.

Think of a good measure as the very means by which you live, because God becomes our food and sustains us through the Sacred Host. His generosity far surpasses ours, so why withhold anything from Him at all? Even our insignificant donation of five loaves and two fish becomes infinitely multiplied through God's generosity.

So don't delay in offering what you have today, because while it will never be enough in your eyes, it will be exponentially blessed through God's good measure.

A TWO-EDGED SWORD

"He made my mouth like a sharp-edged sword, concealed me, shielded by his hand." ~ Isaiah 49: 2

If the sword of the Spirit is faith, does faith have two sides or edges? I imagine a mighty sword of pure silver with two sharp edges that we, as people of faith, carry. I believe it is because we often must slay heresy from one side and sharply, swiftly defend truth from the other.

The two-edged sword also signifies my heart and the state of my interior life, for every vice has a corresponding virtue, and every part of me that longs for what is righteous, holy, and true also battles against the devil, flesh, and the world. But God has equipped me with the sword of His Spirit, and I am to draw upon it every day, for it is both my shield and the source of my fortitude. I am courageous and persevere, undaunted in the wake of war when facing my spiritual enemies.

"For when I am weak, then I am strong," St. Paul reminds me. "For we do not fight against flesh and blood, but against principalities and powers..."

The war, my friends, is not between you and me. It's not purely political, either. It encompasses a broader exchange of battles for our souls; we are the Church Militant, the participants of the eternal and age-old battle between good and evil. The two-edged sword, then, must remain sharp and ready to defend. We do not often defend the noble, true, and honorable ideals of the Lord through our daily lives, but we must.

Now is the time to draw upon the sword of the Spirit with confidence that the Mighty Warrior will give us the words to speak and a magnanimous heart to love Him above all.

BE BRAVE AND STEADFAST

I notice this sinking feeling in the pit of my stomach once again. Am I slipping into the dark abyss? I am afraid – of all that I know and of all that I don't know. My life is consumed by ravaging fear. The unknown is somehow attacked in my mind and filled with all of the disastrous "what ifs" or "if/thens," and my heart is subsequently burdened with dread.

Is this happening, because I've suffered torment before? The pain, the losses – even the memories of what has long past – is too much for me to bear. I have always reproached suffering, avoided it, and when it afflicts me (regardless of my attempts to evade it), I sink into discouragement.

Am I being chastised? Every thorn, every pierce feels like I am abused relentlessly. Could it be that You are blessing me, and I have missed the hidden grace that is present in these trials? Today You tell me boldly, confidently, "Be brave and steadfast." The words Moses spoke to the Israelites as his life was drawing to a close haunt me today, for they are foreign to my thoughts.

Scripture is so hope-filled, reminding me hundreds of times to not be afraid, for You are with me. But I don't feel Your nearness. I don't see You or hear You. The once sweet spiritual consolations were long ago replaced with a hollowness that agonizes me as I desperately attempt to clasp You in the darkness.

Be brave and steadfast. The words almost seem like a warning, a foreshadowing of greater suffering still, and I am too weak to want a heavier cross. I want to be like everyone else – happy, content, comfortable.

But You have called me to something more, something beyond all the riches and wonders of Earth. The raging waters will not consume me, yet they still thrash around me. I am not brave or steadfast. I am crumbling and falling apart.

Lord, save me! I cry to You with only an echo as response. But somewhere in a latent part of my heart, something stirs in me. Could it be hope? Courage? Yes, it swells greater now, and I realize at once that it is You. You have been sleeping in me – in the darkest parts of me – but You never abandoned me. You are my hope. You are my courage.

CHRISTIAN CONSTELLATIONS

"One might say that the saints are, so to speak, new Christian constellations, in which the richness of God's goodness is reflected."
~ *Pope Emeritus Benedict XVI*

The saints are as numerous as the stars in the sky, so their legacies remain sparkling day after day, illuminating the darkness. Indeed, their witnesses shine in the dark nights of our journey. They are the clusters of paradise pinned above us, which point and direct us heavenward.

When we lose our way or begin to doubt our call to holiness (and most assuredly we will be tempted to doubt it), we can recall the Christian constellations of saints. They, like us, are merely pinpricks of light that, together form the unfathomable, enchanting image of the promise that awaits us when we someday die.

For us, death is not the end of life but merely the beginning of our eternal, and thus *real*, life. It is our hope to one day become part of the starry tapestry of Christian constellations, each of us uniquely woven into the Kingdom of Heaven based upon the fulfillment of our earthly mission, which was ordained by God.

Look to the sky on a clear night, and you will be dazzled by the array of light. These are the Christian constellations, the people who have lived valiantly and gained Heaven. The stars remind us that, as countless as they are to the human eye, so it is in Heaven – a constellation of numerous saints who reflect the Light of the World.

CLOTHED WITH JOY

"You changed my mourning into dancing; you took off my sackcloth and clothed me with gladness. So that my glory may praise you and not be silent, O Lord, my God, forever will I give you thanks."
~ *Psalm 30: 12 – 13*

"Your joy is my strength." Nehemiah (8: 10) said it first and best, yet I have only begun to realize this hidden truth: hidden, because I have been blinded with distraction by my suffering and have become self-concerned as a result.

"When I am weak, then I am strong." St. Paul (see 2 Corinthians 12: 10) turned irony into a beloved and timeless verse that both theologians and laypersons alike appreciate. Joy does not equate happiness, or more accurately, happiness is not a necessary quality of joy. Joy is a spiritual gift that supersedes fleeting emotions like happiness. The world has it wrong when it implies that happiness is our ultimate goal in everything, because we will only be supremely happy in the afterlife (for those who enter the beatific vision).

Joy frustrates the plans of happiness, because it is present in the midst of trials, sorrow, and long-suffering. Joy is in our hope of clinging to God in our weakness and realizing His strength alone is what carries us intact through our struggles. In this we are clothed with God, because He cloaks us with His gift of joy.

COMFORT THE AFFLICTED

Suffering does not discriminate. It is the one aspect of life that defines the human condition and prepares the soul for death. If we never felt pain or knew our limitations, would death be even more difficult to face than it already is?

When we offer someone else our comfort, it's true that some form of self-denial will be necessary, because our focus will go from self to other. But in the consolation we extend to a person who perhaps has no source of consolation, we may find that our act of charity brings about healing within us.

Comforting others seems an easy and even menial offering in the grand scheme of other, more glamorous or exorbitant ways to help someone. But neither is this easy or menial. Sometimes, when all we have to give is an open heart, an attentive ear, or a healing touch, comfort becomes a profound agent of hope in someone's life.

We often underestimate the true value of spiritual works of mercy, which far surpass corporal works, in that the soul is the recipient of each act, and the soul has the potential to be eternally altered.

COVERED WITH SMALL CROSSES

"The road of our earthly existence is covered with small crosses."
~ *St. Maximillian Kolbe*

It is foolish for me to assume that my life is only a journey to the largest cross – the Crucifix – where all that is "I" must end and all that is "He" must remain. Truthfully, all of life is an accumulation of smaller, triter crosses – the minor irritations, frustrations, exhaustion, and so on.

Life is not a journey without the small crosses that greet us along the way. I cannot enter the gates of Heaven without the triumph of cross to crown, and this only occurs when God's grace matches the cross I am currently carrying.

But I happen to believe that His grace exceeds my burden, because He cannot be outdone in generosity. His mercy abounds, but will I reach out to Him? Or am I too focused on self?

The pain of this present moment is, in fact, drawing me out of myself and toward the other – the stranger, the foe, the invalid, the widow, the child, the aggrieved, the elderly, the lonely, and ultimately to God.

God's kisses are covered with small crosses.

CROSS WALK

I traverse this lonely road, Lord, with little to call my own. I carry on my shoulders a light pack, but the heavier load is the one hidden in my heart. I set out at Your command, for You beckoned me, "Come to me, you who are weary and burdened, and I will give you rest, for my yoke is easy and my burden light." I responded favorably, because my burden has been holding me back. I am shackled by sin and unnecessary struggle. The promise of a lighter onus enticed me, so I set out on a new path, leaving behind the weighty baggage of my old life.

You promised, "For behold, I make all things new." I walk this lonely road in the hopes I might be made new, for I am a worn and weary pilgrim, a mere pauper's traveler. I do not wander so much to meander aimlessly but more so to seek You wholeheartedly.

And up ahead on this dusty road is a "crosswalk." I pause for a time, bewildered and dazed from traveling so long without reprieve. A choice stands before me; which direction shall I select? I desire the one that leads to You, to eternal life, but my heart is rendered silent in this moment of waiting.

Then I hear You say, "I will direct your paths and show you where to go, whether to the right or to the left." At once, I pay heed to Your command, but then I realize the crossroads was truthfully the final leg of my personal journey to Calvary.

It is truly my cross walk, for I walk to Your cross, now carrying my own crude wood of sanctification. You are right, Lord, as You always are – Your burden is easy and now my yoke is lighter, for I have abandoned the sins of my youth and the old habits of living. And now I sojourn on this cross walk, in which I am both led and carried by You. Yes, it will lead to my interior crucifixion, but ultimately it will result in the gain of Heaven, where the yoke vanishes altogether, and I am finally – at last – free for eternity.

Help me stay the course of this cross walk, so that I may not falter, despite the obstacles, hurdles, challenges, and temptations. Be my guide, O Light, lest the darkness enshroud me in confusion.

Remind me always that the humiliation of the cross leads to the humble admission into everlasting life with You.

DAYS OF GLADNESS

"Now consider what he has done for you, and give thanks with full voice." ~ Tobit 13: 6

I choose to praise God in this storm of my life. As the tempest roars and wails about me, I will respond by confidently thanking God for all. Joy, as love, is an act of the will at times, as well as a fruit of the Holy Spirit. If I choose to praise and bless the One who is all goodness and longs for my wellbeing, then days of gladness will shower me.

To live in hope and exude joy may come naturally to some, but not to me. I am an eager pessimist (sadly), and my fallen nature is tempted daily to abandon the call from God. How I wish it were easy to follow God's call! It is simple but not easy. It's simple, because all that's required of us is resignation to His will in all things, as well as complete trust and confidence in His providence.

Choose to dwell in days of gladness. We don't have to be happy all the time, but let's make the best of all circumstances by seeking the sunshine rather than the rain.

Today I'm looking for the rainbow, too.

ENDURANCE IS OUR PORTION

There's always been a storm in my heart. As a child, I was feisty and fiery, prone to zealous outbursts for the sake of justice. But I never weighed the value of charity and mercy. My spirit had not yet been tempered, because I was spiritually petulant. When I felt convicted, I immediately responded to that conviction, because I errantly believed it was for the sake of righteousness, for the Kingdom of Heaven.

The Lord has been good to me, because He could have chastised me the way I did everyone else: with bold, brazen, caustic blows to the heart. But instead, His discipline has been tender and gradual, and I am changed by His constant mercy.

Because of necessary trials in my life, I've learned the value of endurance over impulsiveness. Endurance is taking a large portion – a call, perhaps, or a mission – and making steady, rhythmic strides over time. It is watching, waiting, and carefully maneuvering so that the fires of righteousness are calmed only enough to become mighty acts of charity.

Endurance is perseverance: in the faith, through spiritual aridity and holy darkness, chronic illness, or prolonged grief. It is running the race and fighting without losing hope or giving up when all appears futile. It is that quiet virtue that evolves over time to create a lasting movement in us toward Heaven.

HOLDING MY HAND

"Yet I am always with you; you take hold of my right hand."
~*Psalm 73: 23*

Lord, my stamina is waning with each passing day, though no one notices. At times I confront my apparent weakness, and I am gravely tempted toward discouragement. How can my afflictions draw out greatness for Your glory?

I know You purposefully select the weakest ones to do Your greatest work, and when I am out of my home and in the world, I see clearly how weak I am and what little I know. I am no expert, so why would You bring people to me – to read what I write, listen to me speak, or seek counsel from me? These questions taunt me every day, and I have become battle weary.

Everything about the state of my life screams that You have left me, that I am forsaken. And most days I can see why: I fall and fail far more than I succeed. There are days, in fact, when I credit no gains, only loss after loss. Shame and sorrow consume me, and I am left to wallow in the darkness, the nothingness once more.

But today I begin anew, and my eyes are opened for the first time to the truth that I was always in Your presence. You use everything for my good, the good of others, and the advancement of Your kingdom. Yes, You even and especially use my faults and frailties, for I am always in Your presence when I walk by faith. You hold my hand, though I neither see nor feel Your grasp.

You are my stronghold as my body fights to shut down, to give up. Somehow, somewhere Your spirit surges in me and instantly recharges my strength for the moment, for the day.

If I am truly in Your presence always, then nothing is lost and all is gain, because Your might and power are manifested through my emptiness and nothingness. Since there is no evidence of my own capabilities to complete the mission to which You have called me, then You alone are necessarily magnified and glorified.

And all is well today, because I was always in Your presence. Though I see not, nor hear, nor feel, I know You are leading the way to victory. Help me to stay the course.

HORIZON OF THE IDEAL

"Christians live...without being scandalized by their own mistakes or by betrayal...but continuously recovering the horizon of the ideal." ~ *Servant of God Luigi Giussani*[xiv]

What is the ideal? For most of my life, I've been accused of upholding high expectations, so my heart always sinks when I consider the ideal. Is it just another lofty expectation to desire Heaven? If we, as Christians, seek what is perfect and holy, the only perfection that is even remotely attainable is Heaven. And Heaven is the ideal.

Are we on the horizon of Heaven? It would seem so, for we are on the cusp of a new Heaven and new Earth. We see Heaven in the distance like a long-awaited sunrise, but it is still somehow a bit too far out of our reach.

Is Heaven – the ideal – attainable in this life? Again, it seems so, because thousands of saints who have gone before us have been caressed by Heaven's gentle touch upon their souls. The miraculous and generous spiritual gifts of the saints are a tangible, hopeful reflection of Heaven. Saints personify the ideal for which we strive.

And since Heaven is on the horizon for many of us – while others have reached the Kingdom already – we carry the hope of dawn, the perseverant faith that is undaunted by trials. The horizon of the ideal is our goal and so we must stay the course, fight the good fight, and remain steadfast until we have reached Heaven.

LET NOTHING DISTURB YOU

"In the world you have trouble, but take courage; I have conquered the world." ~ John 16: 33

My heart is troubled, Lord, for my body grows weak in stature, and my soul realizes its frailties by nature. I am like Martha most days – troubled by many things, anxious, fretting about trite frustrations. Most of the time I allow myself to wallow in this state of fear, but I have learned that my peace must never be disturbed.

It's difficult to fathom how my life can be in such tumult and yet I hear the whisper, "Let nothing disturb you." My finances are in disarray, and we have medical bills piling up, but I hear another word from You, "Rest in my peace." I'm frantically trying to hold together our household while rushing from appointment to appointment, but there is something else beckoning me, "Take courage; It is I. Do not be afraid." Our support system is shifting, and I receive less and less help. Here you tell me, "Do not be troubled or afraid."

How can it be that, regardless of the chaos and uncertainty encircling me every day, my heart remains placidly hopeful? How can this be? I long for it, strive for it, but so far this unfaltering interior tranquility is shaken at the slightest irritation or motion of upheaval.

Your words ring hauntingly true, Jesus. If I were even infinitesimally humble, even remotely confident in You, my peace would never waver but instead remain steadfast through the storms of life. I pray that my faith may grow to the size of a mustard seed and that my heart may rest in You, come what may.

LIVE WHAT YOU RECEIVE
Do I exude the joy I've been given? Am I at peace within, regardless of my circumstances? Do I praise God in the midst of uncertainty and loss?

Life as a Christian, especially as a Catholic, must be attractive to those who watch, listen to, an encounter us. Otherwise all of our theology is moot to them. I hear the beckoning today: *Live what you receive.* I have been given all from above, an inheritance to eternal glory, yet my countenance droops, and my spirit sinks. I do not live the joy, because I still worry. Still, I beg for the grace in spite of my weakness, and God scoops me up again.

To live what we receive quite simply means we must trust God enough to never be disturbed and to always respond to Him with gratitude. As the world becomes increasingly confounded with the problem of suffering, we must be the solution to that problem. We are witnesses of the Resurrection. We are a Resurrection people.

MAKE ME CONSTANT AND TRUE

There are many days (most days) when I can truthfully declare that I have no one upon whom I can rely. I have no earthly person I can trust or know with certainty will be available to help me in my greatest need or darkest hour. Sadly, or perhaps providentially, this truth has crept into my awareness with biting, stinging clarity.

I have no one but You, Lord. There is no person who can care for me as I care for my family, and of course, even I fall short of that. So make me constant and true as You are. Make me steadfast in my resolve to nurture and care for others, despite my hidden suffering. I acknowledge my fallibility and inability to be perfectly accountable to this constancy. But You are my constancy. You are ever-faithful and offer me unfailing help.

You guard me from the foe, as well as the enemy's discouragement and the committee of others berating me about doing too much or too little.

I ask for help and find none, except Your saving hand to pick me up when I've fallen. Will You not rescue me once more today? Even in times when my intellect knows You are my fortress and refuge, my will falters in its frail faith.

Make me constant and true in the thick of my weakness and sickness, that I may be undaunted by life's certain crises, that my faith in You and love for others stands tall in the midst of the uncertainty, skepticism, and unbelief that surrounds us all. For when I am weak, then I am strong.

MAKING DECISIONS

"What you decide shall succeed for you, and upon your ways light shall shine." ~ Job 22: 28

If I do as I please, will You grant me Your favors? It may be so that You are asking me to lean into You in order that I might discover what pleases You instead. Making decisions is always a feat, because I vacillate, second-guess, doubt, and ruminate. How can I be sure my plans will succeed, as You have aptly promised?

I must walk in Your ways every moment and not lose sight of You, which is so often the case. I'd rather meander off the path You've selected for me, following some distraction that pulls me away from decision.

Lord, keep me near You. Remember that I am Your wayward toddler, exploring and seeking and getting into everything without knowing what will help or harm. My motives are innocent, but my actions are petulant. I need You to guide me, loving Father, away from the world and all that diverts my focus from You.

All I need is to know You are with me, closely leading and gently guiding, and I know my decisions cannot fail in light of this love. My gaze must forever be upon Yours, and I will do nothing apart from Your will. Keep me close, and I will follow You to the end of my days.

MOURNING INTO JOY

Even if we are immersed in and surrounded by sorrow, though we grieve now, we have the promise of our pain becoming joy. This is our hope. We cleave to this promise when we begin to capitulate to despair. The truth sheds light on this time of our lives.

We must remember that everything has its season, which is to say that everything we experience has a purpose of good in it. When we are in a period of deep regret or sadness, we know logically that a time of celebration will one day be upon us. Everything is cyclic.

We need the rhythm of life and death, loss and gain, sorrow and joy to balance one from the other. Each time of struggle draws us out of our comfortable lives and invites us to grow and "become what we already are." Then God grants us a reprieve, however long or short it may be, so that we can rest and recuperate for the next challenge.

The promise of God ultimately is this: We are not guaranteed happiness in this life, but we can live our lives in such a manner that we will enjoy eternal bliss in Heaven. That is God's promise, and that is our joy.

OUR DESTINY AND LONGING

I wish I could say all of humanity shares a common destiny. It's true that our shared home is Earth, but sadly, we do not all long for Heaven – nor do we all attain it. But those of us who share this longing seem to wholeheartedly desire that one destiny and one end, the only goal in sight: Heaven. In all its glory, we wait with the groaning of Earth, and we cry along with it, cognizant of the countless consequences of sin.

In order for our destiny to be reached, or rather our *destination* to be reached, we must first fulfill the longing to *be* God's Kingdom on Earth. It is the season of hope and mercy, so we must not succumb to our frustrations and the inevitable irritations that impede our goal. Instead, we must remain focused and draw souls near to God through our love of Him and love of neighbor.

Perhaps the greatest roadblock I must face and overcome is myself. I often block the grace available to aid me in my mission when I doubt. Today I will choose to be merciful to myself, forgiving myself and starting anew, because today is the beginning of my destiny and longing.

REJOICE LIKE A CHAMPION

If we are fighting the good fight and running the race, we are on the road to championship. We do not yet have to reach the goal – Heaven – only to see it or even envision it in order to keep on the path. Our rejoicing begins here, now, because we have set our feet and our sights on the track where God has placed us.

Even if we began the journey today, let us rejoice. With the graceful stride of an experienced runner, let us not lose our stamina. Rejoice if you are in the middle of your race and find yourself weary or wanting to give up. Rejoice if you are nearing the end of the race, for the last stretch is often the most trying.

We are all champions in Christ, the first Victor. He won for us the prize that awaits us, and we can only claim it through His victory over sin and death. So He has given us this championship, and for this reason alone, we must always praise and thank Him.

Gratitude is the foundation of rejoicing, for a dejected heart can easily be uplifted through thoughts of gratitude and praise to God. If this is so, then we all must rejoice through every struggle and celebration of life.

RUNNING THE RACE

"Therefore, since we are surrounded by so great a cloud of witnesses, let us rid ourselves of every burden and sin that clings to us and persevere in running the race that lies before us while keeping our eyes fixed on Jesus, the leader and perfector of faith. For the sake of the joy that lay before him he endured the cross, despising its shame, and has taken his seat at the right of the throne of God." ~Hebrews 12: 1 – 2

Jesus, my eyes are fixed on You. You are my ultimate end, my purpose and goal, my finish line. These days I admit I do not want to run, for every part of me aches and cries out to You in pain. It is no longer subtle but now all too noticeable how truly weak and incapable I am.

So I have now passed the crossroads, and You no longer want me to look to the right or to the left. Now my focus must become more intense on running without ceasing, and I must never – for one instant – take my eyes off of You.

Jesus, I need You to recharge my drooping spirit, because I can tell I am on the cusp of either defeat or victory. There is no middle ground in this race. I have come so far by the guidance of Your hand.

You alone have served as my mentor, coach, counselor, friend, physician, father, brother, advocate, and publicist. I am virtually unknown, and yet You have invited me to join this race, to overcome the most difficult feats. As a result, I have been tried and tested in unfathomable ways. Am I not permitted to rest a while? No, I must press on, for the hour draws near when the race itself will end. I must make it to You, the finish line, no matter what may come or become of me.

Do I possess enough fortitude and perseverance – even the drive – to forge ahead? Yes, I must. I have run too far to turn back or quit. The end of this race is approaching, and then, Lord, I will finally collapse in Your arms, full of relief and in need of respite. For I only have a limited reserve, and this race is pushing every limit I've got.

Though I often want nothing more than to altogether quit, I hear You call to me, "Stay the course," and so I must. The trail is long, but I know I cannot go back or be who I once was. Jesus, catch me when I reach the end, lest I fall to the ground. I am drained of my capacity to love and, at times, my will to live. But to You I look, and I will not succumb to defeat. May You be glorified in my nothingness.

SLAVISH VERSUS REVERENTIAL FEAR

All my life I've lived in constant fear and dread: fear of what may (or may not) happen, fear of the unknown, of change, of trying (and possibly failing at) new things, and on and on. Fear crippled me at times, preventing me from that vulnerability of risk. I never considered the possibility that I may grow or gain through that risk. This was slavish fear.

Slavish fear is of the enemy. It ensnares and paralyzes us

into inaction. We feel disturbed, restless, and anxious as a result. We should rebuke this fear always, recognizing its source. This is the fear that prevents us from loving and fully embracing life.

Reverential fear, however, is an incredible spiritual gift. We are left pondering in gratitude the infinity and greatness of our God – His goodness, too – while concurrently acknowledging our nothingness. There is no shame in this fear, only joy, gratitude, and a greater love for God. Reverential fear releases us from the chains of slavish fear.

We are free at last in this spiritual gift. Let us lift our hearts to the Creator, and remember we are that which is created. Knowing that His perfect love casts out all slavish fear from our lives draws us away from ourselves and closer to God.

THE OFFERING OF A MEAL

When a meal is presented as a gift, it may appear overly simplistic or menial to the typical individual. Meals are often offered as a gesture of hospitality following serious diagnoses, surgery, chronic illness, or the birth of a baby. It's an overlooked blessing by many, because it has become the go-to, proverbial response to the aforementioned situations.

But a meal – in all its simplistic presentations – is far from an insignificant offering. A meal is a gift of the hands and heart, for with loving kindness a meal is prepared for its recipient. The rhythm of preparation mirrors the soothing mantra of a latent prayer, silently petitioning to God that the food will bless those who receive it. In this way, a meal is also a gift from the heart.

Food is the one necessity of the body that caregivers often neglect in an influx of crisis. We are immersed in updating medical records and financial information, post-operative instructions and follow-ups. We seldom consider what we take into our bodies. It becomes mindless chewing, without care or conscious deliberation for nourishment.

So a home-cooked meal nourishes the caregiver's body, but more than that, it heals the soul. Sitting down after acute or chronic stress to a thoughtfully prepared meal centers the caregiver's thoughts to those of intentional eating. The rhythm of preparation transforms into the rhythm of nourishment.

But as we consume our meal from a neighbor, friend or family member, we receive the sustenance and fortification from healthy meals that propels us to continue fighting our battles with perseverance.

Meals warm the heart, as well as the body. They speak a profound message of love, hidden in the midst of ingredients and spices. Meals enliven and refresh our weary, aching bodies after a long stint at the hospital. They rejuvenate both our spirits and our resolve to forge ahead.

Somehow the simple offering of a meal profoundly reminds us that we are not alone or forgotten, that we are loved and supported through the consideration of others who help us care for our basic needs while we care for our loved ones. Meals are simple, common, and organic, yet they are far from commonplace. They are offered as a reminder to the caregiver to stop and rest a while, to recline and dine at the table, break bread and give thanks to the One who supplies us with all our needs, both temporal and spiritual.

THE UNFADING CROWN OF GLORY

"And when the chief Shepherd is revealed, you will receive the unfading crown of glory." ~ 1 Peter 5: 4

O King of Glory, You alone wear the unfading crown of glory. I am not worthy of such an honor. I do not seek the interests of others in lieu of my own, and I am selfish, poor, and spiritually bereft. I am a wretch. Can a wretch like me wear the crown of glory?

One day my hope is to reach Heaven, though its heights seem so far from where I am now. My vice is all too evident, while virtue is nonexistent. I am to grow in virtue and be rid of vice, but all I notice are the aches and pains of my constant sinning.

It is by Your mercy alone that I have a chance at the unfading crown of glory – the crown of the saints, the crown of victory. And it is hope that leads me to believe this crown is possible, even for me. When my life seems so filled with sickness, I cannot see the saints' crown for myself. I am inclined toward unbelief and despair.

But keep the eyes of my heart fixed on Your beautiful cross, Jesus, for then all this suffering will translate into the victor's crown of eternal joy. I cannot claim the crown without first encountering the Cross.

THE WEIGHTIER THINGS OF THE LAW

"Woe to you, scribes and Pharisees, you hypocrites. You pay tithes of mint and dill and cumin, and have neglected the weightier things of the law: judgment and mercy and fidelity. [But] these you should have done, without neglecting the others." ~ Matthew 23: 23

Why is following the law for some people so onerous and tedious? For others, the law is used to manipulate and brand the masses, or often to justify one's own behavior. Why, then, does the law bear such tremendous weight in our lives?

There is the law of man and the law of God, and the two are not the same. Which are we to follow: the rules of the road or the guidelines of God? It seems that this is where a well-formed conscience comes into play. This is an issue of moral discernment, for most things in life require careful reflection rather than impetuous impulsivity.

Certainly I am required to obey basic traffic laws, noise ordinances, and other local legislation that bears no weight on my moral beliefs. But when human law forces me to subsidize contraception or abortion through taxation, I am then commanded in good conscience to refute that law. In essence,

God's law trumps any man-made law.

The law of God must be written on my heart in order for it to be authentically lived in my life. Then I am equipped to decide rightly what man-made laws are just or unjust.

THIS DAY

Jesus, only for today, help me to bear wrongs patiently, respond charitably to others (especially my family), and strive for holiness.

On this day, remind me that Your joy is my strength, and I have all the grace I need...just for today. This day is all I have been given, yet I complicate my life by dwelling on past misfortunes or fretting over future frustrations.

This day is Your gift to me. It is a blank slate, upon which I choose to write my story. Will I succumb to the promptings of acedia or remain steadfast in the true movements of Your Spirit?

At times the bigger call of my life leads me to a holy tension, because this day remains ordinary when I see such extraordinary things on the horizon. This day is much like yesterday and days gone by that turn to weeks and perhaps months. How can I miss the possibilities that this day offers me? By dwelling on what has been and what appears to be impossible.

This day You've shown me that all things are possible for and with You. All I need is to cling to You, Jesus, just for one day. Today it's enough for me to take one more leap of faith, to trust just a bit more, because one day – *this* day – is manageable with Your grace.

UNSTAINED BY THE WORLD

"Religion that is pure and undefiled before God and the Father is this: to care for orphans and widows in their affliction and to keep oneself unstained by the world." ~ James 1: 27

The world and all of creation is good, for You have made all things holy, good, and unblemished. But lately I am burdened by the effects of sin that have tainted the world: acid rain and chemicals in our air, water, and soil. There are increasing diseases – chronic illnesses – and everywhere I turn all I notice is fast-paced, impatient, distractibility.

I long to be unstained by the world, and to somehow leave the world in better condition, to make positive changes and yet not really be so deeply affected by the world's perspective of doing rather than being.

To be unstained by the world is nearly impossible these days, yet I imagine a refuge in uninhabited woods or wilderness, a cabin in the midst of tranquility, clean air, and water. Even to retreat in a place like this would be delightful, but I know it is sinful for me to opt out of the world altogether and somehow subsist instead in a distant land without interruption from its sleepy existence.

You remind me to stay awake, and part of this vigilance is doing, which results from being. You beckon me to rest a while, in order to prepare me for the next battleground, where I must encounter the gravely ill, the wounded, the lost and lonely, and the refugee.

Keep me, then, unstained by the world while I dwell among the sickness and sin in order to bring forth Your healing and hope.

WAITING

Waiting…
…for a miracle,
A chance,
A breakthrough,
Time to dance.

Waiting…
…to finally see,

To hear with open ears,
To find
How God is reaching me.
Or is it
I reach Him Who's always there,
I've got a chance.
I've prayed my prayer.

The time is now.
The time is here.
The waiting is the answer.
It is near
My time to end this wait,
To cease the fight,
To abdicate my tension,
And release this tight
Grip on nothing.

It's the nothing I'm in.
The waiting, the wandering,
I can't see or feel Him.
But I know He is with me
This day and the next
To deliver my heart from agony
And all that leaves me perplexed.

WALK IN HIS WAYS

"Blessed those whose way is blameless, who walk by the law of the Lord. Blessed those who keep his testimonies, who seek him with all their heart. They do no wrong; they walk in his ways."
~ *Psalm 119: 1 – 3*

I have sought truth nearly all my life: truth in the form of a divine Person, for He who saved the world saved me in and by truth. Walking toward "Him whom my heart loves" led me to the narrow path, which soon became darkened.

Now I move forward, pressing on, yet in darkness. I cannot see what lies ahead or if I have strayed from truth. He no longer holds my hand but has now illuminated only one step at a time for me, for His word is "a light unto my path."

The darkness invites doubt and discouragement every day, because I no longer see clearly a straight road. I see nothing at all. I am encouraged only to trust the One who set my feet on this dusty, worn trail. Most days it is a lonely journey as I traverse forward, uncertain of my movements getting me anywhere at all.

But the desire to walk in His ways remains paramount, which grants me some sense of relief. I know He would never lead me astray, so if a darkened road is His will for me to travel, I will follow it, for He shows me whether I am to "walk to the right or to the left."

WALK OF TRUST

Learning to trust God entails movement forward. We never stand perfectly still if we walk in trust, because we know He is always leading us somewhere beyond where we are today. So we walk as sojourners, always forward and never looking back in regret. Trust accompanies us in faith today and keeps our eyes fixed on the One who calls us.

This movement of trust can sometimes feel old, and we begin to doubt or grow discouraged. If we walk at a steady pace for a long time, life may seem to be drudgery. It can be quite cumbersome to continue forging ahead, trusting that one day God will fulfill His promise for our lives.

Perhaps, then, the lesson in learning to trust is not so much the fulfillment of what we anticipate in hope, but instead in the journey itself. The walking with God, toward God is the lesson we must learn – not in the looking back or peering ahead, but in the small, steady steps we take as we follow God's lead.

We walk by faith and not by sight, so we walk in trust.

WE CONQUER OVERWHELMINGLY

"No, in all these things we conquer overwhelmingly through him who loved us. For I am convinced that neither death, nor life, nor angels, nor principalities, nor present things, nor future things, nor powers, nor height, nor depth, nor any other creature will be able to separate us from the love of God in Christ Jesus our Lord."
~ *Romans 8: 37 – 39*

We fall and rise again, but what makes us fall and what makes us rise? In order to fall, we give way to our ever-present concupiscence, and sin invades our souls. To rise is to look heavenward, and, in desperation, reach up to grab God's outstretched hand. His grace upholds us always.

When we conquer, it is because we are in a state of grace and call upon the name of Jesus. We do not overcome the enemy, the world, or ourselves alone. But there is power and true freedom in calling upon His name with confidence and hope when we are slandered, spiritually attacked, or oppressed by our life circumstances.

In these moments, we conquer *overwhelmingly*. This gives rise to courage, which may be latent when we exist in bondage. And courage (a small segment of fortitude) gives way to perseverance, then hope. Hope lifts us up to a place of faith, which is deepened by charity.

We conquer overwhelmingly when we love and embrace the One who is Love. To love overwhelmingly is to die daily so as to rise with Him who conquers all and is all through and in us.

WORKING THROUGH WHISPERS

"He is struck by something, be it only a whisper, for the Lord works even through whispers." ~ *Servant of God Luigi Giussani*

The world is looking for a shout, but God provides the whisper. We notice what is flashy and frivolous, but God hands us what is simple and plain. The wisdom we seek cannot be overcomplicated or overstated, because wisdom is quiet, needing few words, and profound.

God works through our whispers, too. He may have a message for others that seems subtle and goes unnoticed. We may sulk or scoff at the possibility that no one will hear, notice, or care about the inaudible whispers he speaks to others through our gifts.

Never underestimate the power of a whisper. There is someone, somewhere who is inspired, touched, and transformed by your faithfulness to God. We do not see or understand the "whys" of what we do, but if we are called to do them, God brings beautiful fruit from our *yes*. He multiplies our meager fish and loaves exponentially. This is how His whispers move gingerly and rhythmically through the world, marking His presence in our hearts.

WRONG EXPECTATIONS

I think I've gotten my life all wrong. To become disappointed, one must expect that which never comes to fruition or perhaps never existed at all. I've traded hope for expectation, falsely assuming the two are synonymous in every sense.

But my expectations differ from God's. Do I hope in Him or myself? In Him or the world? I've hoped for what I do not see, yet believe. I've hoped, however, for people to be as flawless as God is, and, because of that, my spirit is often crushed by this delusion.

I cannot trust man's word. I can only trust his actions. Sadly, I do not wish to be an indecisive person who cannot commit or keep my word. Yet only God does this perfectly. Do I expect Him to fulfill His promises? At times I have not, but His word never fails.

My hope is only in God. He strengthens me with His breath of clarity, uplifts me through Sacrament and Word, finds me when I am wretchedly lost, and draws me back when

I have erred. In God alone I hope, and I shall not be disappointed.

YOUR LAW IS MY DELIGHT

"I will ponder your precepts and consider your paths. In your statutes I take delight; I will never forget your word."
~ *Psalm 119: 15 – 16*

If I am to be bound by any law, let it be Yours, for Your statutes are sweeter than any form of human obedience to government. That's not to say I am rebellious against my governing councils, but that often their ways are so dismissive of the citizenry that they neglect relationships with their constituents altogether.

Human laws can be impediments to life, but Your laws are life-giving and life-changing. You free humanity through Your commandments, for at the root of both following Your laws and passing them on to future generations, is love.

Love is life-affirming and looks foremost at the person, not the rule or ordinance that was or wasn't adhered to correctly or perfectly. Your laws and ways are simple and true, drawing us nearer to You through growth in virtue.

Man's laws are often complex and unnecessary, trailed by paperwork inches thick. It becomes a chain that binds both the oppressed and the oppressor, because the authentic encounter with a person is lost amidst the details.

Your law is my delight. I revel in it and relish it as my primary motivation for the way I choose to live this life You have given me.

CHAPTER THIRTEEN

Discovering Mission

A DIVINE LEGACY

"Rather, God chose the foolish of the world to shame the wise, and God chose the weak of the world to shame the strong, and God chose the lowly and despised of the world, those who count for nothing, to reduce to nothing those who are something, so that no human being might boast before God." ~ 1 Corinthians 1: 27 – 29

I've been pondering lately if life is worth living only to pursue bodily comforts and pleasures. Al my life I've been a dreamer, wistfully imagining a life of luxury: lavish, annual vacations, a beautiful home, contented surroundings, and tranquil scenery.

That dream long ago vanished, but I find myself on occasion returning to the "what ifs," longing for a life without turmoil, uncertainty, and suffering. The temptation usually intensifies during times of reacquainting myself with an old classmate who is the CFO of a large corporation or even CEO of an internet company, easily raking in millions per year.

I then question: What have I done with my life that's worthwhile?

It would be humiliating (and humbling) to admit my constant struggle with finances, health concerns, and the tense climate within our family and home. What do I have to offer the world? In a sense, a divine legacy.

It isn't so much that my life has to glimmer and shine to the world, but rather my heart must be pure when presented to God alone. In the end, it is His opinion of me that matters.

To leave a divine legacy may very well entail more loss, more stripping of selfish ways, and even a call to simplicity through evangelical poverty. The world will never understand this call. It seems foolish and radical. But the world doesn't have to understand.

God's ways appear foolish to the world, but they are wisdom beyond wisdom that lead us to eternity. The road to sainthood requires a refining of my heart, a perfecting along the way so that, in the end, perseverance, tenacity, and fortitude will prevail.

A divine legacy isn't about me at all. It's about leaving a trail behind me that speaks of Jesus, an attraction to Heaven, and holiness that others cannot resist. My divine legacy must display the road to eternity as one of sweet surrender in the sufferings and uncertainties of the here and now and hereafter.

A MANTLE OF ZEAL

"He put on justice as his breastplate, victory as a helmet on his head; He clothed himself with garments of vengeance, wrapped himself in a mantle of zeal." ~ Isaiah 59: 17

I was born with a fiery spirit, driven to defend the defenseless and to act on behalf of justice. Zeal, it seems, was a spiritual gift granted to me at my Baptism, and I longed daily to fight for good, resist evil, and purge myself of all my wrongdoing.

The counterpart of zeal, however, is often pride in the form of impulsivity or presumption. I had to learn, often through mishaps, misunderstandings, and misfortunes, how to temper my natural inclination toward truth and justice with the softness of compassion and mercy.

Today I am reminded of being bathed and clothed under a mantle of zeal: zeal for God's house, His will, His purpose and plan, His truth. How do I know I am working for His will and not mine? Yes, that is the age-old question. I know, as St. Bernard of Clairvaux said, "by the revived activity of my heart" rather than any sensory perceptions of His presence.

When vice is destroyed and holiness is cultivated in me, then I am cloaked in zeal for God's house.

A MEAGER OFFERING

As a child, I approached You with my basket of a few loaves of bread. Instead of rejecting my meager offering, You blessed it and distributed it to hundreds of people. Now, as an adult, I have nothing but an empty basket to offer You, and though I am ashamed, I give it to you, anyway. You smile and take my face in Your hands. In this moment, I know You will fill my basket to an overflow of freshly baked loaves so that I may go out as a missionary and feed the spiritually impoverished among me.

These loaves will feed thousands in my lifetime and countless more after I have gone to my eternal reward. This is what it means to bear fruit for Your kingdom: to first become so lowly that no one and nothing else could be more wretched – and then in faith and hope – hand You this mess of myself so that You might be glorified in and through my life's work.

Mess though I am, take this meager offering and miraculously multiply it, Lord, because even my emptiness and nothingness belong to You. Then, when I have not even my empty basket left, then and only then will the blessings abound.

COMMUNITY OF ISOLATION

People today are lonelier and more depressed than ever before, yet we are so busy that we scarcely allow ourselves time to breathe, let alone think or pray. It seems that, while we may be surrounded by a plethora of people on a daily basis, we are not truly loving them. By loving, I mean making contact with their hearts and meeting them in their loneliness. What we have built in this Information Age is an empire of forgotten souls, swimming in a sea of isolated babble.

This is our community of isolation: we see but do not encounter, and we hear but do not listen. We no longer invite others into our world with any level of authenticity or gratitude, because we're in too much of a hurry. Most importantly, we have somehow shut out God with our mindless and incessant busy work. At the end of the day, we must face this emptiness within, but instead we escape into television, our personal devices, and video games.

Life has become a distraction rather than an enjoyment, and along the way, we've not only lost connections with God and other people, but we've also lost ourselves in the process.

To reclaim a genuine sense of community, we must discipline ourselves to set aside time for silence and prayer each day, time to think and reflect about who we are, what we've done, and where we're going. A person who is content with his or her own company is more suitable to journey with others who have lost themselves or their way.

At the center of community is our God, Who fills us when our well has run dry, Who directs our paths and guides the words we speak. When we are lonely, we turn to Him, Who never fails to completely satisfy. A soul at ease is one who returns to God on a daily basis instead of living in seclusion.

CROWNED WITH EVERLASTING JOY

"And the ransomed of the Lord shall return, and enter Zion singing, crowned with everlasting joy; They meet with joy and gladness, sorrow and mourning flee away." ~ Isaiah 35: 10

We are not promised a life free of ills, betrayal, sickness, sadness, or death. Essentially, we all experience the ongoing consequences of sin – our own and those of others. But we are all called to a sort of martyrdom, and with that we await our crown of everlasting joy.

On the road to Heaven, we reach a point of accepting this martyrdom or rejecting it: Will we sacrifice ourselves to the point of death, be it death to self-love and ambition or bodily death? If we answer "yes," we proceed onward with newfound strength and surprising peace.

Martyrdom isn't exactly how the world presents it. In many ways, to be called a martyr is an insult, especially to the ego. We view martyrdom as some archaic, radical measure of faith, and so it is in many cases radical, but it certainly is not outdated by any means.

Another type of martyrdom, a sort of interior death or white martyrdom, is not necessarily literal (though it can become a red martyrdom), but it is more of a constant dying to self. In turn, the heart is wounded and aggrieved by sin and strife, ever turning itself to the One Who became sin as an appeal to Divine Mercy.

Martyrdom is a choice we all must face if we truly desire the crown of everlasting joy in Heaven. We cannot expect to share eternity with the Prince of Peace if we are unwilling to give Him all in this life for the sake of all in the next. And this gift of all essentially leaves us with nothing of our own accord. We are stripped. We are spiritually exposed. And this is when Jesus swoops in and takes over, filling us with His Spirit so that our nothingness translates into the gift of everything – victory – in Heaven.

CROWNED WITH MARTYRDOM

All of us will be crowned with martyrdom by the time we reach Heaven. I used to believe that martyrdom was an elite call to a few privileged saints, and from what I learned of it, I was in no way drawn to be slaughtered, burned alive, or beheaded. But I did not know that martyrdom is not exclusive to heroic sainthood. Martyrdom is the call of every faithful Christian, for it requires a dying to self.

Some of us may be asked to sacrifice our temporal existence for the sake of faith; indeed, many Christians are earning the crown of martyrdom as I write this. But still others of us – perhaps more – are asked to bear a white martyrdom, a crucifixion of the heart that is hidden, silent, and a wound of love. This martyrdom does not appear to be valiant to others, but instead requires a quiet, humble submission to the call from God.

This call is a slower, steadier death than red martyrdom typically is. It often begins with a question to the heart: "Will you suffer for Me?" With an affirmative response, we begin the path to purgation, and we are eventually stripped of all earthly and even spiritual consolations. Interiorly, there is no difference between a white or red martyrdom, because the martyr's heart has relinquished all to Jesus as an act of love. Martyrs are never victims, but rather they are always willing participants in the Final Victory.

Martyrdom, then, is a universal qualification for us to enter Heaven. To die to oneself and rise anew with Christ is the epitome of our common destiny.

EARTHEN VESSELS

"But we hold this treasure in earthen vessels, that the surpassing power may be of God and not from us." ~ 2 Corinthians 4: 7

My treasure is in Heaven, Lord, with You and all the angels and saints. Yet I live in an earthly body. My soul is encased in flesh, and I am but an earthen vessel – earthen, because I was created from dust and ashes, and a vessel, because I am but a harbinger of Your love to the world. I carry Your message in my heart, but You are our ultimate end.

My treasure, then, is captured in the earthen vessel of my body, because my soul is what is elevated to the heights of Heaven. It guides my will and intellect toward my eternal destiny.

I imagine myself as an earthen vessel – crudely made of clay, simple and plain, without frivolous embellishments. I am worn from decades of use, because I am carried in Your loving hands. You pick me up and bring me to a new journey, but You never let me go. Yes, I am simple and poor, a mere clay pot, but I carry a treasure so rare within. It cannot be visible on the exterior, but what is hidden reveals the gem of Your love.

ENDURE LIKE THE SON

"May his name be forever; as long as the sun, may his name endure." ~ Psalm 72: 17a

We tend to think our lives are delicate and fleeting. While we are but dust and dirt – here today and gone tomorrow – we are meant to endure, to persevere, and to remain in some form for all eternity. Knowing that we are reflections of God, made in His image and likeness, we are more inclined to endure rather than to give up altogether or give in to acedia. Our lives are meant for one purpose: to know, love, and serve God in all we think, say, and do.

Though the sun is not always visible to human eyes, it remains, sometimes in the shadows, behind clouds. Even in the darkest night, the sun has not vanished but only moved, rotated, never settling in one place for too long. So, too, must we emulate the sun's movement: always forward, never backward, and around the center of the universe, namely God. Our progression in movement belies our zeal for mission rather than complacency. And sometimes our works are visible and illuminative to others while, at other times, our love is meant to be veiled from view and only revealed in hidden and humble ways.

No matter, we must persevere, dear Christians. Our lives must emit the heat of the Holy Spirit's flame that consumes all for the sake of love. We also must reflect the Light of Christ, Who shines in and through us. Like the sun, our lives must leave a lasting imprint in whatever way we are called, a divine legacy that is both fruitful and indelible.

Yes, life on Earth is but a flicker of time for us, but the

impression we leave behind for our progeny is the blueprint of God's work throughout time. The sun shines day in and day out, never fading or faltering. So must we carry on with passion and purpose so that the Kingdom of Heaven might be manifested in our lives.

ENVOYS OF GOD

God does not exist within the context of time, though we do. As such, He reached into a particular moment in time to be born as one of us, among us. The Living God has always been, however, present, if not visible and tangible. And we, though countless in number throughout the beginning of our creation, are also placed in a specific epoch with a specific mission to complete.

As envoys of God, we are conduits for His grace to touch those we encounter today. Today is my opportunity to be His vessel, to allow Him to use me for His glory and my gain of Heaven. As envoys and vessels, we are the shells that remain motionless without God. We are not able to propel ourselves forward. It is God – alive in us, here and now – Who chooses to act in and through us. It is His Spirit Who moves us to action.

So we, though existing in this time and place, somehow mystically participate in Jesus' mission, which is one that existed before and outside of time. We enter into His mission, but it is fluid and simultaneously constant. The ways in which we respond to His call are varied and vital, but all are unique to the charisms we receive.

Our goal as envoys is the same, regardless of means or our cultural influences. Our end is always Heaven and striving to bring souls to eternal happiness with us. In this, we participate in the Church's united mission. In this, we exist in solidarity with every Christian who strove and struggled to reach the gates of Heaven.

EXISTING FOR THE SAKE OF ANOTHER

"Amen, amen, I say to you, unless a grain of wheat falls to the ground and dies, it remains just a grain of wheat; but if it dies, it produces much fruit. Whoever loves his life loses it, and whoever hates his life in this world will preserve it for eternal life. Whoever serves me must follow me, and where I am, there also will my servant be. The Father will honor whoever serves me." ~ *John 12: 24 – 26*

A few days ago, I was casually walking our dog on a humid summer's eve. It was a typical evening for me: contemplating the day, waving to the neighbors as I passed them, and silently reciting my Rosary. As I neared a familiar corner, Jesus unexpectedly awoke in me. He said, "You no longer belong to yourself."

I nearly cried, because this truth resounded so deeply and intimately in my heart. I knew long ago that my life was not my own, yet I continued living as if it were: fighting everything that came to me unbidden – like illness, pain, financial strain, and marital hardship. Nearly my entire life I have fought for the Lord. On the one hand, I prayed fervently to become solely His, and on the other, I refused to budge from the life I knew.

Now nothing is comfortable anymore, but instead of yielding gracefully to the struggle, I have once again responded with resistance. In that moment I heard Jesus's invitation, I knew He wanted more from me, though I felt so poor and small at the time.

How could He want more, I thought, when He has taken almost all I know? Then I realized: He wanted my resistance, to, for I had withheld myself from Him as a free, total, faithful, and fruitful disciple. He knew my heart and requested that, too.

I wondered if all the decades of bitterness, resentment, frustration, and fighting against God had caused my mysterious ailment. My body was speaking to me for a long time to slow down and heed the call to discipleship: a call to be for another and no longer exist for myself. And now it has reached the point of giving up because of my stubbornness and fear. It has begun to fight me back in defense, and I cannot defeat the inner agony that remains undefined.

But Jesus's invitation awakened in me something that I had forgotten and even believed was completely gone: that I am His and because of that, all that happens to me is used for my sanctification. My only job is to yield to my cross, and then my commissioning to be His love-light to others will, at last, come to fruition.

FROM MAINTENANCE TO MISSION

How do we move from a place of stagnancy to growth? We must admit the times in our lives that require waiting, but this waiting is purposeful and valuable. Unlike the latent periods of spiritual discovery, complacency is a sort of sloth, a bland maintenance to which we subscribe. We somehow become comfortable with the status quo, unwilling to put in the effort for the very petulant parts of ourselves that necessitates challenge and change.

Pain, while disconcerting and uncomfortable, indicates the need for movement in our lives. It would be nearly impossible for us to unravel and engage in our life's calling without it. And mission is the very essence of that quintessential question, "Why am I here?" We all ask it, some at young ages and others in our senior years, but everything we are as people stems from that one nagging, pressing thought – that we were created for more than comfort and mediocrity. God's plan for each of our lives includes brilliant and even valiant opportunities to change the world and honor Him.

When we stumble upon or discover our mission, it's not enough to know about it, because we will be unsettled and incomplete until we embark on that journey of fulfilling our mission. This is not an easy task. Mission involves perseverance, because many impediments will attempt to dissuade you from your calling, including people, circumstances, and personal doubts, among others. Do not heed the false voices that try to lure you away. Keep your eyes and heart on the gifts you've received that equip you to bring to fruition all that God has created for you to do and be.

But do all in a spirit of service, of humility. Never forsake the reason you press on, which is to glorify God by your life. Do not lose sight of this, or you will find that insolence has replaced genuine zeal for advancing God's kingdom and saving souls.

When you are weary, you will be tempted to abandon your mission and return to a life of mediocrity and maintenance. Find and call upon that flame within you, and God's Spirit will intercede with groanings when you find no words or reason to keep on. Over time, your mission will become a part of your identity and then your legacy.

Work for mission, and you will never feel lackluster or worthless in your life.

GREATER THINGS THAN THIS

"Jesus answered and said to him, 'Do you believe because I told you that I saw you under the fig tree? You will see greater things than this.'" ~ *John 1: 50*

We need the promise of this message in our world today, which is so full of uncertainty, apathy, unrest, and blatant evil. We are witnesses to and of the message of Jesus to Bartholomew/Nathanael: "You will see greater things than this." What could surpass seeing Jesus face-to-face? Going forth to spread the encounter with Jesus worldwide? This is the call and mission of every Christian throughout the ages.

Some are called to very hidden lives, which are more contemplative or monastic in nature. For them, the cross exists in their invisibility, yet this is also their witness and joy. Others have been commissioned to publicly declare the wonders of God, and their cross is in the accountability of living what they preach to others.

Preaching, however, does not need to be proselytizing. Preaching at its best is reaching others through our spiritual charisms (at times subtly and at other times boldly). We preach through the lives we choose to lead, and eventually we hope to see Jesus welcome us as His own one day.

To see greater things is to respond to His call – that *we* might become greater and overcome indifference through love.

IN THE VALLEY OF DECISION

"Crowds upon crowds in the Valley of Decision; for near is the day of the Lord in the Valley of Decision." ~ Joel 4: 14

I've been in the thick valley, fumbling through mud and sand for a long time, perhaps most of my life. On occasion I shift my gaze from the earth to the sky and marvel at the towering mountaintops beyond my reach. Though I was born in the valley, it no longer is a place that suits me. I've been yearning for more, dreaming of a life atop the mountains, which appear so strong and certain – unlike me, a timorous and insecure child still awaiting my destiny.

As time progresses, I realize evermore that I am called to ascend that mountain, and with this understanding comes a deeper wisdom. The mountain climb will be treacherous, tedious, and terrifying at times. This call will not arrive, then, without great effort manifested through perseverance and fortitude.

So I dwell in the valley of indecision. Should I chance the impossible and potentially become more than I am now, or should I remain a child in the valley with little more than dust at my feet?

There is much to delight in the valley, especially the opportunity to contemplate this dilemma. But I know I must leave the valley behind and dare to face God's dream for me. What lays beyond the mountain for me persists as a mystery for now, but I decide to abandon the valley of decision and embark on the mission that is my destiny. Somehow I know the view from the pinnacle will bring my life's purpose together in a splendid view from the heights.

KEEP MOVING FORWARD

"Keep moving forward." ~ *St. Junipero Serra*

I am at a crossroads yet again – more obstacles and frustrations blocking and impeding me from seeing Your ultimate vision and my ultimate goal. I am impatient, and, as time passes and I continue to wait here, doubt creeps in. Time has become my enemy, and it taunts me with nervous wrestling. *It's all a farce,* the voice rasps. *Nothing is happening. There's no point to this.*

For a time, I am strongly tempted to turn away from where I came. It is safe and certain there. I can easily return to a quiet life without constant struggle. It is truly what I desire: safety and anonymity. If I turn back, no one will remember me, and I am no longer accountable to the world for my behavior.

But I am accountable to God. And His voice of truth tells me to forge ahead. I resist, because I cannot move without direction and purpose. Do I wait with my eyes fixed to the future or behind me to the past?

Here and now is a lonely and arduous place to be, but somehow I know I must carry on, moving ahead when the Spirit prompts me. I am past the point of no return, too entrenched in what lies ahead. Mission is not far off, so I must never give up and turn away from the calling that beckons me through the thickest, densest fog. It is there, and I hear God's voice saying, "This is the way. Walk in it."

PERSEVERE IN GOOD WORKS

"…who will repay everyone according to his works: eternal life to

those who seek glory, honor, and immortality through perseverance
in good works…" ~ Romans 2: 6-7

I'll never forget my dear friend, Sr. Theresa Marie, telling me to
"make sure to do God's will, not necessarily His work." Labor,
of course, is both a necessity and a consequence of original sin.
And we are blessed by honest, hardworking ethics in our daily
labor.

Our labor can – and should – be an offering to You, so that
the work of our hands will both bless and be blessed by You.
Toil can be drudgery, cumbersome, and tedious. We may
suffer in our jobs. But we are also called to be witnesses of
Your love in the workplace.

However, I think sometimes we mistake work for Your
will. Busyness has become much more comfortable for us than
being. Solitude and contemplation may be misinterpreted as
sloth, but there is wisdom in discerning whether You are
calling us to action through good works and labor or to a state
of waiting and being, which is equally (and sometimes more)
important than action.

Doing God's will means that sometimes He will ask us for
hard sacrifices, toil, and sweat, but at other times rest and
recuperation from life's struggles.

RECALLING YOUR TEARS

"I yearn to see you again, recalling your tears, so that I may be
filled with joy." ~ 2 Timothy 1: 4

Each time I recall my own tears, I most certainly am not filled
with joy. In fact, recalling sorrow often leads me back to
sorrow, and a new wound opens in the remembrance of such
sadness. Perhaps Timothy was speaking of tears of joy, those
tears that flow without reserve from the face of one who has
finally come to truth. Tears of conversion are always cause for
celebration and thanksgiving, and Timothy knew those tears –

healing, baptizing – would somehow strengthen his resolve in the mission of evangelization, his specific calling, however trying it was at times.

We know that all who follow in the footsteps of Jesus often emerge in a similar condition to the first apostles – persecuted, taunted, ignored, ostracized, and even martyred. Timothy was no stranger to persecution, yet he drew upon the memory of those radiant faces, filled with tears and a tranquil smile, to keep his mission alive. The transformation of those who came to know and follow Jesus was affirmation enough to suffer the masses who rejected Jesus and thus punished Timothy.

Throughout our personal call to mission, we can be assured of the struggle, whatever it may be. We may doubt or wrestle with fear or feelings of shame. We may come to believe we somehow got it all wrong and should change course. But we, too, will recall something significant – like those beautiful tears of conversion – that reminds us of the need God fills through our work. We must think often about what kinds of spiritual fruit results from our daily work. The response should confirm or deny that we are following a path that is right and good.

SAYING YES TO GOD

"However many are the promises of God, their yes is in him."
~ *2 Corinthians 1: 20a*

Sometimes our wholehearted, resounding yes means saying no to human pressures. It always means our hearts are open to whatever, however, and whenever God beckons us to do or be – to retreat into solitude, to reach out to others in need, or to spend more or less time with others, to name a few examples.

When we say yes to God, we realize He may ask more of us than what we believe we can handle or are capable of accomplishing. He may permit us to suffer or endure more than what we have ever suffered or endured before. But it's always as a result of our gift, our yes to Him. He gives us more, because He is asking us to depend on Him entirely rather than ambivalently. This is why we may suffer more – because our generous yes has been compounded by God into a more generous question. The more He asks of us, the more we respond affirmatively. And the more we respond positively, the more likely we will be asked to give more and more of ourselves until nothing except God remains.

We say yes, because we love God and trust Him with our lives, so truly there is nothing we desire to withhold from Him. We long for total union – perpetual, permanent communion – with Him, which requires a total and unreserved offering of self.

Our yes to God always necessitates action from the heart, but we know our yes closes other doors in our lives, perhaps of good and noble causes or opportunities, so that we can give ourselves more freely and fluidly to Him rather than our self-serving wants.

Yes to God always means one door closes, but another opens. It always involves no – to our sensory pleasures, to what others are calling us to do, or to hoarding our time rather than generously giving it to God with sincerity.

But yes is always fruitful and joyful when we affirm it daily as our offering to the One who said yes as a ransom for our souls.

THE GIFTS AND CALL OF GOD

"For the gifts and the call of God are irrevocable."
~ *Romans 11: 29*

When you are convicted in the heart, it is as if you are lanced with love. God's call is love, and it is a burning desire, a longing, and a particular pain to do His will wholeheartedly and irrevocably. Love of God's call produces zeal, and zeal, action.

This is why God bestows specific gifts to you and me. He

wrote His plan on our hearts at our conception and knows, therefore, the strengths and charisms we require for the fulfillment of this call. Nothing and no one else can serve the Lord in the way you were called to serve Him.

Zeal is the fruit of this burning love to do God's will. Love increases in us at the first planting of the Spirit's seed in our hearts until it blossoms and matures. But love is aware that it cannot remain still, or it will become stagnant and wither into oblivion. So zeal enters into one's heart in conjunction with love (which was present long before), so that you might put into practice the call you have received in love.

Perhaps we move through life as pilgrims of love, but it is zeal that continues to move in and through us. If we live as people of active love, God wastes not a second of our time that is spent for advancing His kingdom.

THE GREATEST MARTYRDOM

"Are my measureless desires only but a dream, a folly? If my desires are rash, make them disappear, for these desires are the greatest martyrdom to me." ~ St. Therese of Lisieux

I am a young soldier with a warrior's heart. As a child, I pined to do great things for God, and this zeal only intensified as I grew older. God prepared, pruned, and molded me for my mission, and I've never taken my eyes off of the goal: fighting the good fight and winning souls for Heaven.

I awaited the day I would finally train for battle, and eventually it arrived. Young and naïve, I entered the spiritual boot camp that would further refine my skills for mission.

And now I am ready. I'm waiting for my Heavenly orders, I stand with fervor, armed and equipped.

I am ready for my mission.

And I can see it far off in the distance. I draw nearer and notice the details coming together, aligning with precision, blessed by God.

But He does not send me out yet. I see others go, one by one, some who have trained before me or with me, others after me. I eagerly wait for my cue, expectant and vigilant. I am not sleeping but wide awake. "I am ready, Lord! Send me!"

But He does not send me forth.

Like the enemy, I feel crushed and defeated, so the adversary swoops in to attack my vulnerability. I doubt. I question a lifetime of yearning to accomplish great things for God's Kingdom. I second guess my training and even consider returning to my former life – quiet and simple.

And this is my agony: waiting for my mission and now equipped for it, but it doesn't arrive. I can see it so clearly, but I am merely permitted to view it from afar rather than enter into it.

This is the greatest martyrdom: to burn with desire for God's glory and want nothing more but for these dreams to be fulfilled, yet they remain ideations that fizzle and fade.

Only they do not entirely fade away but somehow grow stronger each day, and I am left with a heart torn, broken, and wounded for a Love unfulfilled. When will it be my turn to give back to God? Maybe today. Maybe never in terms of what I've envisioned. But He will fulfill His promise in ways I cannot foresee. For now I wait in the agony and ecstasy of love.

THE KINGDOM WITHIN

Some days I spend inordinate amounts of time building a castle and acquiring wealth and prestige. "This is my kingdom, and it needs to fall," says popular contemporary Christian music artist Colton Dixon. Somehow I've lost perspective of what matters most: my life and all of my dreams, or God's will and His dreams for my life?

The truth is, God does want me to possess a kingdom, that is, His kingdom within my soul. But I know His kingdom doesn't include the things I falsely believe will make me deliriously happy, so I am tempted to flee and never look back.

God's kingdom is a refuge for the weary, weak, lost, and brokenhearted. It is a hospital for sinners and a haven for saints. God's kingdom requires tireless work for the outliers and outcasts rather than falling at the feet of the educated and elite.

Is this what Jesus meant when He said, "You are not far from the Kingdom of Heaven?" Yet the Kingdom of Heaven does not yet reign supreme in a heart so full of self and vanity. The Kingdom must make me poor in spirit, reduced to nothing, so that God may rule freely and without constraint. Then, and only then, will the Kingdom of Heaven be visible in and through my life's work.

THE ONE HOPE OF YOUR CALL

"…one body and one Spirit, as you were also called to the one hope of your call; one Lord, one faith, one baptism; one God and Father of all, who is over all and through all and in all." ~ Ephesians 4: 4 – 6

We are created for mission. God's definite purpose for our lives often negates our own, yet our mission can only be fulfilled in hope – the hope of our call.

Where is this hope, or better yet, *who* is this hope? Mission is nonexistent without the flame of hope, and the One who ignites our passion and surging ahead is Jesus. We cling to Him, keeping our gaze locked with His. This focal point keeps us anchored to Him, and in this anchoring, we go forth into the world, realizing – actualizing – the burning yearning perhaps present from birth, or developing in our youth. Our call to mission is fed by hope as we continue following Jesus wherever He leads us.

Sometimes we are led to where we do not want to go. When we become disillusioned or doubt our call, Jesus is our hope. He returns the longing of our hearts to Him, and we are reminded that life is not truly lived unless we dwell within this call, this heavenly mission. In fact, all of life is flat, bereft of joy and meaning when we lose sight of our call. Living our call is both life-changing and life-giving, and this is our hope.

WE WALK ON FIRE

O Holy Spirit, Your fire consumes me, Your flames allure me. At once, my heart is ablaze and You gesture for me to walk on the flames of Your love. They are as a blanket to my feet, and at times I am terrified of their power to obliterate and incinerate me into ashes.

But You have called me out of apathy and into the fire. So I must navigate with deliberation on these flames – the flames that burn with an icy-hot sting, the flames that refine and purify, and the flames that consume.

Sometimes I feel the fire of Your love will overwhelm me with the pain of purgation, but I am enticed by Your love that burns for me and for a wounded world. When I walk on Your fire, I am changed. My heart of stone becomes one of flesh, and I rediscover my capacity to love without resignation or apprehension. I am new.

I am mesmerized by You, O Holy Spirit, for I am humbled by the flames' ability to kill me or to transform me. Is this the crucible of suffering? How is it that an earthen element can both destroy and make me new? I do not desire to be burned, but I walk on Your fire in trust, abnegating my fears to Your all-encompassing flames.

When my heart is finally ablaze with zeal, I long to lure others toward You, O Spirit of Fire, where I know You will illuminate and warm them before You begin to purify their souls! My aspiration has become a permanent sign of Your Spirit, emblazoned within me, and nothing can now destroy it – not fear or even death will eradicate this love for You.

And so my mission has now become one of passion – to draw others to Your flames of love through my witness of living my own passion with holy indifference, joy, and peace.

May we never fear You, Holy Spirit, but instead will ourselves to be completely consumed by You so that our hearts may be as one.

WHAT IS IMPOSSIBLE

"For human beings this is impossible, but for God all things are possible." ~ Matthew 19: 26

I have my sights set on Heaven. Is it possible for me to one day realize my dream? I long, too, for God to fulfill grand things in my life for the sake of others, but at times I wonder if my dreams are too outlandish and frivolous.

Today I am reminded that nothing is impossible for God. Could it be that my faith can soar to new heights? Can my confidence in God grow in enormity, enough to boldly proclaim that, yes, God will fulfill the longing in my heart and much more?

The longing itself was planted by God long ago. Why would He choose to leave it unfulfilled? What is impossible for me to fathom – the "hows" and the "whys" – He orchestrates flawlessly and with impeccable precision.

My confidence must remain not in what God can or might do, but in what He has already achieved and promised me. I must await the promise to transform into mission and action, for He Himself has said, "I will not let my seed return to me void."

YOUR LIGHT AND YOUR FIDELITY

"Send your light and your fidelity, that they may be my guide." ~ Psalm 43: 3a

I know You are a faithful God. I know what You promise, You fulfill. But I am facing yet another interior crisis, and this time doubt has overshadowed what little faith I possess. Did I hear Your call correctly, or am I yet again foolishly pursuing an empty dream?

A year ago, the call seemed so clear I would have given anything to anyone who asked me about it. But today I am second guessing all of it myself. The voices from my past are trying to convince me to abandon ship and turn in the opposite direction.

This year has been one of incredible blessings. Your light has shone on me over and again through some of the bleakest, blackest hours. Trials, too, have been many, challenging what I've believed to be my mission, and now I'm not so sure.

I have no more money to invest, no time, and my health is waning. Will You not multiply my meager offering? I need a miracle of the fish and loaves, Lord. Today. Yes, it may be weak and selfish of me to ask once more for Your light and Your fidelity, but I am drowning in darkness.

I do not want to give in to despair.

This grief I have long lived with has become my enemy once again, or at least the weak entryway to the adversary. Now I am utterly lost, and the dreams, the call, the hope have faded into oblivion.

Where are You, O Light? Return to me, and bless my efforts to glorify You.

CHAPTER FOURTEEN

Encountering God

A HEAVY BURDEN

"You tested us, O God, tried us as silver tried by fire: you led us into the snare; you bound us at the waist as captives...but then you led us out to freedom." ~ Psalm 66: 10 – 12

I feel crushed by the weight of Your love. Sometimes, Lord, it is so suffocating to be loved by You and to grow closer to full union with You. I've come to believe there are two main reasons that Your burden exists for my sake: as holy discipline through refinement and as a foretaste of how vast and unconditional Your love is for me. If I were to experience or understand the depth of Your love in its immense and immeasurable capacity, I would die of Love's affliction. I cannot bear Your infinite love for me, so it often crushes me in my littleness and fragility.

Of course, it is for love's sake that You chastise me, as well. But love in any form hurts, Lord. It hurts to be picked, poked, and pruned. My pride is plucked from its interior throne, and the rest of my body remains wailing at the void of such vice. But this is because my concupiscence leans toward sin and all that comforts. You bid me to something greater, which is love.

In order for love to reign in me, all aspects of self must cease. I must be entirely empty, which is the first step in Love's Wound. It is the wound of self-death. Then, when I have nothing left within me to claim as my own, You begin to fill me with Yourself, and I come to know that pure, authentic love cannot exist without constant self-giving. Sacrifice of my desires and plans hurts, too, Lord. Yet this wound begins to afflict me sweetly over time, until it no longer is a gaping gash but a sealed heart embodying Your love.

AN ENCIRCLING WALL OF FIRE

Lord, You protect me, though I often do not feel safe in the midst of interior turmoil and exterior strife and chaos. I want to retreat, but You encase me with Your Spirit, and I am called to enter the war zones of life in order to evangelize to those who are spiritually ill or dying.

Your fire, O God, is my delight. I am warmed and softened by Your love. I am also refined by it, and all is illuminated by its glow. Now, however, Your fire extends outward as a wall of protection and shield in the battles of life.

Where is my trust? When Moses led the Israelites out of Egypt and they arrived at the edge of the sea, there was nowhere else for them to flee from Pharaoh and their captors. But Moses raised his staff, and Your fire descended from Heaven as a wall to delay the onslaught of Your people.

I am not oppressed in this way, but I am one of Your chosen ones, however unworthy I may be. No one deserves Your protection, yet I am given it through such extraordinary grace. I believe Your encircling wall of fire will pave my path to Heaven, just as you paved the way for the Israelites to daringly walk on the ocean floor as the fire wall prevented their deaths.

BELOVED AND CHERISHED

"Beloved and dear, separated neither in life nor in death, swifter than eagles, stronger than lions!" ~ 2 Samuel 1: 23

We do not know how beloved we are. We are in the midst of a cloud that constantly divides us, especially as we grieve or suffer betrayal or bodily maladies. We do not believe He loves us as He really does, as His beloved and cherished ones, each individually, yet also collectively, cradled in His bosom. Oh, how God longs for us to believe this, to embrace Him as He does us, despite our faults and failures. We often view Him in light of a humanly father, perhaps tyrannical or critical, dispensing love based on conditional requirements.

But our heavenly Father is quite the opposite. He loves us with an everlasting, unchanging love. We are the ones who hide from Him in shame. We allow healthy guilt to become fear and shame, thus blocking ourselves from His embrace.

But He waits for us as His beloved and cherished children. We are always His and have always belonged to Him, yet we adopt the lies from the enemy that God only accepts us based on what we do for Him. This is not true. In the depths of our misery, He is present. In our wailing and thrashing of sorrow or our fits of rage – even toward Him – He is holding us.

Our God loves us the same, because He never changes. He is the same yesterday, today, forever. When we believe first in His love, then we begin to notice our hearts melting into His. We rest our heads on His shoulders, free to weep or laugh or sigh. Only those of us created in His image (e.g., humans) can confidently claim to be His beloved and cherished, because we are a part of God just as a child is a part of his mother and father.

So God awaits our yes, our "I believe," and our drowning ourselves in His mercy. He simply waits for us to accept His love, perhaps even before we are able to fully love Him as He loves us. What a treasure! To know we have been loved before all time and until the end of time is a priceless gift. It is a gift that heals all ills and transforms hearts. It is the only gift we will ever receive without conditions.

CHRISTIAN FRIENDSHIP

"Whatever is true, whatever is honorable, whatever is just, whatever is pure, whatever is lovely, whatever is gracious, if there is any excellence and if there is anything worthy of praise, think about

these things." ~ Philippians 4: 8

We would be wise not only to think of such things but also to incorporate them into our friendships. Life without genuine friendships ends up hollow. God wants us to draw nearer to Him through human relationships, and vice versa. It's only one of many ways and reasons He became one of us. Through Jesus, we are finally able to see and touch the eternal, Triune God, so we also recognize His face through those we meet along our life's journey.

Christian friendship is so valuable, because it is so rare. We often foster relationships based on small talk or similar hobbies and interests. These aren't sinful reasons to forge or maintain friendships, but they are sorely incomplete. Jesus wants our relationships with people to be a reflection of our relationship with Him. In Him there is no duplicity, no falsehood, and no façade. So we must be authentic and honest in how we relate to people, allowing God to move and direct our friendships to the depth He desires.

At some point, we all will encounter uncomfortable moments with our friends. Love sees truth, but love also exists for another in spite of sin. Authenticity requires openness to God's movements, which aren't always smooth and predictable. God may request something of our friendships that we aren't prepared to give: loving the other so much that we want what's best for him or her. When we desire good for a person, he or she may see it as an act of rejection or judgment rather than an act of love.

But love, in a genuine, God-infused sense, cannot exist apart from this encounter. We encounter Jesus when we cultivate our friendships in and through Him. The gift of friendship produces the fruit of holy conversation. Love, then, draws us nearer to Heaven by way of our friendships. We are made better – *more* – because of the friend who loves us enough to steer us away from sin and toward Truth. And we do the same when we look to Jesus for an example of how to be a good friend, a friend who loves.

Look to love as your beacon, and your friendships will become reflections of that love. Remember mercy, too, and love will be fulfilled in your relationships and in all your affairs.

CONSECRATED IN TRUTH

"Consecrate them in truth. Your word is truth." ~John 17: 17

You speak to my heart in Sacraments and through sacramentals in the inspired words of others and in Your Word of Scripture. What You spoke then – be it in verbosity or total silence – You speak today. Your Word is truth, but You are truth.

Consecrate me in Your truth. Seal me as Your own, that I may be protected from both receiving and proclaiming falsity. Unite my mind and heart with Yours, that they may be as one as You are One in the Father, Son, and Holy Spirit.

O Spirit of wisdom and word, breathe life into my stony heart, grown cold and sterile by life's storms and struggles. Warm it and rekindle the unadulterated zeal that once called my heart its home.

The world today has become callous and apathetic due to narcissism that fuels a frenzied lifestyle. But You are the Eternal Word; no indifference lies in Your indwelling. I ask for Your pity upon us. Rather than spitting out and smiting the lukewarm majority, I implore You to breathe new life – a life enriched by Your love and presence – into our stony hearts. Consecrate and rededicate us to Your truth.

Make us witnesses of truth in this Information Age, and draw us nearer to each other and to You through our common desire to serve You. Draw us nearer to You still in Word and Sacrament, that we, in turn, may draw others to Your mercy and love.

DEAF TO BEAUTY

"Our busyness yields us to hardness of heart."
~ *Pope Benedict XVI*

Our society places high value on beauty, that is, aesthetics. Everything that is worth success and praise in this life centers around such exterior beauty. Advertisements appeal to our senses: teeth whitening products, body slimming programs, tanning packages, stylish clothing, etc. It seems the world equates glamor to true beauty.

Yet the Lord does not concern Himself with what we present to others on the outside. We must remember when Jesus admonished the scribes and Pharisees for demonstrating their shiny, clean cups while at the same time concealing the filth on the inside of their cups.

What matters more in the end: a clean soul or a clean body? We have become a people deaf to beauty, to what truly counts, because we concern ourselves with superficiality and frivolity while neglecting virtuous living.

True beauty always reflects God, not mammon. It elevates the mind and soul to Heaven. Consider masterful works of art in music, paintings, and performances, the ones that are timeless and have withstood all of the other trends and fads that come and go. True beauty remains.

When we fail to appreciate the gift that one's heart presents, we neglect to recognize beauty, and we ourselves become hardened. In time, we do not see with the eyes of our hearts, but only with the calloused gaze of one who has pushed away the vulnerability necessary to value what lies within a person, beyond exterior pretenses. When we have become deaf to beauty, we have become deaf to God.

HIS POWER IS CONCEALED

"His splendor spreads like the light; rays shine forth from beside him, where his power is concealed." ~ *Habakkuk 3: 4*

I ponder the tiny host before its consecration. It is to become Your body – the Living Host, illuminated, radiant, resplendent. Yet You choose to remain hidden there in a small wafer that fits neatly into my hand.

I realize now that Your power is often concealed – not because You are inept or incapable of superb, extraordinary miracles, but because You have deliberately opted to remain hidden. Perhaps all true power, then, is concealed! Perhaps this is the ultimate meaning of humility: seeking to remain invisible and unknown, yet to do great things because of a pure heart.

Great acts do not have to be acknowledged and in fact, when they are, we tend toward pride and self-aggrandizement. It's not necessary for us to accost ourselves, but maybe we should ask for concealed power in order to seek You more honestly and definitively.

In essence, when I consume Your Body and Blood, You are transfigured in every holy act I offer, whether clandestine or evident. You permeate me, and I am then configured to You in a mystical union of hearts. Then I become Your living host as a place where You dwell and rest, a place where Your power is manifested through the zealous movements of Your Spirit and the quiet contemplation and offering of my excruciating interior afflictions.

But true power, the power that comes from Heaven, is concealed, so that we may relentlessly pursue You and never cease until we have, at last, reached You.

I SAW THE FACE OF GOD

I saw the face of God today in the eyes of a child who turned into a beautiful young lady. She was different: a girl born with a disease doctors predicted would conquer her life long ago, an incurable malady.

But tonight I met her, and I saw God's face as she smiled and said, "There's no one in the world who loves you like God loves you." For a split second, I saw a flash of every person who was born with special abilities. I saw the pain, the suffering through every surgery, and a lifetime of therapy. But I also saw the love transcending the pain, a rare wisdom found in such a young soul.

She looked up and said, "To the moms of kids with disabilities, God chose you as special moms. I know it's hard to love us through the difficult moments." Then I saw Jesus and realized that we are Simon the Cyrenian when we assist Him to His crucifixion by carrying His Cross.

How can I refuse Him? When I care for my daughters, walking with them through the hard times, I am carrying Jesus' Cross on my shoulders. I am the unsuspecting bystander who has suddenly become an instrumental figure in history. But I don't do this. It blindsides me. I'm just passing through, on my way to live a fairly innocuous and inconspicuous life, but God had other plans.

The Cross can be cruel, but in its cruelty lay a hidden sweetness. How many of us are asked to be Simons? Not all of us are summoned to this unique and arduous task, but those of us who are must acknowledge the substantial and severe importance of what we accept.

Do I accept this out of love or obligation? It must be love that drives my obedience. I will carry Jesus in the form of my daughters. It's the one gift God has presented to me in such a painful and horrific form, but it's a gift nonetheless. Caregiving is a unique cross, but it ultimately is a participation in the journey to Calvary.

I must remember that this life leads to Resurrection.

JUDGING BY APPEARANCES

"You judge by appearances, but I do not judge anyone."
~ *John 8: 15*

We've all heard the adage, "Beauty is in the eye of the

beholder" or "Man judges by appearances, but God looks at the heart." What is it about physical beauty that allures us, or at the very least makes us prefer the company of some over others?

Sarah recently asked me a poignant question: "Why do we have a face?" Ironic as it may be, I told her the three-year-old answer, "Well, so that we can see, hear, taste, talk, and smell." But clearly this child of God, whose face is the imprint of a disguised beauty, will one day know the simplicity of her question. Beauty, though often defined by symmetry, is truly a reflection of one's soul. My daughter is proof of that.

But when – *if* – we truly believe this, we will have to train ourselves to look more carefully at a person and dismiss our initial, superficial assessment of them based on appearances alone. We will need to learn to read a person's heart, reaching them heart-to-heart. If we do this, we will be profoundly humbled by all that the suffering or disfigured people have to teach us about life and love. Their view is often deeply entrenched in wisdom and gratitude, for their cross is visible to all. They've learned well the price of vulnerability, and we would do well to learn from them.

Beauty is what elevates the soul heavenward, be it a literary work, musical composition, or artistic masterpiece. Let's try to consider the people whose faces aren't symmetrical as artistic masterpieces of God's hand. The face of beauty is not defined by aesthetics, only by the ability to draw our hearts to God.

Redefine beauty by dropping your judgments, or at least handing them over to the One who assesses the heart.

LIFE AND LIGHT

O Lord, You are my Life and Light.
You carry me through the abyss of night
And all the travails of my plight.

You are my Life and Light,
Keeping paths straight and crooked ways right.
Though my worries are many and often quite trite,
You fill me with wonder at every Heavenly sight.

You are my Life and Light,
And my heart is humbled and contrite
When I consider Your mercy, cloaking me in white.

O Lord, You are my Life and Light
Shining as bright
As the stars of night,
Finding my love ever so slight
That You sweep me away as my heavenly Knight.

O Font of Life, O Font of Light,
Bring me back home through the wings of the flight,
Through the sparrow's song and the lion's might,
So that all in my soul may be made right.

LIKE A PARCHED LAND

I wonder how many people's wells have run dry. I'm speaking of their life source – the Living Water – and all that is life-giving. It seems that many of us are merely existing, just going through the daily motions of life without too much thought of anything spiritually substantial. I know I have felt like this quite often, especially when my mind is swarming with thoughts of the girls' many developmental needs, paperwork, phone calls, and appointments.

When I begin to feel as if I am sinking or even drowning, I find the cure to be scheduled, deliberate quiet time – for rest, for prayer, for spiritually enriching reading. Prayer, too, has changed over the years from specific and regimented novenas or litanies to mental prayer-time, entering into that sacred space of solitude to listen to and be with God.

Space doesn't always need to be filled, even with chattering to God. When we are parched, our entire beings cry out to God for some sort of reprieve, and our lamentations never go unheard or unanswered. We must acknowledge the very deep and ongoing spiritual needs – our need for God and connection. There is nothing that will snatch away our very lifeline more than withdrawing ourselves from the necessary and life-giving connection first to our Source and then to others.

When we regularly do this, our spirits are rejuvenated. We awaken the Holy Spirit in us so that we who are thirsty receive boundless and copious amounts of life-giving Living Water. May our wells never run dry.

LISTEN TO HIS VOICE

"Oh, that today you would hear his voice: Do not harden your hearts as at Meribah, as on the day of Massah in the desert."
~ *Psalm 95: 7b – 8*

Do you hear God's voice? Do you recognize it among the other, unnecessary voices around and within? God's voice is clear and sure, unwavering and gentle – but firm. When He speaks, the body is at rest and the mind clear. The heart swells with confidence and renewed hope and purpose. Peace and joy remain with the soul when God speaks.

To listen, however, requires much more than to merely hear. We hear all sorts of sounds and noises every day, and we cleverly filter them without concern or consciousness. But when God speaks, we must know Him so intimately that, whether subtle or overt, His voice makes us pause to listen with our hearts.

God doesn't typically speak to us at convenient times, but if we are trained in the way of love, we will not be put off by His calling and His invitation to encounter. When we listen to Him, we always respond with love and action. For a heart that loves God cannot ignore the opportunities placed before it to love Him more.

LIVING IN NAZARETH

Because little is recorded in Scripture or historically about the time Jesus spent in His formative years and youth, we can ponder the value of His time living in Nazareth. It was a time of growth, yes, but quiet and hidden growth. Living in Nazareth was a period of solitude and rest before Jesus became a public figure or person of controversy and contradiction. We can learn much from this unknown and perhaps secluded period of Jesus' life. Its importance and value do not escape us.

For us, living in Nazareth can be the months or years in our lives when nothing seemingly significant is happening. We may lead a very active spiritual life, but we are relatively unknown and fairly ordinary at first glance. We may enjoy this slower pace – a time of settling down and establishing a home career or family – or we may be restless in the quiet we've been given. But dwelling in Nazareth is only one opportunity of many for us to walk in Jesus' footsteps and appreciate all of life's seasons, from waiting to discovering our mission. Even within seasons of activity, we find pockets of rest and recreation; likewise, we may have a burst of action during the more latent lengths of time we spend with Jesus in Nazareth.

When Jesus calls us to live with Him in Nazareth, He is asking us to enter into His childhood and adolescence, to rediscover the meaning of family and to pursue quiet conversations of carefree timelessness with Him. We can engage these times of waiting by spending them in purposeful listening and contemplating the gift of childhood, especially its innocence and purity.

Living in Nazareth is living in the here and now. We dwell with Jesus today. We wait with Him and for Him, now.

MY HIDING PLACE

"You are my shelter; you guard me from distress; with joyful shouts of deliverance you surround me." ~ Psalm 32: 7

All my life I've preferred to be invisible, content with anonymity and comfortable with a small, predictable way of being. For a time this served me well, but this is the problem: It served *me* rather than God. So naturally He called me out of myself and all that was familiar to stretch me in a most distressing way.

Then I was naked, exposed for all to see my flaws: anxiety, temper, selfishness. You see, I preferred a secluded life so that I could preserve my ego and serve myself. Then I wouldn't have to face the hard truths about myself. I wouldn't have to change.

But God shattered my pride, and today I am grateful for His loving discipline. No longer do I dwell among the shadows, for what was once concealed by darkness has been revealed in the light of truth. And, at last, I am truly free. My soul is liberated from deception and falsehood, even protecting me from my own ego.

Ironically, God offers me a hiding place, a refuge, a shelter from the madness of the world. He is my hiding place, where I can retreat for a time and receive a bit of nourishment from Him before reentering the public sphere. The One from whom I once shamefully hid has now become my hiding place.

RECEIVING THE HOLY SPIRIT

"If you then, who are wicked, know how to give good gifts to your children, how much more will the Father in heaven give the holy Spirit to those who ask him?" ~ Luke 11: 13

As a child, I believed I could ask God for a toy or magical powers and be granted them based on this passage. Eventually I realized God didn't operate that way, but I still tried to bargain with Him: *If You do this for me, then I will do that for You.*

Today I look at this popular Scripture passage with fresh eyes. "How much more will the Father in Heaven give the *Holy Spirit* to those who ask Him?" It is the Holy Spirit we must ask to receive, seek to find, and knock to be answered. He never fails to respond favorably to our longing for Him. I realize now that when I seek God alone and truly love Him, my desires are not apart from His will for me. Somehow I no longer desire material things or special abilities; when I love God, I desire *Him.*

If we truly long to become citizens of Heaven, then we must seek the path where God walks, a path He lays before us to follow without reservation or resignation. If we ask for good gifts of His Holy Spirit, we will receive them through the necessary purification of our souls.

But He will never deny us Himself if we seek Him alone, above all.

REVELATION

I see You
> At dawn
> In the sunrise,
> At night
> In the darkness.

You are near.
You are here.

I see You
> In the sky
> Moving listless clouds into oblivion –
> Sublime opening of Heaven's gate.

You are near.
You are here.

I see You

In a baby's smile –
Innocent, sweet, pure, open.
In the dying man's dream –
Ready, eager, coming home.
In the suffering soul –
Wounded by love, struck by death and joy.
You are near.
You are here.

Man's eye does not have to wander far
To see with clarity the revelation
Of the God-Man.
We seek You and find You with our hearts.
You dwell within.
You dwell beyond.
You are near.
You are here.
You are everywhere.

SHARING OF HIS SUFFERINGS

"...to know him and the power of his resurrection and [the] sharing of his sufferings by being conformed to his death..." ~ *Philippians 3: 10*

It is true that our afflictions constitute the fulfillment of Jesus' Passion. What He suffered was complete, of course, but we are extensions of Jesus as the Mystical Body of Christ. We are the little living Christs that have been planted here and now for the purpose of loving Him enough to die for Him. Our afflictions, then, are a continuation of this act of love. They are our participation in Jesus' mission, for "when one part suffers, the entire body suffers" (see 1 Corinthians 12: 26).

Suffering is not our end but is only the means to our end, which is Heaven. We cannot become true Christians without walking the path to Calvary and following in Jesus' footsteps.

When we suffer, then, Jesus walks alongside us, for He's been there before and chooses to accompany us in our own scourges and crucifixions.

This is the fulfillment of love: to suffer with someone without reluctance. We prefer to accompany those we love through their pain, however grievous that pain is for us, as well. We do this for love and only love, because love never abandons one who is lonely, ill, or in pain.

It's not that pain itself is love, but rather, God's grace is infused in our interior afflictions, so that pain is transformed from something ugly and undesirable to something sweet and preferred. This is the fruit of such supernatural grace: that we do not run from the Cross as revealed in our little crosses, but instead run toward it with every hope and joy, no matter the cost.

This is why the Cross remains our symbol of solidarity in love and a sign of what our love should exemplify. It is our beacon, an icon of strength, and a promise. We love the Cross, because we love Jesus, who first loved us.

THE ART OF ACCOMPANIMENT

"The 'art of accompaniment'…must be steady and reassuring, reflecting our closeness and our compassionate gaze which also heals, liberates, and encourages growth in the Christian life."
~ *Pope Francis*

Take my hand, and I will follow where You lead. Then I must go and seek the lost and lonely, weary and wounded, sick and suffering – taking their hands and accompanying them on their journey to Heaven. I walk side-by-side, encouraging and comforting, but still I follow Your lead.

I cannot lead without Your directive and sure guidance, though I daily follow You on an unknown path. In order to lead others, I must be trustworthy. Others must have faith in me as I have in You, so that they are willing to step away from the familiar and venture into foreign lands in order to be eternally rewarded.

Somewhere on this journey of accompaniment, they will no longer see or hear me – only You. I will teach them to recognize Your voice, to know You – not just *about* You – to relish the budding relationship between Father and child.

The art of accompaniment requires a delicate balance between holding someone's hand for a time and knowing when to let go.

THE DESIGN OF HIS HEART

"The Lord foils the plans of nations, frustrates the designs of peoples. But the plan of the Lord stands forever, the designs of his heart through all generations." ~ Psalm 33: 10 – 11

My designs and plans are many as I arise each day. I have so many things I need and wish I could accomplish that sometimes I lose sight of what God is asking of me: to stop and pray, to play with my children, to spend some time in silence, to contact someone in need, to take a nature walk, etc. God's designs for me make my plans seem like folly, just fillers in the day. He is beckoning me to examine what truly matters in life, because His will remains strong and steadfast when all the plans of countries and people have withered away.

We are invited to enter into God's design for us, which necessitates stepping away from our own. We cannot have one foot in our world and another in God's. He is always asking us to choose, always. Will we follow our own inclinations or trust Him enough to follow His lead, wherever He may take us?

And we know His will is stitched in His heart – the designs of His heart – so His will must be permanently branded in our hearts, as well, since we reflect His image and likeness. This is what pleases God and proves our love for Him! It's not so much the drastic, one-in-awhile changes we make out of obligation, but rather it is the process of conforming ourselves to His heart, little by little, that proves how much we love Him.

A heart conformed to God is a heart reformed.

THE DIALOGUE OF LIFE

I recently saw a somewhat clichéd quote on a local bible church that read, "God doesn't just want weekend visits. He wants full custody." This, of course, was in reference to the now-commonplace terminology referencing how divorced couples divvy up time between homes for their children. But the point, although a bit off-base, overall made sense: God doesn't just want us to set aside time to worship Him on Sundays. This is important – vital even – but it's not the be-all-end-all of our relationship with God.

Relationship implies that there's an ongoing dialogue between persons – one speaking, the other listening, and vice versa. Relationships must include daily, even moment-to-moment, encounter in thoughts and conversations. Our relationship with God, then, should imitate this value of ongoing communication. Ultimately it's a conversation of hearts – not always spoken, but ever-present – between God and us.

Love is the underpinning of every good motivation in our relationships, whether human or divine. God doesn't want us to simply give Him fragments of ourselves in scheduled chatter, which is what we often do in prayer. On the contrary, our entire lives – our breath, our being – should involve this dialogue of love, always elevated heavenward. It's sometimes occurring on a subconscious or semi-conscious level, but our hearts are always speaking to God and listening to Him.

This is the depth of true prayer and a vibrant love relationship with God: to make a perpetual conversation with Him of every aspect of our lives.

THE FIRST PRINCIPLE AND THE LAST END

You are my First Principle, for You thought and breathed me

into existence. Out of ash and dust was I created, and only to dust shall I return. Therefore, You are my Final End, the Home for which I long and will ultimately find eternal rest.

But what of everything in between the beginning and end of my life? I must question how I've spent my time and whether or not I've lived a life worthy of the end I seek. If I am but dust, then I must consider my nothingness each day and how I might reach for You – my all-in-all – so that my life today may reflect Your presence.

It's the living in between birth and death that we so often neglect, or at the very least ignore, because time appears to us to be a commodity, a luxury. But time, unlike our belief, is not always on our side. It is a gift, and the only possible way to our heavenly end is by making the moments of time we are given to matter somehow, whether great or small.

As the Little Flower said, if I do all things with great love, then my life was lived well, and I shall one day see eternal light.

THE HIDDEN COUNSELS OF GOD

"They knew not the hidden counsels of God." ~ *Wisdom 2: 22*

We tend to categorize and stereotype everything, including God. Somehow, because we define ourselves by labels, we think we can easily label God, too. But there is danger in trying to cram the fathomless depths of God into a tiny, predictable box.

When we grow in the fear of the Lord, we begin to sever those labels, and God's essence becomes Mystery. It's not that He hasn't revealed Himself to us, because we know Him as our Father, Redeemer, and Sanctifier. But we must confront His infinity with our limited lens of life. As we encounter the God of mystery, we realize how small we truly are, which also increases humility in us.

We would do well to ponder often His greatness and

vastness. We honor and praise God when we recognize and worship Him in totality, including that which is hidden from the human eye and mind. It is often in those clandestine crevices of ourselves where we find God and thus love Him evermore.

THE KINDNESS OF GOD

As a child, I imagined God to be distant, punitive, and tyrannical, yet my heart was drawn to the Father. Somehow I knew my Creator loved me, and love is not distant or cruel. It's true that God's love is disciplinary, but there is a sweetness and gentleness in that correction.

God's mercy abounds. He cannot be outdone in generosity, though we often place limits on Him as if He were a created being rather than timeless Creator. Each new day, then, is rich with His love for us – personal and also universal. Let us seek His kindness and emulate the goodness of God in our daily lives.

Do not be duped by the enemy's lies about our loving Father. Would a heartless dictator design innumerable varieties of animals, plants, flowers, and trees, all of wildly gorgeous colors and shapes? The creation all around us is God's gift to us.

Our heavenly Father blesses us with His peace each new day before the dawn breaks when all is still and silent. He rests in us and invites us to rest in Him. We are together in this moment of stillness, and He fills us up with His graciousness and kindness. All is well when we rest in Him.

THE MYSTERY OF DEVOTION

"Undeniably great is the mystery of devotion, who was manifested in the flesh, vindicated in the spirit, seen by angels, proclaimed to the Gentiles, believed in throughout the world, taken up in glory."
~ *1 Timothy 3: 16*

True devotion to Jesus isn't merely trite affection or distant fondness. It isn't following the fickle path of feelings, wistfully blowing in one direction and then the next. No, devotion is not contingent upon fluffy emotions or fleeting moments of happiness.

True devotion is a mystery. It requires fortitude, perseverance, strength, and much hope in the midst of holy darkness. If I am devoted to Jesus, I love Him as an act of the will, even and especially when it appears as if He has forsaken me. I remain faithful and recall Timothy's second letter, "He remains faithful, for He cannot deny Himself."

So my fidelity, though it falters frequently, is a meager offering of the conditional love I hold for God. But God is faithful in the midst of the tempest and through the darkest, blackest hole in my life.

I can neither see nor feel Him, but I still follow Him. I know nothing of what He is doing with, in, or through me, but I continue to cling to hope. In essence, true devotion to Jesus is how we learn to trust Him wholeheartedly.

THE WISDOM OF THE WORLD

"Where is the wise one? Where is the scribe? Where is the debater of this age? Has not God made the wisdom of the world foolish? For since in the wisdom of God the world did not come to know God through wisdom, it was the will of God through the foolishness of the proclamation to save those who have faith."
~ *1 Corinthians 1: 20 – 21*

The wisdom of the world tells me to abandon my faith in pursuit of narcissistic pleasures, to run from this suffering – the invisible cross – that has consumed me. To be wise in a secular sense means I must seek happiness in the form of worldly comforts rather than keep my eyes fixed on eternity.

As time passes, I realize increasingly how foolish I must seem to the world. I listen to people's theories about the law of attraction and how abortion clinics are selling baby parts, and I wonder how far their false wisdom has brought them.

Yes, the Cross is a contradiction, and I have been tempted many times to forsake it, but it's the only certainty for me in this spiritual darkness. The Cross has become my beacon, my fortress, my sanity for all the nonsense that continues to swirl around me. Is that foolishness?

It must not be foolish to believe in the One who redeemed me by His blood and who long ago invited me to pick up my cross, following Him to Calvary. It would be foolish only if no Resurrection awaited me. But, alas, the foolishness of Christ far surpasses the false wisdom of the world, so I will follow His foolishness all the way to eternity.

THE WORK OF YOUR HANDS

I am the pen; You are the author.
I am the vessel; You are the Maker.
I am the ship; You are the Captain.
I am the seed; You are the Gardener.
I am the instrument; You are the Musician.
I am the leavened bread; You are the Baker.
I am the bridge; You are the Engineer.

For all I have done, I have truly not done,
Except by Your doing,
Your making,
Your creating.
Without You, I am merely a hollow shell.
But You have created a masterpiece in and through me.

I am Your slave; You are the Master.
I am Your candle; You are the Light.
I am but dust and dirt; You make a path.
I am a lowly worm; You transform me into a butterfly.

Truly my life is not my life,
But it is Yours in me.
You breathe into my soul,
And I come alive.

TRUE DEVOTION

"Whenever you...do what God tells you, then you are growing in the love of God, no matter what your feelings may be."
~ Fr. Gerald Vann, O.P[xv]

When I live according to the whims of my emotions, I never truly grasp what it means to love – to love myself, God, or others. Feelings seem to drive the behavior of many in today's society: "If it feels right to you, go for it" is the message we constantly are bombarded with. "How do you feel about that?" is another moniker coined from famed psychotherapists. Surely feelings must be evaluated and validated, but they should not contribute definitively to the choices we make or be the motivating reasons behind how we choose to live.

Defying our emotions can, at first, seem to be a betrayal to oneself. "I have to be true to myself" is another cliché we have perhaps convinced ourselves is true. But isn't it more valiant to be true to *God?* In so doing, we kill the self – not in identity, but in egocentrism, selfishness, and sin. We remain constant in our unique personhood, yet we choose, as an act of the will, to defy our emotions when we devote ourselves entirely to God.

That's not to say we never feel, on occasion, the love associated with devotion. God does grant us periods of time when we are renewed in both the will and heart to maintain our obedience and fidelity to Him, but we must not expect these moments to last. They are gifts of grace provided to strengthen our resolve, possibly because new challenges face us on the horizon.

But if we press on through every trial and emotional or spiritual aridity, we begin to understand – and live – the virtue of perseverance, which fosters fortitude and forges devotion to God, come what may.

WHATEVER YOU ASK OF GOD

"Even now I know that whatever you ask of God, God will give you." ~ John 11: 22

St. Martha is not portrayed positively in Scripture: she complains, doubts a bit, and frets too much over the details. She's busy in body and spirit, to the point of frustration. In essence, St. Martha is a relevant saint. She is much like me: weak in nature and openly so.

But her confidence resides in God rather than in her own capabilities. She laments, yes, but immediately the true perception of her faith emerges: "Whatever you ask of God, God will give you." Jesus recognizes this confidence and blesses her. "Your brother will arise...Do you believe this?"

Sometimes I, too, need Jesus to ask me: "Do you believe this?" Even if I display an insignificant act of confidence in His prevailing Providence, doubt may creep in. Jesus sees through this and wants my assurance of faith. "Do you believe this?" "Yes, Lord, I believe You are the Savior and that you can do anything."

I pray this along with St. Martha, because the second profession of my faith, following Jesus's question, requires intentional effort on my part. I pause for a moment and interiorly reflect: "Do I believe?" Yes, Jesus! Oh, yes, I believe! It becomes more than mere lip service due to habit. It is a reflection of my heart, an awakening of love to Love.

Despite my visible weaknesses, faults, and foibles, I can – and do – say wholeheartedly and without evidence that yes, I believe Jesus can do all things and that whatever He asks of the Father, He receives. This is a declaration of divine mercy, which I am greatly lacking.

Jesus, I am desperately in need for You to do great acts of

mercy in my life. I do believe You and all that You promise. Help, then, my unbelief and rise again in me with new hope and trust in Your unfailing love.

WHO IS "I AM?"

If we philosophize what it means *to be*, or exist, we could conjure everything that does not exist, too – trolls, gnomes, fairies, and aliens, to name some. But to exist is something entirely different, because we're speaking of what is real rather than imaginary.

When God calls Himself I AM, He is saying much. He means that He's always existed, with no beginning or end. He exists outside of time, though He chooses to enter it for our sakes. He encompasses everything good – grace, benevolence, mercy, and love. He is all of these and more.

We must consider, then, that we "are not." If God is "I AM," that is, everything – all – then we are not everything. God is Creator, we the creation. God is infinite, we are finite. In light of God's immensity, we receive the opportunity to humble ourselves in gratitude before Him, to love our humanity enough to depend entirely on Him.

"I AM" is with us, we who sin and have limited capacity for learning and love. Ponder the wonders and works of His hands, so that you may grow in holy fear of the Great I AM.

YOU ARE MY CHAMPION

"The Lord is with me like a mighty champion."
~Jeremiah 20: 11a

What is a champion? A victor, a winner? Is it possible that a champion stumbles and even succumbs to death? Yet You did this, Jesus, and scandalized our hearts, shaking our faith. At times this reality reawakens doubt in us – about You being who You say You are, about the real victory of conquering sin and physical death.

Yet You truly are my champion. You run the race, fight the battles, and pave the way for my victory when I am approaching defeat. When I am teetering on the edge of giving up, You sweep in to rescue me.

You are a mighty champion in the condescension of the Cross, in the dying and rising again. I now know that true victory requires death of self and a poverty of spirit in which I possess nothing in order that I may gain all.

CHAPTER FIFTEEN

God's Mercy & Grace

A DWELLING PLACE OF GRACE

"Behold, I stand at the door and knock. If anyone hears my voice and opens the door, then I will enter his house and dine with him and he with me." ~ Revelation 3: 20

Lord, I have long closed the door to my heart. It once was open to all, but it quickly became bruised and abused, worn thinly by fear, anxiety, and uncertainty. The sting of betrayal was the final act to shut my heart.

But again today, as every day, You gently knock. I've lived far too long behind the façade of security, in my inner chamber where all is safe and certain. But I've also yearned to open this door and to, in fact, remove it altogether, because I want no barriers between us.

This world has truly befuddled me. I can no longer comprehend the motives behind particular celebrations in our society. The world leaves me confused, so I long for You all the more.

Jesus, make my heart a dwelling place for Your grace. Today I open the door to my heart at Your beckoning. Today I invite You in – wholeheartedly, holding nothing back from You. Come, dine with me and I with You. Let us break bread together, that I may consume You, Bread of Life and You, in turn, may consume me with Your Spirit.

Then remove the door of my heart – all of the barriers I've permitted to thicken as life has grown more challenging. I want to hold nothing back from You, only to give freely and totally myself to You and for the salvation of souls who, like me, were once lost and afraid, shackled by sin. At long last will I be free!

AN UNEXPECTED DELIGHT

Life drudges on for days, weeks, months, or even years without an obvious answer to our petitions. God hears each word we utter – our prayers never fall on deaf ears – but, as time passes, we are inclined to believe He will not respond. Then suddenly, unexpectedly, drastic changes occur, and things effortlessly fall into place. Life resumes its light-filled vigor, and we delight at all the goodness and beauty surrounding us.

We must learn to live with gratitude for both the lulls and the movements – even the setbacks – of our lives. Life has a cadence to it that, if we allow it, becomes quite an orchestra that God conducts. He never makes mistakes, so the times we begin to doubt whether He will find favor in us, we should recall with fondness and appreciation all of the moments in the past when blessing upon blessing has been showered on us. The times of paucity and even darkness are opportunities for perseverance in our fidelity to God, who never wavers in His love and care for us (even when we are fickle).

Consider the quiet periods when the Spirit sleeps as times of rest for you. Move with God, and your rhythm will become harmonious and smooth.

Do not stumble over God. These are awkward movements we create by resisting His period of rest and blessing. Trust when nothing seems to be happening. Trust, because God moves in secret ways of which we are not privy. He is always moving and working for our good, so we must allow that work to naturally unfurl in the unexpected delights that surprise us with plentitude and happiness. Wait in the frustration, and the reward will far exceed the suffering.

APPEALING FOR DIVINE MEDICINE

Lord, I am ill in so many ways. Only now has my body finally reached a point of revealing the depth of my spiritual malady. I know the body, mind, and soul work in harmony and so also become broken in unison. So many people advise me on what to do and how to heal and repair myself. Is this truly possible, or are You perhaps teaching me to entrust this unrevealed affliction to You as my Divine Physician?

That's not to say I will neglect finding the proper remedies to help myself heal. There is so much truth to the rudimentary ways of healing: rest, adequate sleep, unscheduled time spent outside among nature, nourishing foods, and lots of clean water. Much can be restored through these natural gifts and remedies and, at times, in conventional medicine.

But I am sad to admit that conventional medicine has merely labeled me as a diagnosis – sometimes an erroneous one – because some traditional physicians cannot humble themselves to say they don't understand certain human complexities. I am more than a diagnosis and treatment plan. I am a whole person, and I need healing to occur on all levels.

Yet I am skeptical of alternative medicine, simply because some practitioners use sneaky New Age methods of healing, and I don't want to expose myself to the enemy out of desperation to feel better. I suppose my goal isn't really to feel better, anyway, only to function at a place where Your Spirit overcomes my flesh.

I cannot continue the pattern of life this way. It has lost a soothing rhythm and has somehow become discordant. You are my Divine Physician, so I appeal to Your mercy for Your divine medicine. Only You can heal me, whether it is through the hands of a good health practitioner or through other, extraordinary means.

But I am so desperate for You to advise me, Lord, that I may see and hear clearly which route I am to take in all of this. Many purport to show the way to true healing, but You know me best. You know what I need and what is garbage. Send me to the people who know You and will listen to me, helping me heal in entirety, not just one symptom at a time.

BORN OF WATER AND SPIRIT

It saddens me how few people are baptized these days, including older children and adults. It not only saddens me, but it also frightens me, Lord, because I cannot imagine the sense of loneliness and lack of purpose these wandering, lost souls must carry inside their hearts.

Being born of water and Spirit is our first official claim as adopted sons and daughters in the Christian family. I receive my anointing as priest, prophet, and king to share in Your heavenly portion, Lord. And I am indeed made an entirely new creation by the mercy of this Sacrament of Initiation. How, then, do so many neglect the beauty and beckoning of this gift of rebirth?

If we are offered a life of vibrancy, a life fulfilled, a life of eternal joy, why do we deny the simple gift of water and Spirit? Breathe life in me, Lord, that I may bring life to the world through You.

CALLED AND CHOSEN

"We know we have been called; we do not know whether we have been chosen." ~ St. Gregory the Great

Scripture states, "Many are called, but few are chosen." What does this mean exactly? It means each of us is born for God's purpose and design. We are brought into this world through His will and made in His image. Therefore, we are *called*.

We are called to fulfill God's dream for us, whatever it may be, and ultimately to spend eternity with Him. And this is where *chosen* comes into play. To be chosen means that we have actually ended our lives worthily and well, fighting vice and temptation while simultaneously growing in virtue.

Being chosen means we responded to God's call and remained faithful, residing in His grace to the end of our earthly existence. As St. Gregory points out, some of us heroically follow Christ but end up abandoning Him, while others live very sinful lives in the beginning but then faithfully serve Him before they die.

Many are called, but few are chosen. How can we respond to God's call, yet also never waver from fidelity in the face of temptation? To begin, we must never presume we are among the few chosen. So pray first for humility, and you will be encased in an unknowing that protects you from falsehood and pride.

To be *chosen* means we awake each day with the sincere intention of serving Jesus, and *when* we sin (not if), we immediately make amends to both God and man with contrition and repentance. Therefore, Confession is our Sacrament of Humility and Mercy. It is where we become more self-aware with brutal honesty, yet we receive the inexplicable mercy of Jesus.

I am loved by Him. I must never forget this in order to remain on or return to the narrow road. If I do not believe this at all times, I will more easily and swiftly be deceived by the adversary in other matters.

So I must always cling to God's love, and every day beg for His grace. With sincerity, humility, and contrition, I will follow where He leads, even on an unknown path. My goal is Heaven, and though I can never be assured of it in this life, I can be certain of God's love and desire for me to be with Him forever.

CONVERSATIONS OF MERCY

"Jesus loves to connect lives." ~ Fr. Dan Scheidt[xvi]

Though I love people and find that getting to know them nearly always enriches my life, I still tend to shy away from conversing with total strangers. Everyone has a story, and human life is always interesting, but I'd rather avoid entering into that story. It's too risky. It's too painful. I'd rather avoid eye contact and move on.

But that's the response of most people, isn't it? We retreat into our shells where it's safe, comfortable, and predictable. We've built invisible walls around our hearts in an effort to both conceal what's ugly about ourselves and to prevent any real encounter with another person.

We live in a world that craves authentic encounter, however. Now, more than any other era in history, is about disconnection being more prevalent than real conversation. Jesus invites us to stretch beyond what is known or familiar and reach out to others who are dying inside from lack of connection.

Having an extroverted child provides a daily opportunity for me to speak to others – people I would have otherwise ignored or passed by with simply a smile. But Sarah says, "Hi" to everyone in such a way that she's eagerly awaiting a conversation. It's not mere courtesy for her; she wants to *know* people. Because of that, her efforts pay off in grand ways.

I've realized that people are just starving for someone to notice them, to care about their suffering, to listen. When we do these things, however awkward it may feel for us, we're presenting the mercy of God to a world so lacking in real love. Let's have these conversations of mercy today.

I AM WHAT I AM

"By the grace of God I am what I am." ~ 1 Corinthians 15: 10a

We may say with feigned resignation or indifference, "It is what it is," but when we say, "I am what I am," it's usually a poor rationalization for our character defects. Here, however, St. Paul looks at his life, and in all humility, states, "I am what I am" because of God's grace. He's not making excuses; rather, he's giving God both the credit and glory for making St. Paul such an incredible witness of the Faith. He does not neglect to acknowledge his unworthiness, but he's telling us and the people of his time that any good deeds they see or preaching they hear from him is purely given to him from God's grace.

The same is true for us. We can say, "I am what I am" out of pride, or we can say the same out of immense gratitude for all God has done in and through our lives. The dismissal of our sins is one way to maintain mediocrity in our spiritual life, but to admit that all we have accomplished is a blessing from the One who bestowed these gifts upon us is the true test of a heart that fears God.

We seek God outside of ourselves, but God wants us to see Him in our very core – "I am what I am" – only because of God's mercy and love, nothing else. I have become someone new, someone better, because God has changed me.

MERCY TRIUMPHS OVER JUDGMENT

"For the judgment is merciless to one who has not shown mercy; mercy triumphs over judgment." ~ James 2: 13

So much of my life has been wasted on anger and presumption. I've squandered the mercy I've received and instead cast people away by throwing stones at the first offense. I have not displayed mercy, because justice always mattered more to me. But I see a bit more clearly now that mercy is an act of love, of true charity. Mercy requires forgiveness and kindness.

Would I not hope for the same treatment each time I hurt, offend, or sin?

Is mercy the warmth of Your Spirit that melts the hardened wax around my heart? I do not want to be calloused and emotionally barren, but too many betrayals have left me feeling jilted and jaded. At times I feel I cannot risk vulnerability or trust when I've been let down more often than not.

But Your mercy showers my brokenness like gentle and cleansing rain. It reigns over my harsh judgment and pain. I must do the same then. But how can I trust others? How is it possible for me to forgive and love my enemies? I've come to a feigned acceptance – or rather, resignation – that "it is what it is." I suppose I am called to embrace constant criticism and maligning from others.

My conclusion is that mercy is not easy to offer. It contradicts my human defenses. I cannot extend mercy to others – or myself – without the aid of divine grace. But I know I must immerse myself in Your mercy first and then distribute to others what I've been given and how I've been forgiven.

MY STRENGTH AND MY SONG

"The Lord, my strength and song, has become my savior."
~ *Psalm 118: 14*

People tell me all the time how greatly they admire my inner strength, but my heart is wounded at this for two reasons. First, I wish they would see *Your* strength in me rather than presuming any resilience originates from myself. Second, if only people knew the truth of my weakness! I am such a selfish person, constantly battling nearly every vice on a moment-to-moment basis. Nearly every thought, attitude, word spoken, inclination, or decision I make is fraught with intense discernment, wrestling and struggle against my pride and the enemy's enticement.

No, the truth is that I am quite weak. Another point of evidence about my pride is that I am surprised by my weakness. Over and over again, I become startled when I sin, as if I have already achieved perfection!

My friends, the weakest among us may appear to possess an impressive tenacity, but let us not be fooled. The strength of the weak is the Lord's; He is our strength and our song. When we are infirm, ailing, exhausted, and depleted, let us recall the words of Nehemiah: "The joy of the Lord is my strength."

When I appear to have a particular gift, talent, joy, or strength, I want to be clear that it belongs to God. The origin of all goodness is the Lord's alone. Left to my own devices, I would certainly crumble and meet my demise instantaneously.

Remember this: "I can do all things through Christ who strengthens me, for when I am weak, then I am strong."

Amen. Rejoice in the strength of the Lord!

REMAIN IN ME

"If you remain in me and my words remain in you, ask for whatever you want and it will be done for you." ~John 15: 7

I could ask You for healing for me and my daughters, a new home, or a new life. But does that mean "it will be done" for me? Certainly not. I am no fool to assume that "whatever I want" gives me license to request anything without thought, or rather, prayer.

The operative prerequisite to obtaining "whatever I want" is to remain in You and for You to remain in me. When I am fully dwelling in Your presence and basking in Your love, my heart no longer desires selfish and frivolous things. The desire of my heart is to do what pleases You – at the expense of my own suffering in any capacity.

Love would pull me away from myself and draw me nearer to You. When facing You in the recesses of my heart, I cannot refuse You. I cannot turn away, because I no longer wish for a life lived in narcissism. I no longer am "I," but "we." You are my indwelling.

So what I ask of You is to know Your will for my life – this hour, this moment, this day. It is to beg You, Lord, to fulfill Your dreams for my life and grant me the necessary wisdom to recognize Your will, as well as Your grace, to carry it out each day.

This is when "whatever I ask" is granted – not for anyone, anywhere, any time. It does not mean I ask for my ego to be boosted or to obtain a comfortable life. Only when I choose to remain in You, to dwell with You and You in me, does my heart increase with fervent ardor and the pure longing to ask of You what You want for me.

Then my prayer is granted, and more than I would ask selfishly is fulfilled by Your generosity.

THE BATH OF WATER AND WORD

"Husbands, love your wives, even as Christ loved the church and handed himself over for her to sanctify her, cleansing her by the bath of water with the word, that he might present to himself the church in splendor, without spot or wrinkle or any such thing, that she might be holy and without blemish." ~ Ephesians 5: 25 – 27

Jesus, Your life and death alone have reconciled me to You. Each day I awake to the dawn and am both delighted and discouraged: delighted at the opportunities that await me today, but discouraged at the filth of sin that stains my heart.

In many ways, You wash me anew each instant I approach You with sincere contrition and in the Sacrament of Mercy. I am bathed by both the cleansing waters of Baptism and Your Eternal Word. Instead of a mere sprinkling of mercy, You thoroughly cleanse me in entirety so that my soul is rid of the dirt and grime; all of it is gently showered until the gleam of my soul is fully revealed in its natural condition through Your redeeming grace.

You created me from Mercy, for Mercy, through Mercy, and to Mercy. Because of this, my soul bears Your image and was created to authentically reflect You. Yet each day I fail in this lofty endeavor, which is why I return to You time and again for my daily bath of water in the Word of Life.

You refresh my soul, and I am made new, which becomes my delight at dawn. I know assuredly of my concupiscence, yet I also know I must run into Your arms with gratitude and a remorseful heart. Then I am renewed by Your spirit and bathed in Your light.

Jesus, You are the purifying, Living Water for which I thirst. Only You can quell my parched heart and clothe me in the cleansing waters of refreshment. Refresh and revitalize me in Word and Sacrament today.

THE BOUNTY OF YOUR MERCY

"And now we follow you with our whole heart, we fear you and we seek your face. Do not put us to shame, but deal with us in your kindness and great mercy." ~ Daniel 3: 41 – 42

I heard a fire-and-brimstone explanation of world events from a Protestant who believed the Rapture is coming soon. It's true that we live in horrific, unprecedented times. I cannot bear to imagine the overt evil of which we hear in daily news, but it is real – and it is evidence that our amoral society has become the devil's playground indeed.

But what of God's mercy? It seems an error to focus entirely on God's wrath *or* His mercy. It's true that our wanton ways have warranted God's justice, but I will never stop appealing to God's mercy. I cannot stop reminding Him – or myself – that He is Goodness and Truth. He is Peace and Protection. Mercy is the solution to the world's madness – not ire, division, or fear.

And we cannot delude ourselves into thinking we will escape the times ahead, which are filled with heavier crosses and unknown sufferings. Where would our mercy for the souls of the lost be if we did not show the world the loving face of Christ?

God tells us His mercy is bountiful. We must never forget His generosity in dispensing mercy. When we plead for it, we do so not out of expectation or fear of His anger or out of a sneaky desire to weasel our way out of important and necessary consequences.

No, we plead for mercy from a deep longing to be healed and made new, which originates from humility. It is humility that softens God's heart toward our petitions and lamentations. And humility emerges from the acknowledgment that I am small and weak while God is great and strong.

God desires us to show the world His mercy, too. Therefore, since we have been recipients of His generosity in love, we, too, must dispense mercy liberally to ourselves and others. I imagine that mercy and love will conquer the stifling madness of our world and the prevailing sickness – one soul at a time.

THE COLORS OF GRIEF

When you look at me, you see the white light of goodness, but when I see myself, all is black. You see a vibrant rainbow with every hue of the spectrum, but I am surrounded by darkness.

Do not pity me, because, most of the time, this darkness is my friend. It is God's protection, His way of keeping me for His own and seeing that I do not stray from Him. Still, I'd like to see as you do, only I can't. I see your colors – the gifts you share, your virtues in deeds, and the hand of Providence upon you. But my colors ran dry long ago, when I lost myself somehow in the thick of a spiritual awakening. God took hold of me, but He wanted me to see myself as I really was – nothing, vacant, void of substance.

While this aggrieved me for a time, I was assuaged by the knowledge that God is everything. I must first believe – that is, to see interiorly – that I am bereft in and of myself of goodness, before the Light of All can be revealed through my own life. His everything – His colors – replace my nothingness, and I am, at last, a person of beauty, one with purpose and fulfillment.

Remember this when you speak with me or view my life

from your lens: I do not see myself or my life as you see me or it. I know I can do no good thing without His grace, which revives the colors you see, but intensifies the blackness I see.

I must decrease. He must increase.

THE LORD OUR JUSTICE

"Look! I am bringing the city recovery and healing; I will heal them and reveal to them an abundance of lasting peace."
~ *Jeremiah 33: 6*

St. Louis de Montfort says in *Preparation for Total Consecration,* "You are mine by mercy, and I am yours by justice."[xvii] We often think of justice in tyrannical, overbearing terms. Justice seems to necessarily overlap with judgment, which is true. But justice is more closely related to mercy, contrary to what we know or believe of both.

Mercy is what melts the ice of justice, but justice hardens mercy so it does not become too soft. Too soft or too hard – either way is perilous for one's interior development, though it can be said that one should err on the side of mercy. In other words, mercy cannot truly be overdone.

Why, then, is God our justice? He justifies us to Himself through the cruelty of the Cross, but once again, we can only view this act of justice through the lens of mercy. Were it justice alone that kept Him on the Cross, we would never be fully transformed and converted. Instead, love kept Jesus hanging there, exposed. It was mercy in conjunction with justice that kept Jesus there.

Moreover, we do not deserve God's mercy, only His just judgment. This is why He belongs to us out of mercy and we to Him out of justice. It is truly "right and just" for us to give Him our all, since He suffered all for our sakes, for love's sake.

THE SHADOW OF YOUR WINGS

"In the shadow of your wings I seek refuge till harm pass by."

~ *Psalms 57: 2b*

Hide me in Your shadow, Lord, for in my invisibility, You cloak me with Your darkness. And Your darkness shelters, protects, and defends me under Your wings. Even as You sleep, Your wings enshroud me with the gift of a holy darkness, a refuge and haven in which no predator or enemy is permitted to harm me.

I was swept away at once by Your might – the power and strength of the eagle. Your graceful gliding across the vast blanket of earth and sky captivated me. So I made myself vulnerable to You. I made myself visible to You, knowing and hoping that You would capture me.

And now I nestle safely under the shadow of Your wings, soaring to inimitable heights quite impossible for me to scale alone. You carry me to unknown territories, yet my heart and soul are elevated by the mystery of Your darkness, the abyss of Your love, which knows no limits and cannot be quenched by my sadness or sin.

Hide me in Your shadow, Lord, under Your wings, where I dwell safely and am transported by Your mercy to a place of peace, the indwelling for which I long. Keep me hidden in Your darkness, Lord, for I find strength there.

I am changed. I am made new. I am transformed under the shadow of Your wings.

THE SUN OF JUSTICE

"But for you who fear my name, the sun of justice will arise with healing in its wings…" ~ *Malachi 3: 20a*

Who is man that You are mindful of him? But You breathed life into us, making us whole and illuminative reflections of Your goodness. When we chose sin, we damned ourselves eternally, but then You arose – the Sun of Justice – and conquered sin and death on our behalf.

St. John Paul the Great has said that mercy and justice cannot be separated, so as the Sun of Justice You also came as the Sun of Mercy. If You had not risen on the horizon and high above the earth and clouds, our lives would be fruitless and meaningless.

Come, then, Sun of Justice and Mercy, come and be born in me. Rise in my heart day after day. Though You take refuge at times in my soul and sleep softly while I wait for You, still You faithfully rise like the daybreak and bring forth Your light to conquer the shadows that temptation and sin have invited into my heart.

Shine anew, then, Sun of Justice, and throw out the old, rising in me again and again.

THE TIME OF MERCY

"Do not be afraid of this executioner, but be worthy of your brothers and accept death, so that in the time of mercy I may receive you again with your brothers." ~ 2 Maccabees 7: 29

We cannot expect to defeat evil through retaliation; "an eye for an eye" was long ago abolished through the New Covenant. Because Jesus Himself is Mercy, we, too, must be agents of mercy to others. Violence may beget violence, but for the devoted Christian, violence is met with mercy. We do not capitulate to evil, but rather we courageously confront it through the arms of love. Only when others see the radical love in our hearts – that which we are willing to die for – can the possibility of conversion happen.

We are the possible channels of conversion for those who have falsely acceded to the time of evil. The time of mercy – a new era of hope, resurgence of life-giving love, and a renewal of our Christian commitment – is now. We are called to respond to all acts of evil with love, which is sometimes manifested as patience, at other times self-control, and still others, kindness.

Love conquers all. Love, indeed, is enough, because Love Incarnate enshrines, envelops, and enshrouds us with Himself. In the ultimate goal of unitive love, our hearts beat in unison with His. Mercy is upon us. Mercy is with us.

THIRSTING FOR RIGHTEOUSNESS

"Christ has the answer to this desire of yours. But He asks that you trust Him. True joy is a victory, something which cannot be obtained without a long and difficult struggle." ~ St. John Paul II

Dwelling in true freedom means I choose what is right in the face of life or death. Righteousness leads to life, while injustice, malice, sloth, etc. lead to eternal death. Righteousness is not a self-righteous attitude, which is truthfully pride incognito. That is more comparable to a sanctimonious flair rather than thirsting for truth and seeking it earnestly, humbly.

None of the beatitudes exists in the vacuum of vice. Righteousness is living in harmony with the Righteous One, the One who calls us to true freedom from sin, from the voice of the world. When I thirst for righteousness, I pine for it – an aching, a longing that cannot be satiated except by the means of sanctification through faith.

But we come to righteousness by way of great struggles and intense battles. We must enter willingly into the death of sin and selfishness before experiencing resurrected joy in righteousness. Let us seek righteousness, then, and live it in every facet of our lives. Let us stop standing around reading and proselytizing, but instead move forward in holy action. We are propelled into acts of service by the fulfillment of our hunger and thirst for righteousness, namely, through the Sacraments of Reconciliation and Eucharist.

We are a resurrection people. Therefore, we are a righteous people, but our righteousness isn't a birthright. It is an honor and privilege for living and walking in holy light – in the light of love and truth. May Jesus alone quell our thirst for this righteousness, and may the Holy Spirit anoint and commission us with the Living Water of Mercy, that we, too, may be the face of Mercy to a world devoid of mercy and righteousness.

USED FOR LOVE

"Nothing is too small, pathetic, or shameful to be used for love."
~ *Sr. Ruth Burrows*[xviii]

Shame and guilt are common side effects of those living with chronic grief. In fact, many people silently bear the pain of shame, without revealing their brokenness to another soul.

We all feel small, pathetic, and shameful from time to time – some more frequently than others. This self-pity can become self-destructive if I permit it to engulf my identity as a son or daughter of God.

Shame and guilt can also lead me closer to God. When I realize that He can use me, despite my faults and failures, I am humbled. I no longer see myself as disposable or dispensable. I am somehow restored by grace.

But I must will this interior change, so that guilt and shame no longer define who I am or where I am headed in this life. It cannot thwart my mission and purpose. It must only lead me to greater self-knowledge and deeper love for the One who restores all to Himself.

Restore me, Lord. Make me a new creation. I am pathetic and pitiful today, but You make all things new. Even in my wretchedness, I know You can and will use me if I only ask You.

WE MAY LOSE GOD'S GRACE BUT NEVER HIS LOVE

When the enemy gets ahold of my thoughts, I tend to focus on my shame – "not good enough" – and all of the ugliness in my life is somehow imbued with this message of fear. So I recoil from the sting my sin has caused, and the guilt and shame certainly follow suit. The committee in my head runs a tape that loops on these negative messages, so that I stay downcast and heavy-hearted.

In these moments, I accept the fallacy that the mistakes I've made, my obvious sorrow, and the outbursts of anger or jealousy cannot be used for love. What a fool I am to believe this! Everything is grace, as St. Therese of Lisieux reminds me. All things work together for good, says St. Paul in his letter to the Romans (8:28). Yes, it's true that my imperfect choices and bad attitudes have some merit, if only that God takes what I've broken and puts the pieces back together by grace.

Only it isn't the same as before. If I have shattered the porcelain cup of my friend's heart through a hurtful comment, God repairs it with His love, but the jagged edges of my damage are still visible. We receive cuts and wounds so deep that scars remain long after they have been healed. God makes all things new, which essentially means that the substance of what once was has been entirely transformed into an altogether different substance.

Perhaps when God takes my mess – mere unleavened bread – He, through the touch and words of love, changes it into something greater, which is His Body and Blood. When I unite all of myself, including my ugliness and sinfulness, to Him, He uses it for the good of my soul and for His greater glory. My brokenness serves as a tool, a vessel where imperfection meets the only Perfect One. He takes it all, and for the sake of love, makes it whole in and through love's touch.

CONLUSION

Life's struggles, though many, are not the end. In choosing victory, we choose to love and embrace our crosses. Along our personal journeys to Calvary, we encounter Jesus – the God who is Mystery – and we walk alongside Him, if only for a time. This is our gift *from* God, as well as our gift *to* God. It is a gift from God, because only through suffering can we gain Heaven. Suffering refines virtue in us and defines our character. The gift to God is, of course, the love we return to Him by accepting whatever He permits for our greater good, including trials.

As you continue your life's journey of discovering your mission, encountering God, learning about God's mercy and grace, and living in the midst of mystery through silent contemplation and prayer, remember that your faithfulness in times of darkness is the greatest gift of love you can offer the One who created you and loves you still.

I am particularly fond of this poem by St. Frances de Sales. May it leave you with sublime thoughts and longings for the God who created Heaven and Earth.

HOW TO FACE THE STORMS IN LIFE

Do not look forward in fear to the changes in life;
Rather, look to them with full hope that as they arise,
God, whose very own you are,
Will lead you safely through all things;
And when you cannot stand it,
God will carry you in his arms.
Do not fear what may happen tomorrow;
The same understanding Father who cares for you today

Will take care of you then and every day.
He will either shield you from suffering
Or will give you unfailing strength to bear it.
Be at peace,
And put aside all anxious thoughts and imaginations.

ACKNOWLEDGMENTS

I couldn't have completed this work without the aid of so many. Unless one is an author, one doesn't realize the extent to which such credits are due for making a manuscript come together cleanly, professionally, and beautifully.

First, I must thank my husband, Ben, who sacrificed so many hours of his free time, so that I could complete this manuscript. His love and dedication mean the world to me.

Next, I must extend deepest gratitude to my editor, Eric Postma, who swiftly completed his edits and offered many thoughtful suggestions for where I could improve.

My dear friend and amazing artist, Ruth Smucker, offered her talent with the cover design, which was no small feat. But what I envisioned, she put to life magnificently, and I am grateful she was willing to take on a new project.

The Lord inspired me to write this devotional, day by day, month by month. Though it doesn't boast of exactly 365 or 366 reflections, the ones selected here seemed to be most important for those who are stuck in a place of discouragement or deep anguish. This book is for them, from my heart.

ABOUT THE AUTHOR

Jeannie Ewing believes the world focuses too much on superficial happiness and then crumbles when sorrow strikes. Because life is about more than what makes us feel fuzzy inside, she writes about the hidden value of suffering and even discovering joy in the midst of grief. Jeannie shares her heart as a mom of two girls with special needs in *Navigating Deep Waters: Meditations for Caregivers* and is the author of *From Grief to Grace: The Journey from Tragedy to Triumph.* Jeannie was featured on National Public Radio's *Weekend Edition* and dozens of other radio shows and podcasts. For more information, please visit her websites lovealonecreates.com or fromgrief2grace.com.

[i] Pope Francis, *Welcoming Jesus: Advent Reflections by Pope Francis and Henri J. M. Nouwen* (All Saints Press, 2015), 9.

[ii] Pope Francis, "Meditation of the Day," *Magnificat,* January 1, 2016, 26.

[iii] Some may argue that Jesus was capable of complex reasoning as an infant by virtue of His divinity. Because Jesus was fully human and fully divine, His fully humanness meant that He learned everything according to developmental milestones that every person would reach.

[iv] Paraphrased from Advent homily on December 15, 2015 by Fr. Dan Scheidt at St. Vincent de Paul Catholic Church in Fort Wayne, Indiana.

[v] Quoted from homily on January 10, 2016 by Fr. Dan Scheidt at St. Vincent de Paul Catholic Church in Fort Wayne, Indiana.

[vi] Pope Emeritus Benedict XVI, "Mass opening," *Magnificat,* March 22, 2016, 61.

[vii] Caryll Houselander, "Meditation of the Day," *Magnificat,* June 3, 2015.

[viii] Quoted from homily on September 13, 2015 by Fr. Dan Scheidt at St. Vincent de Paul Catholic Church in Fort Wayne, Indiana.

[ix] Caryll Houselander, "Meditation of the Day," *Magnificat,* March 4, 2016, 70.

[x] Quoted from homily on February 2, 2016 by Fr. Polycarp at St. Vincent de Paul Catholic Church in Fort Wayne, Indiana.

[xi] Jacques-Benigne Bossuet, "Meditation of the Day," *Magnificat,* March 2, 2016, 44.

[xii] Luis M. Martinez, *When God Is Silent,* (Sophia Institute Press, 2014).

xiii Jaime Garcia, *15 Days of Prayer with Saint Augustine* (New City Press, 2008), 77.

xiv Luigi Giussani, "Meditation of the Day," *Magnificat,* June 16, 2015.

xv Fr. Gerald Vann, O.P., "Meditation of the Day," *Magnificat,* March 9, 2016, 151.

xvi Quoted from homily on February 28, 2016 by Fr. Dan Scheidt at St. Vincent de Paul Catholic Church, Fort Wayne, Indiana.

xvii St. Louis de Montfort, *Preparation for Total Consecration* (Montfort Publications, 1984), 44.

xviii Sr. Ruth Burrows, O.C.D., "Meditation of the Day," *Magnificat,* February 20, 2016, 300.

65417168R00157